# REUTERS

# SPORTS

## IN THE 21ST CENTURY

REUTERS

# SPORTS
## IN THE 21ST CENTURY

with 766 color illustrations

Thames & Hudson

PAGES 2–3 Mexican Laura Sánchez dives during the women's three metre springboard final at the XIV Pan American Games in Santo Domingo. Sánchez finished in fourth place. 8 August 2003, Jorge Silva.

Conceived, designed, edited and produced by
Thames & Hudson Ltd, London

For Reuters:
Executive director Monique Villa
Project director Jassim Ahmad
Picture editors Catherine Benson, Hamish Crooks

First published in 2007 in hardcover in the United States of America by Thames & Hudson Inc., 500 Fifth Avenue, New York, New York 10110

thamesandhudsonusa.com

Library of Congress Catalog Card Number 2006940570

ISBN 978-0-500-54341-2

Printed and bound in China by C&C Offset Printing Co., Ltd.

# CONTENTS

# Sport in the 21st Century

## Introduction by John Mehaffey

Steam rises off the head of soccer player Mikael Silvestre of Manchester United.
6 January 2002. Michael Regan

# Sport in the 21st Century

Perched in Tiananmen Square in the centre of Beijing at the top of the steps leading to the Museum of China stands a giant rectangular digital clock. Less than a month after the 2004 Athens Olympics' closing ceremony this public timepiece started the countdown to the 2008 Beijing Games, the latest staging of the world's most spectacular sports festival.

Beijing's 91,000-seat Olympic stadium has been nicknamed the Bird's Nest because of its complex intertwining metal girders. The 17,000-capacity National Aquatic Centre is designed in the shape of an ice cube. Together they form the heart of a complex which enshrines the present, commemorates the past and anticipates the future.

All great civilizations have built stadiums to honour athletic achievement, with Ancient Olympia in Greece the most celebrated. Not just sports fans but also philosophers, poets and politicians flocked to the sacred grove to applaud the fleeting glory of athletic perfection.

The legacy of the Ancient Games, which endured for approximately 1,000 years, was recalled in 2004 when the modern Games returned to Athens for the second time and the shot put was staged in the original stadium at Olympia. This simple, timeless action, a striving for the perfect athletic combination of strength and speed, helps illustrate the singular quality of sport, whose essentially primitive rituals still entrance millions through television, radio, print, the Internet and photography.

In the opening decade of the new millennium, young men and women with no advantages over their contemporaries other than physical gifts can captivate millions and gather handsome rewards, parading upon a global stage where the boundaries of time and space vanish. Live sport and news about sport is available 24 hours a day. Some is dross, the product of a proliferation of television channels with endless hours to fill. But much is compelling viewing, attractively packaged.

Sports junkies in any part of the world can watch a Tour de France stage race climax in the Netherlands. Random flicks through the channels bring tennis from Monte Carlo, athletics from Oslo, one-day cricket from the Caribbean, rugby union from Cape Town, baseball from Chicago, soccer from Barcelona, a triathlon in Sydney. Fans can relive their experiences through television replays, specialist publications and a dizzying array of websites, as well as the expanding sports sections of daily newspapers.

The impact of television and the vast sums of money it generates cannot be overestimated. Two of the more prominent global sports – and two of increasing appeal to China's growing middle class – have been significantly altered by the special demands of the networks.

Match play, the most exciting form of golf, pits one player against another over 18 holes and was used in two of the four tournaments when Bobby Jones won the grand slam in 1930. But because a match can end suddenly when one player wins 10 holes, bringing a premature close to television coverage, it was abandoned for standard tournaments in favour of stroke play, in which the lowest aggregate score over four completed rounds of 18 holes wins.

Tennis had an opposite problem. Under rules in force until the early 1970s, players had to win a set by a two-game margin, culminating in the 112-game two-day epic between Pancho Gonzales and Charlie Pasarell at the 1969 Wimbledon championships. To keep matches from stretching to eternity, the tiebreak was introduced at the 1970 U.S. Open, employed when a set is tied 6–6. Similarly, soccer devised the penalty shootout.

A security guard stands in front of the Olympic Aquatic Centre in Beijing. 26 September 2006, Reinhard Krause.

A cruel but undeniably dramatic device, the shootout concludes matches unresolved after extra time which would otherwise present the headache of scheduling a replay.

Night baseball neatly combines the interests of the schedulers and the majority of its fans who need to clock in at a regular job during the day, an approach copied by cricket with its day–night limited overs matches. Other sports have lost out in the television age. Squash, a game of skill and finesse but played with a tiny ball flying at great speeds, has declined dramatically in significance because of the difficulties in translating the action to a television screen. Television cameras also fail to convey the full drama of downhill skiing, where competitors fly down such sheer inclines as Kitzbühel's Streif course, regularly touching speeds of 130 kilometres (80 miles) an hour.

During the winter Olympic Games it is figure skating, with its combination of spectacular routines and popular tunes, that attracts highest viewing figures.

Athletics, although still central to the Olympic Games, is a sport struggling to keep its place in the global spotlight. This is despite biennial world championships and a new generation of excellent sprinters, including world 100 metres record holder Asafa Powell of Jamaica.

Another sport slipping out of the limelight is boxing. Mike Tyson is the last man to command the same aura as the great prize fighters of the 20th century, when the excitement of a heavyweight title fight featuring the likes of Jack Dempsey, Joe Louis, Rocky Marciano or Muhammad Ali would ripple throughout the sporting world.

## Sport's essentially primitive rituals still entrance millions through print, radio, television, the Internet and photography.

Tyson combined ferocity with an intelligent appreciation of his vicious trade and was on course to join his heroes in the heavyweight pantheon when his life imploded after a rape conviction in 1992. Over the next decade he became an increasing embarrassment as his life spun out of control. It came as a relief when the underrated Briton Lennox Lewis, widely disparaged in the United States for his refusal to do any more than he needed to win, systematically exposed the American's faded credentials in 2002 with an eighth-round knockout. Two years later Lewis wisely retired to enjoy his riches with unscrambled brains, becoming only the third man after Marciano and Gene Tunney to step down while still heavyweight champion.

Boxing provokes mixed emotions even among its devotees. In Ali the sport produced possibly the greatest sportsman of the 20th century; but it was also responsible for the head injuries that imprisoned one of the liveliest minds of his time within the frozen

mask of Parkinson's syndrome. The decline in quality in the U.S. heavyweight ranks has become so precipitous that for a brief period in 2006 each of the champions from the four competing bodies hailed from countries who were once part of the former Soviet Union.

Motor racing may be the supreme fusion of television, technology and sport, whether in Formula One or in stock cars on the American NASCAR circuit. The daredevil days of the old Grand Prix circuit, when drivers were the earthbound equivalents of World War fighter pilots or the early supersonic test aviators, may be long gone. But so too are the frightening casualty rates. Instead of designing cars to go as fast as possible, designers now balance speed with safety.

A cameraman stands in front of posters promoting the five cities bidding to host the 2012 summer Olympic Games. In the IOC vote held on 6 July 2005 in Singapore, the Games were awarded to London over long-time favourite Paris. 3 July 2005, Luis Enrique Ascui.

The dominant figure in Formula One until the ascent of 2005 champion Fernando Alonso was German Michael Schumacher, who won his first drivers' championship in 1994 with Benetton after Brazilian Ayrton Senna was killed on the Imola circuit in Italy. By the time Schumacher retired in 2006 he was the most successful driver in the history of the sport, winner of seven championships, including five in a row for Ferrari, the Italian team whose name is synonymous with the sport. But he also infuriated his critics who recall a collision with Briton Damon Hill in 1994, when he won the title by a point, and an incident three years later when he tried to barge Canadian Jacques Villeneuve off the track.

Formula One is a striking example of a global modern sport whose protagonists command the attention and salaries of their counterparts in the music and film industries. In an entertainment-fixated society, sport supplies concentrated drama, with athletes displaying often breathtaking skills under sometimes intense pressure. Unlike the theatre, where Hamlet will always die at the end of the final act, the result may be uncertain until the final whistle. Unlike the messy compromises of everyday life, there is usually only one winner.

Another attraction stems from the explosion in the fitness and leisure industries, with sports gear increasingly doubling as casual wear. Spaniard Rafael Nadal, the king of the clay tennis court, could have strolled off a beach with his piratical bandanna, baggy shorts and minimalist tops revealing impressive biceps.

## Against the odds

The popularity of the summer Olympics, with 28 sports staged over two weeks, is rivalled by the soccer World Cup with a maximum of three games on any one day. Certainly the global appeal of the 2006 World Cup was unparalleled since the tournament's stuttering start in Uruguay in 1930.

Zinedine Zidane, the son of an Algerian warehouseman born in the Mediterranean port city of Marseille, acquired his skills on dusty public pitches. He needed no special grants or schools of excellence to become the supreme player of his generation, scoring two headers in France's 3–0 victory over Brazil in the 1998 World Cup final at the Stade de France in Paris. The victory was acclaimed at the time as a triumph

Two Cuban boys face each other during their boxing training at an Old Havana neighbourhood boxing gym. 12 August 2003, Claudia Daut.

Schoolchildren in the northeastern Indian city of Siliguri sign a banner wishing the Indian cricket team good luck in the 2007 World Cup in the West Indies. 21 February 2007, Rupak De Chowdhuri.

And the timeworn maxim that sport is the ordinary person's culture and a potential outlet from obscurity and poverty still applies in a world where national boundaries are dissolving and hordes of people change countries and continents in search of a better life.

'The roads from all the dusty pitches of the world now converge on a satellite feed. The thrill of victory and the agony of defeat is measured in audience share and dollars,' observed the American sportswriter Robert Lipsyte a quarter of a century ago. 'Yet at the heart of it all is the true glory of sports, the individual daring to be better. How society can nurture the dream without cynically exploiting it may be the true sports challenge of the century.'

for a new multi-racial France, depending as it did on a team drawn largely from descendants of immigrants from the former colonies.

Looking old beyond his years, with a tonsure increasingly resembling that of a medieval monk, Zidane emerged from international retirement to recapture the magical essences of his youth and take France to the 2006 World Cup final. After converting an audacious penalty via the crossbar, Zidane was poised to stand alongside Brazil's Pelé as the greatest player ever to play the beautiful game on the global stage.

Those at the Berlin Olympic stadium and the millions of television viewers thought they had seen a destiny fulfilled when, as in Paris eight years earlier, Zidane rose for a header that would surely have decided the match. Instead the consistently excellent Italian keeper

Gianluigi Buffon tipped the ball over the crossbar. In the final minutes, after an insult from Marco Materazzi, Zidane head-butted the Italian defender on the chest and was shown a red card. Almost inevitably France, deprived of their supreme dead ball kicker, lost on penalties.

What demons raged in Zidane, whose onfield behaviour had often strayed beyond the acceptable in between bewitching displays of ball control and an all-embracing intelligence, remains a matter of speculation. It is probable, though, that had he got the ball past Buffon, nothing Materazzi could have said or done would have provoked such an extreme overreaction. A career apparently set to reach its climax on his sport's greatest stage will always have an asterisk attached.

> Sport more often reflects than influences society. However in the field of race relations, it has indisputably helped change the world for the better.

Zidane's impact beyond the confines of the playing field is more complicated. After the 1998 World Cup triumph white Frenchmen praised him as a role model for Muslim immigrants. But large numbers still voted for Jean-Marie Le Pen's far-right Front National party, which disparaged Zidane and his team mates as foreign mercenaries.

Although claims are often made for the superior moral values of sport, in reality it more often reflects than influences society. However in the field of race relations, sport has indisputably helped change the world for the better. At the 1936 Berlin Olympics, Jesse Owens, grandson of a slave, exposed the malign Nazi ideology of Aryan white supremacy by winning four gold medals. Then came the fierce black baseball genius Jackie Robinson, who helped break his sport's unspoken racial barriers while playing for the Brooklyn Dodgers in the early 1950s.

During the turbulent 1960s Muhammad Ali, stripped of his world heavyweight title for three years for refusing to serve in the Vietnam War, became a hero on the unsettled American campuses with his articulate denunciations of racism. An international sporting boycott played a key role in the crumbling of the Apartheid regime in South Africa, where rugby union, chosen sport of the Afrikaner, is a passion.

At the start of the 2000 golf season Tiger Woods, son of a black father and a Thai mother, specifically addressed the racial blight that had afflicted his childhood. 'America is the melting pot of the world,' he said. 'We have all the different ethnic races, religious choices. I just want to make golf look like that.' The American golf club, spiritual home of the white suburban Republican, has been more resistant to cultural change than many other institutions, and Woods, guided and encouraged by his late father Earl, had to break barriers to reach his goals.

Italy's Marco Materazzi (left) falls to the ground after being head-butted by France's Zinedine Zidane during their soccer World Cup 2006 final match in Berlin. 9 July 2006, Peter Schols.

He might not have confronted the same obstacles as Ali, nor those that faced Owens when he discovered his gold medals did not win him a decent job back home. But Woods still had to battle against bigotry in his middle class neighbourhood in Cypress, California. 'I was always treated as an outsider,' he said. 'We were the first and only black family for many years and we had many problems. I've been denied many things because of the colour of my skin.'

Coincidentally, a parallel struggle had been taking place in Los Angeles, where another black American, Richard Williams, coached his daughters Venus and Serena on public tennis courts, accompanied at times by the sound of gunfire as rival gangs took pot shots at each other. Also against the odds, both women went on to dominate their game with their power and aggression.

By the turn of the century Tiger Woods had through willpower, unremitting hard work and pure talent succeeded the Chicago Bulls basketball phenomenon Michael Jordan as the best known sports person in the world.

'Watching him do that had the same aura as watching Nelson Mandela come out of jail,' said black American activist Dick Gregory. 'It was moving to me because I knew what it was doing to people all across the country.'

Golf still meets a certain scepticism. There are those who regard it as a sport played by people who cannot play anything else. To Britain's wartime leader Winston Churchill, it consisted of 'putting a very small ball into an even smaller hole with weapons singularly ill-advised for the purpose.'

Such scorn melts in the presence of the athletic perfection that is Woods at his best. After doffing his cap to the gallery and flashing a smile only slightly less dazzling than the sun, it is all business for Woods, who concentrates the resources of an acute intellect, a gym-honed body and a relentless will to the task of mastering the course and defeating his rivals. Body speed as much as strength gives him length from the tee. His touch is uncanny and he had the humility to take time out and reshape a swing his rivals already coveted.

Above all, his attention to detail is incredible. After the 2001 Masters, the tournament in which he became the first man to win each of the four professional majors in succession, Woods reflected on saving par at the 10th hole of the final round. 'I hit a good three-wood off the tee,' he said. 'Unfortunately I had some mud on my ball and it was on the front right of the ball. And I was thinking, well, if I hit it on the front right part of the ball it usually makes it go a little bit left. And I tried to hit a cut shot to hold it but it took off and it tumbled.'

Woods' only visible weakness has been in the Ryder Cup, the biennial team event that pits the United States against Europe, where he has struggled to come to terms with the format. His presence on the U.S. team did not prevent the Europeans winning the first three Ryder Cup tournaments of the new century.

## Crossing borders

Nationalism is no longer the force it was in the post-World War Two Olympics, when the United States and the Soviet Union viewed the medals table as an extended arena of the Cold War. Yet it still forms a powerful appeal at the summer and winter Olympic Games and at regional and world championships in a host of individual sports where the nature of the competition makes national identity all-important. But the thrill of seeing new and exciting athletes from exotic locales has all but disappeared now that the best perform in all seasons throughout the world.

Soccer has a huge pool of performers crossing borders to play for one club after another in the lucrative European leagues. Many are from impoverished African nations, notably George Weah, the 1995 world player of the year, who after a distinguished career with AC Milan, Chelsea, Monaco, Paris Saint-Germain, Olympique Marseille and Manchester City stood unsuccessfully 10 years later for the presidency of his native Liberia.

In tennis, Russian women have suddenly flourished, their games honed by relentless practice often at American academies. Anna Kournikova, their most notable export, was paradoxically the least successful, playing in only four WTA finals and failing to win one. But, in another reflection of the times, her exceptional good looks nonetheless earned her millions in endorsements.

Africans, primarily Kenyans and Ethiopians, chase each other on the world's running tracks, outdoor and indoor, and across country. The outstanding long distance exponent at the moment, and maybe already the best ever, is the light-footed Ethiopian Kenenisa Bekele, who has proven uniquely adept on any surface.

One interesting side-effect of today's freedom of movement is the steady trickle of African runners moving to the Gulf States and changing their nationality in exchange for money they could not hope to earn representing their native countries. The prime example is the world steeplechase champion and record holder Saif Saaeed Shaheen, who competed for Kenya under his original name of Stephen Cherono but who is now paid significantly more running for his adopted country Qatar.

In a parallel case, Switzerland, a country without a coastline, won the 2003 America's Cup, the world's oldest sporting trophy, thanks to a team of renegade New Zealand yachtsmen.

## Olympic renaissance

The new century opened in a spirit of wary optimism as the global economy rebounded following the threat of a meltdown two years earlier. It was celebrated with New World exuberance at the 2000

OPPOSITE ABOVE  World champion Saif Saaeed Shaheen of Qatar competes in the men's 3,000 metres steeplechase at the Zurich Golden League meeting in Switzerland. He won the race in a time of eight minutes 2.69 seconds. Formerly known as Stephen Cherono in his native Kenya, Shaheen is the most high-profile track and field athlete to change nationality for economic reasons. 19 August 2005, Pascal Lauener.

OPPOSITE BELOW  Chinese basketball fans watch a game in front of cut-outs of National Basketball Association players at a fair in Shanghai organized ahead of the first ever NBA games to be held in mainland China. The Sacramento Kings were scheduled to play in Shanghai and Beijing against the Houston Rockets, powered by Chinese star and Shanghai native Yao Ming. 7 October 2004, Claro Cortes IV.

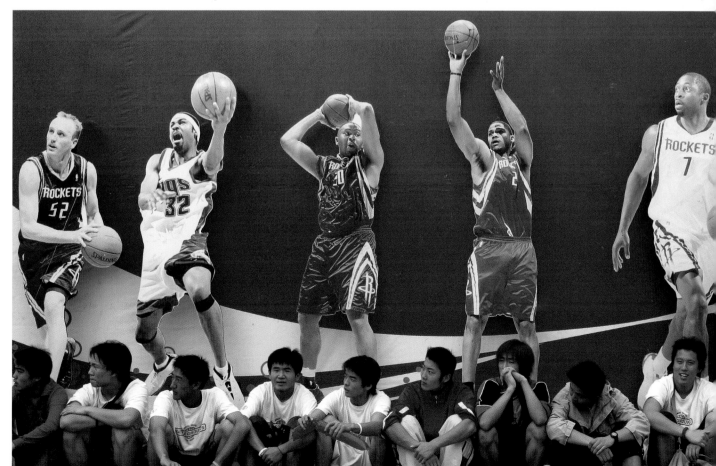

Sydney Olympics, the city which had unexpectedly been awarded the Games ahead of favourites Beijing. A sun-burned continent grasped the opportunity to parade the attractions of one of the world's more vibrant seaside cities set in a country which pursues sports and the outdoor life with unrestrained vigour.

Sydney also provided a perfect tonic for the International Olympic Committee (IOC) following a corruption scandal over the vote to award the 2002 winter Olympics to Salt Lake City. With sponsors threatening to defect in droves after revelations that several members of the unelected body had taken bribes or inducements before the vote, it was no exaggeration to suggest that the future of the Games was threatened.

Australian runner Cathy Freeman speeds to a first place finish in the semi-final of the women's 400 metres at the Olympic Games in Sydney. She went on to claim gold in the final.
23 September 2000, Gary Hershorn.

'The vultures of the sport/leisure industry were waiting in the wings for any signs of weakness that they might exploit, with the potential to entice willing International Federations to create a new multi-sports commercial venture,' wrote Olympic historian David Miller in *Athens to Athens*, the official history of the modern Games.

The IOC survived the scandal after punishing 10 members, six of them with expulsions. Its embattled president Juan Antonio Samaranch was present in Sydney for his final Games in charge which proved both a perfect finale and a template for future Games. The venues were stunning, the organization virtually flawless and the athletes shone in the sometimes uncertain weather of the Australian spring.

In a public relations masterstroke, aboriginal Australian Cathy Freeman lit the Olympic flame as a symbol of reconciliation between the indigenous people and European settlers. Freeman went on to win the 400 metres gold, fulfilling the stifling weight of expectations of a nation which punches far above its weight in most sporting arenas, particularly in swimming, where 17-year-old Ian Thorpe won three gold medals and two silvers.

After the chaos of the Atlanta Games four years earlier, the whole experience moved Samaranch to remark in his closing speech: 'I'm proud and happy to proclaim that you have presented to the world the best Olympic Games ever.'

Global sport and show business have been entwined since the 1984 Los Angeles Olympics, the first Games to set out to make a

In heartening testimony to the progress of women in sport over the course of the previous century, it was Marion Jones who seized the headlines and the magazine covers in the run-up to the Sydney Olympics.

commercial profit, and where Carl Lewis announced he was going to emulate Owens and win gold medals in the 100, 200 and 4x100 metres relay as well as the long jump. Lewis succeeded without to his frustration ever gaining the adoration and applause he craved from the American public.

The year before the Sydney Games, Marion Jones – articulate, graceful and gifted – announced she would go one better. Jones wanted the same four titles as Owens and Lewis, but also planned to win gold in the 4x400 metres relay. In heartening testimony to the progress of women in sport over the course of the previous century, it was Jones who seized the headlines and the magazine covers in the run-up to Sydney.

Women were excluded from the first modern Games in 1896 but took part four years later in Paris, when British tennis player Charlotte Cooper became the first woman to win an Olympic gold medal. Prejudice, though, still permeated the highest levels of sports administration. At the 1928 Amsterdam Games several competitors collapsed at the conclusion of the women's 800 metres. Subsequently, women's races over 200 metres were banned from the Games for 32 years and IOC president Count Henri de Baillet-Latour spoke for the reactionaries when he said that, as in ancient Olympia, women should not take part in the Games at all.

The Belgian aristocrat's views were already out of touch with the times when he voiced them, and by 2000 women were taking part in all track and field disciplines with the exception of the 3,000 metres steeplechase, which was finally introduced at the 2005 Helsinki world championships.

World Cup in Japan and South Korea would go ahead at all. Both did but at enormous cost, with organizers in Salt Lake spending an unprecedented $310 million on security.

September 11 was never far from the hearts and minds of the thousands of spectators who poured into the Utah state capital. A tattered U.S. flag rescued from the rubble of the World Trade Center was flown during the opening ceremony and later that year fluttered over the U.S. Open tennis tournament.

Against this emotional background, Janica Kostelić, a 20-year-old Croatian who began her skiing career while her native Yugoslavia disintegrated in bloody discord, claimed three gold medals and a silver. Despite suffering 11 operations on her battered knees and the removal

Marion Jones of the U.S. crosses the finish line in the 100 metres during the Golden Gala IAAF meeting at Rome's Olympic Stadium. 14 July 2006, Max Rossi.

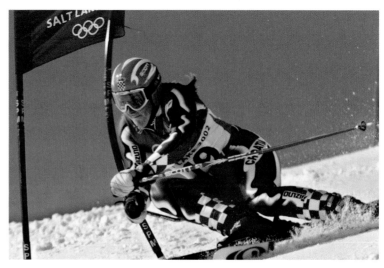

Janica Kostelić of Croatia skis a gate in the first run of the women's giant slalom competition at the 2002 Winter Olympic Games in Salt Lake City. 22 February 2002, Wolfgang Rattay.

In Sydney, Jones completed the first part of her ambitious programme with runaway victories in the 100 and 200 metres. But she faltered in the long jump, finishing third behind a superior technician, German Heike Drechsler. Another bronze in the 4x100 metres relay meant Jones would not equal Owens and Lewis although she went on to win a third gold with an astonishing run in the third leg of the 4x400 metres relay.

Fifteen months later, the global mood had darkened dramatically. The first winter Olympic Games of the new century, staged in Salt Lake City in February 2002, were also the first major international sporting event since the attacks on New York and Washington on September 11, 2001. In the fraught weeks after 9/11, there had been serious doubts in the sporting community that the Games and the subsequent soccer

of her thyroid gland, she was still around four years later in Turin where she won the combined and took a silver medal in the Super G.

## The drugs nightmare

Scientists have changed the face of sport legitimately through improved diets, remarkable surgical techniques to speed up rehabilitation and healing, and novel materials and equipment. The pole vault evolved gradually through bamboo, steel and aluminium implements before it was transported into another dimension by the introduction of fibreglass, which acts essentially as a catapult.

But the chemists have also been busy designing illicit performance-enhancing drugs, without doubt the most serious issue facing sport today, as testified by the establishment of the World Anti-Doping

Agency in 1999 headed by the outspoken former IOC vice-president Dick Pound. The drugs nightmare has haunted the Olympics since Canadian Ben Johnson tested positive after winning the 1988 100 metres final in world record time. And it descended on sunny Sydney when during the Games it was revealed that Jones's husband, world shot put champion C.J. Hunter, had tested positive four times for massive quantities of the anabolic steroid nandrolone during the previous year. The hulking American had pulled out of the Games, citing injury, but he was still present in Sydney and wept openly at a packed news conference while Jones stood stony-faced by her man.

Anabolic steroids, drugs that mimic the effects of the male sex hormone testosterone, produce rapid muscle growth, a corresponding increase in strength and stamina, and sometimes dramatic mood changes. They emerged during the 1930s, when German scientists fed to them to the Nazi storm troopers. In the 1950s they were administered to Eastern Bloc school children in an attempt to build a master race of Olympic athletes. In the following decade they became part of the Californian bodybuilding cult. Steroid use in sport has been most marked in speed and strength events such as sprinting and, in particular, weightlifting, a sport always popular at the Olympics but plagued by periodic drugs busts.

A Canadian government inquiry in the year after Johnson's fall from grace had already revealed in shocking detail the extent of drug abuse in athletics, much of it supplied under oath by the sprinter's coach Charlie Francis. Francis admitted that he had turned to performance-enhancing drugs for his athletes after the 1976 Montreal Olympics, when the medals tables had been dominated by athletes from the Soviet Union and East Germany, where state-controlled doping was rife, as documents released since the fall of the Berlin Wall confirm.

At the Hunter news conference in Sydney 2000, sitting unnoticed among the shot putter's entourage, was a former jazz musician who had played bass with the pianist Herbie Hancock and was now enjoying a lucrative career as a nutritionist. Victor Conte ran the BALCO laboratory in California, and Hunter and Jones, as well as baseball slugger Barry Bonds, were listed among his clients.

Three years later everybody in the world of sport knew the name of Victor Conte following a drugs scandal that still reverberates. The furore erupted after Trevor Graham, Jones's former coach, anonymously sent a syringe containing a previously unknown drug to the U.S. Anti-Doping Agency. Scientists at the Los Angeles Olympic Analytical Laboratory identified and devised a test for the new drug, dubbed tetrahydrogestrinone, or THG, which had been designed specifically to fool the testers.

As a result federal agents raided the BALCO laboratory and a number of athletes, including Bonds, were subpoenaed to give grand jury testimony. Bonds, who had transformed himself into baseball's premier home run slugger, overtook Babe Ruth's home run tally of 714 in 2006, behind only Hank Aaron's record 755.

By the 2002 outdoor season, Jones had separated from Hunter and found a new partner in sprinter Tim Montgomery. In September of that year, Montgomery became the first man to run faster than Johnson, whose Seoul mark of 9.79 seconds had never been recognized as an official world record but had also never been bettered.

In the following year the duo attracted unwanted controversy when they were coached briefly by Francis, who had been banned for life from coaching Canadian athletes. Jones took the rest of the year off to have Montgomery's baby and in her absence Kelli White won the 100–200 metres double at the Paris world championships. Two years later both Montgomery and White had been banned after the U.S. Anti-Doping Agency produced sufficient evidence – the so-called non-analytical positives, based on circumstantial evidence rather than positive test results – to prove that they had taken a frightening variety of banned substances, including THG, supplied by BALCO.

The northern hemisphere summer of 2006 proved a triumph for the drugs testers and a disaster for the devotees of speed and endurance. Justin Gatlin, although he shared the world record of 9.77 seconds with Powell, was by common accord the fastest man in the world after winning the 2004 Athens Olympic 100 metres gold medal followed by the 100–200 metres double at the Helsinki world championships. But just as the world was savouring the prospect of a sprint rivalry to match that between Lewis and Johnson a generation earlier, Gatlin tested positive for excessive amounts of testosterone.

Within days, his fellow American Floyd Landis, winner of the world's most gruelling endurance race, the celebrated Tour de France, had also tested positive for testosterone.

OPPOSITE ABOVE Justin Gatlin of the U.S. celebrates after setting a 100 metres world record at the Qatar Super Grand Prix in Doha, with a time of 9.77 seconds. In July 2006 it was announced that Gatlin had tested positive for unusual amounts of the male hormone testosterone after a relay race in Kansas. 12 May 2006, Fadi Alassaad.

OPPOSITE BELOW Italian Marco Pantani (centre) rides among the pack during the sixth stage of the 83rd Giro d'Italia in 2000. One of the greatest climbers in the history of cycle racing, Pantani won both the Tour de France and the Giro d'Italia in 1998. But the following year he was disqualified from the Giro d'Italia after failing a random blood test. He was put on trial, accused of using the banned performance-enhancing drug erythropoietin (EPO). The trial collapsed but three years later Pantani was suspended for six months after a syringe containing insulin was found in his hotel room. He died of a cocaine overdose on 14 February 2004, leaving a note saying that years of police inquiries and judicial investigations had made him deeply depressed. 19 May 2000, Vincenzo Pinto.

## An irreconcilable dilemma?

The sport of cycling and in particular the Tour de France produced one of the trio of supreme male athletes who dominated the first half of the decade. Lance Armstrong returned to racing after recovering from testicular cancer which had spread to his lungs and brain. At one point he had been given less than a 40 percent chance of survival.

'There was one unforeseen benefit of cancer,' he wrote. 'It had completely reshaped my body. I now had a much sparer build. I was leaner in build and more balanced in spirit.' His reshaped body took Armstrong to seven successive Tour victories before he retired in 2005. In that time his only serious rivals as the most successful sportsman in the world were Woods and Schumacher.

Seven-times Tour de France winner Lance Armstrong of the U.S. cycles down a mountain during the 204.5-km (127-mile) 17th stage of the Tour. 22 July 2004, Stefano Rellandini.

The Tour de France is a remarkable event, devised in 1903 by Henri Desgrange, the editor of *L'Auto*, with the express purpose of selling more copies of his newspaper. Early impressions that the race was an exercise in organized sadism were reinforced when the remote mountain outreaches of the Pyrenees plus the French Alps were added to the three-week endurance race. By the time the French sports daily *L'Equipe*, the best publication of its type in the world, took over the race after World War Two it was a national institution.

Part of *L'Equipe*'s authority comes from its record in breaking doping stories, and in 2005 it devoted four pages to a story claiming Armstrong had tested positive for the blood-boosting drug erythropoietin (EPO) during his first win in 1999, the year before a test was formally introduced at the Sydney Olympics. Armstrong has never failed an official test, and responded by reiterating his consistent denial that he has ever taken performance-enhancing drugs.

The continued popularity of the Tour de France, despite doping scandals in the year before and the year after Armstrong's seven wins, shows that spectators may not necessarily care. But the sponsors, crucial to modern sport, need their products to be associated with glowing health and clean-cut performers, not a sordid trail of needles and vials.

This possibly irreconcilable dilemma is essentially commercial, with the difference between a gold medal and fourth place measured not merely in time or distance. It is also the difference between receiving appearance money and sponsorship worth millions of dollars or

> Sponsors, crucial to modern sport, need their products to be associated with glowing health and clean-cut performers, not a sordid trail of needles and vials.

remaining among the also-rans struggling to earn as much as they can before their bodies begin to betray them at an age when their counterparts in other fields are just starting to make their way in the world.

## Style and substance

Enormous payrolls do not automatically buy success. The New York Yankees shell out around $200 million a year to their players but have not won the baseball World Series since 2000. English Premier League soccer club Chelsea, bought by Russian oil billionaire Roman Abramovich in 2003 for an estimated 140 million pounds ($233 million), have been more successful, with consecutive titles in 2005 and 2006, although they do not have to endure the uncertainty of post-season playoffs.

Much of the money now available to the elite comes from shoe companies, which have been associated with athletes since Adolf

Dassler, the son of a German cobbler, invented a spiked shoe for track athletes in the 1920s. With his brother Rudolph he set up Adidas, which supplied the footwear for Owens in Berlin and also for Ali and Joe Frazier when they fought for the world heavyweight title in 1971. In the following year Adidas was named as the official sponsor for the Munich Olympics.

Twenty years later the American shoe company Nike were pre-eminent, signing Jordan then Woods and also a long-haired tennis player from Las Vegas called Andre Agassi.

To the purists, Agassi's appearance in a Nike advertisement proclaiming 'Image is everything' confirmed style had finally eclipsed substance. The purists were wrong. After making his breakthrough

Outside Paris the Swiss is already a master of his sport. In 2004 he became the first man since Swede Mats Wilander in 1988 to win three of the four grand slam titles, a feat he repeated in 2006, losing to Nadal in Paris after breezing through the first set.

Federer possesses a fantastic variety of shots, speed and imagination, and in full flow his mastery evokes comparisons with Woods. The pair drank champagne together after the 2006 U.S. Open final and afterward Federer said: 'He knows what it is like when you have the feeling that just nothing is going to go wrong.'

Comparisons across the range of sports, with their differing technical demands, are tempting but pointless. Armstrong was supreme on a bike, Schumacher peerless in a Formula One car.

Tiger Woods of the U.S. blasts out of a bunker on the 13th hole during second-round play of the 2005 PGA Championship at Baltusrol Golf Club in Springfield, New Jersey. 12 August 2005, Kevin Lamarque.

Switzerland's Roger Federer hits a shot during the men's singles final against Chile's Fernando González at the Australian Open tennis tournament in Melbourne. 28 January 2007, David Gray.

in 1992 by winning the Wimbledon singles title on grass, a surface theoretically unsuited to his counter-punching style, Agassi worked at his game with puritanical zeal. He shaved off what remained of his once flowing blond hair, married the German women's grand slam champion Steffi Graf, and by the time he retired in 2006 was one of only five men to have won each of the grand slam singles titles.

For much of his career he duelled with another American and even greater player, the supreme serve-and-volleyer Pete Sampras, who retired in 2002 with a record 14 grand slam tournament victories, including seven at Wimbledon, five at the U.S. Open and two in Melbourne, Australia. His only weak point was the clay courts at Roland Garros, home of the French Open, a surface which initially thwarted his lineal successor Roger Federer.

Woods and Federer are the best in their chosen sports – one day they may be the best ever. The entertainment they and their contemporaries continue to provide is incomparable.

John Mehaffey

# Sporting Glory

Courage / Talent / Drama / Triumph

Yuliya Nesterenko of Belarus runs to victory in the women's 100 metres
at the Athens Olympics. 21 August 2004. Shaun Best

## JUMP!

ABOVE German striker Miroslav Klose turns a somersault after scoring against Ecuador in Berlin in the 2006 World Cup. Klose scored five goals from seven matches to win the Golden Shoe award as the tournament's top scorer. It was the lowest winning tally in a World Cup since 1962. He scored two goals against Costa Rica, two against Ecuador and a header in the quarter-final against Argentina, bringing his total tally in World Cups to 10. 20 June 2006. Shaun Best

RIGHT Chelsea fans applaud Frank Lampard as he celebrates with team mate Damien Duff after scoring a second goal in a Premier League match against Aston Villa at Stamford Bridge in London. Lampard, a powerful midfielder with a savage shot from long range, was a key member of Chelsea's 2005 and 2006 Premiership winning sides. He was runner-up in the 2005 European and world player of the year awards but had a disappointing 2006 World Cup, where he failed to reproduce his club form for England. 24 September 2005. Dylan Martinez

## THE LINE-UP

LEFT Italy captain Fabio Cannavaro challenges for the ball Ghana's Richard Kingston (third left) and Michael Essien (second left) during their 2006 World Cup group match in Hanover. Awaiting the outcome are Ghana's Eric Addo (centre) and Samuel Osei Kuffour (second right), and Italy's Daniele De Rossi (third right) and Alberto Gilardino (far right). Italy won 2–0 with Andrea Pirlo scoring in the 40th minute and substitute Vincenzo Iaquinta sealing victory in the 83rd. Italy went on to win their fourth World Cup. 12 June 2006. Shaun Best

BELOW Argentine players (left to right) Ariel Ortega, Javier Zanetti, Gabriel Batistuta, Juan Verón and Diego Simeone protect themselves against a Jay Jay Okocha free kick in their 2002 World Cup group F match against Nigeria in Ibaraki, Japan. The Argentines, among the pre-tournament favourites, edged Nigeria 1–0 but then lost by a similar margin to England after a David Beckham penalty and were eliminated after a 1–1 draw with Sweden. 2 June 2002. Ruben Sprich

## STRIKER

BELOW Italian striker Francesco Totti in action during the 2006 World Cup semi-final against Germany. This consistently entertaining match between the eventual champions and the hosts, which went 90 minutes without a goal, exploded in extra time. The Italians hit the woodwork twice but still seemed set for penalties, a German speciality, until Fabio Grosso beat keeper Jens Lehmann with a minute to go and then Alessandro Del Piero chipped into the net with the last kick of the game. 4 July 2006. Kieran Doherty

## DEFENDER

OPPOSITE Tigres' goalkeeper Edgar Hernandez grimaces as he dives after the ball during a Mexican championship match against América at the Azteca stadium in Mexico City. The Tigres are one of the most popular teams in Mexico. 13 August 2006. Henry Romero

## WILKINSON'S WORLD CUP WINNER

England flyhalf Jonny Wilkinson strikes the drop goal that broke Australian hearts and took the rugby World Cup to the northern hemisphere for the first time. Both Wilkinson and England had struggled for form during the 2003 tournament in Australia until the rain-drenched semi-final against France. The final in Sydney was tied 17–17 in the final minute of extra time when Wilkinson, a natural left-footer, let fly with his right boot. 22 November 2003. Kieran Doherty

## RUGBY RAMPAGE

TOP New Zealand's All Blacks perform the haka before the rugby test against Italy in Rome. In 2006, the All Blacks upset rugby's authorities by including a throat-slitting gesture at the end of the haka. 13 November 2004. Tony Gentile

ABOVE Stephen Hoiles of the Waratahs receives a hand to his face from an Auckland Blues defender during a Super 14 rugby match at Aussie Stadium in Sydney. The Waratahs, who went on to reach the semi-finals, won 43–9. 24 March 2006. Will Burgess

TOP Bulls winger Bryan Habana dives over the line to score against Stormers during their Super 14 rugby union match at Newlands in Cape Town, South Africa. The Bulls went into the playoffs with a 43–10 win. 13 May 2006. Howard Burditt

ABOVE Trevor Woodman of England is tackled by Keven Mealamu and Carl Hayman of New Zealand in the second test at Eden Park, Auckland. The All Blacks won 36–12 to complete a 2–0 series win against the world champions. 19 June 2004. Andrew Budd

## FIELDS OF PLAY

LEFT New Orleans Saints fans cheer as their team takes the field to play the Atlanta Falcons in the first National Football League game at the Louisiana Superdome since Hurricane Katrina devastated the city. The Superdome, the largest fixed dome structure in the world, was used as an emergency shelter when the hurricane struck in August 2005. The Saints, who had spent the previous season on the road while the Superdome was restored, brought some much-needed relief to a crowd of around 70,000 with a 23–3 victory after a pre-game show by rock groups U2 and Green Day. 25 September 2006. Tami Chappell

BELOW A rainbow arcs over the pitch at an African Nations Cup qualifier in which Rwanda (in yellow) beat Liberia 3–2 in Monrovia. 8 October 2006. Christopher Herwig

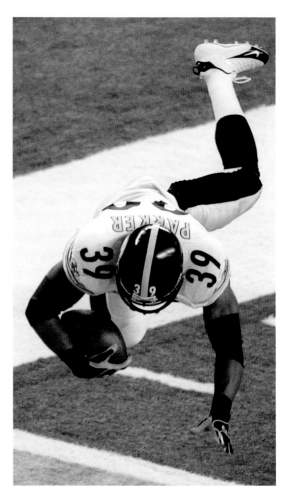

# GRIDIRON GREATS

OPPOSITE ABOVE LEFT  New Orleans Saints running back Reggie Bush (25) breaks a tackle by Atlanta Falcons Darrell Shropshire (71) during the second quarter of their NFL game in New Orleans at the newly restored Louisiana Superdome, 13 months after Hurricane Katrina had ravaged the city. 25 September 2006. Sean Gardner

OPPOSITE ABOVE RIGHT  Michigan defensive back Jashaad Gaines (29) keeps Notre Dame wide receiver David Grimes from making a catch during the first quarter of their college football game in South Bend, Indiana. 16 September 2006. John Gress

OPPOSITE BELOW LEFT  New England Patriots kicker Adam Vinatieri (4) kicks the ball to score the winning field goal in the dying seconds of the game against Carolina Panthers in the fourth quarter during Super Bowl XXXVIII in Houston. New England defeated Carolina 32–29. 1 February 2004. Richard Carson

OPPOSITE BELOW CENTRE  Indianapolis Colts quarterback Peyton Manning calls a play during the second quarter of the NFL's Super Bowl XLI football game against the Chicago Bears in Miami. The Colts won 29–17 to take their first NFL title since 1971, when they were based in Baltimore. 4 February 2007. Mike Blake

OPPOSITE BELOW RIGHT  Pittsburgh Steelers running back Willie Parker dives into the endzone to score a touchdown on a 75-yard run against the Seattle Seahawks in the third quarter of the NFL's Super Bowl XL in Detroit. It was the longest touchdown run from scrimmage in title game history. 5 February 2006. Rebecca Cook

RIGHT  Seattle Seahawks wide receiver D.J. Hackett fails to reach an incomplete pass in the endzone from quarterback Matt Hasselbeck as he is guarded by Pittsburgh Steelers cornerback Bryant McFadden in the first quarter of the NFL Super Bowl XL in Detroit. Pittsburgh won 21–10 for a record-equalling fifth title. 5 February 2006. Lucy Nicholson

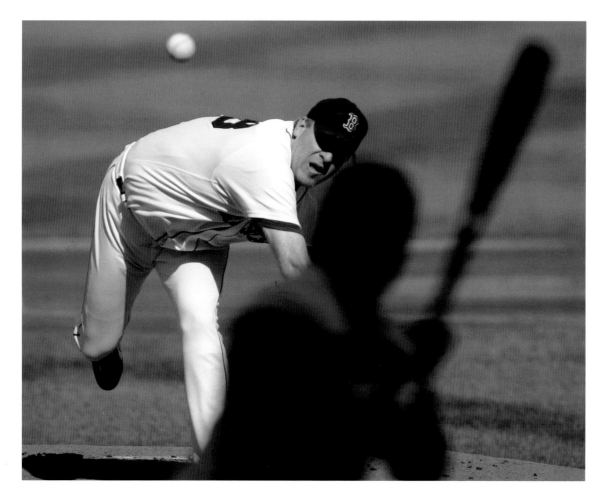

## DIAMOND HEROES

LEFT Curt Schilling of the Boston Red Sox pitches to New York Yankees batter Gary Sheffield during their game in Boston. The Red Sox won 10–1 to earn the American League wildcard playoff spot. 2 October 2005. Gary Hershorn

LEFT Boston Red Sox players celebrate after clinching their first World Series win since 1918 with victory over the St Louis Cardinals, in St Louis. 27 October 2004. Mike Blake

RIGHT Detroit Tigers' Craig Monroe breaks his bat as he grounds out in the third inning against the St Louis Cardinals during Game One in Major League Baseball's 2006 World Series in Detroit. The Cardinals won their first MLB title in 24 years with a Game Five victory. 21 October 2006. Rebecca Cook

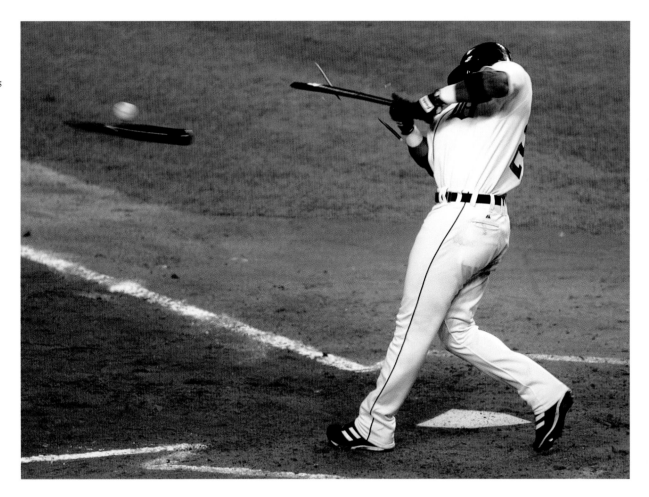

RIGHT Seattle Mariners' Ichiro Suzuki tips his cap to the crowd as he leaves the field for the season, in the eighth inning against the Texas Rangers, in Seattle. Ichiro finished the season with 262 base hits, surpassing the 84-year-old record of 257 held by George Sisler of the St Louis Browns. 3 October 2004. Andy Clark

## PLAYING TO THE CROWD

Andre Agassi stretches into his serve during the
final match of his professional career against
Benjamin Becker at the 2006 U.S. Open. Agassi,
36, who needed four injections during the week to
relieve the pain in his aching back, lost in four sets
to the 112th-ranked German qualifier in an emotional
farewell to Flushing Meadow, New York. 'I don't
take pride in my accomplishments,' the eight-times
grand slam winner told the crowd. 'I take pride in the
striving.' 3 September 2006. Mike Segar

## EYE ON THE BALL

OPPOSITE Andy Roddick serves during his quarter-final against Russia's Nikolay Davydenko at the Australian Open in Melbourne. The American was leading 6–3 7–5 4–1 when Davydenko retired injured. Roddick lost in the last four to Lleyton Hewitt. 26 January 2005. David Gray

TOP Marat Safin lunges for a backhand as he helps Russia to win the Davis Cup men's team trophy for the first time with a 3–2 victory over France in the Paris final. 29 November 2002. Philippe Wojazer

ABOVE Australia's Lleyton Hewitt returns the ball to American Justin Gimelstob during his straight-sets win in the third round at the Wimbledon championships in London. Hewitt lost to eventual champion Roger Federer in the last four. 24 June 2005. Dylan Martinez

TOP Gustavo Kuerten of Brazil stretches for a return from Sjeng Schalken of the Netherlands in the fourth round of the U.S. Open in Flushing Meadow, New York. Kuerten lost 3–6 6–7 7–6 6–7. 3 September 2002. Shaun Best

ABOVE French Open champion Rafael Nadal hits his way to victory over Italy's Filippo Volandri in a playoff in Santander to put Spain into the 2006 Davis Cup world group with a 4–1 win. 24 September 2006. Victor Fraile

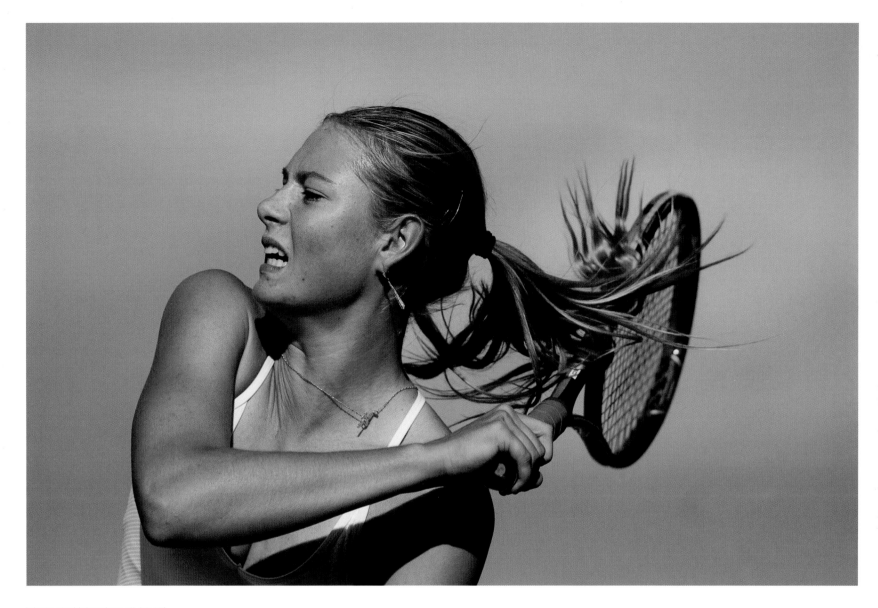

## TOP OF THEIR GAME

OPPOSITE ABOVE LEFT Lindsay Davenport hits a forehand to Maria Sharapova of Russia during the WTA Tour Championships in Los Angeles. The American, who won three grand slam titles, quit at the end of 2006 to have a baby. 10 November 2005. Lucy Nicholson

OPPOSITE ABOVE CENTRE Justine Henin serves to Amélie Mauresmo of France during the Australian Open final in Melbourne before she was forced to retire with a stomach upset. The Belgian reached the final of all four grand slam events in 2006. 28 January 2006. Tim Wimborne

OPPOSITE ABOVE RIGHT Amélie Mauresmo returns the ball en route to beating Justine Henin in the round-robin stage of the WTA Championships in Madrid. Henin got her revenge two days later when she defeated Mauresmo in the final. 10 November 2006. Andrea Comas

OPPOSITE BELOW Belgium's Kim Clijsters stretches to return the ball to Lindsay Davenport during the fourth round at Wimbledon. Clijsters, who went on to win the U.S. Open the same year, announced plans to retire at the end of 2007. 27 June 2005. Dylan Martinez

THIS PAGE In 2004, at the age of 17, Maria Sharapova became the third youngest champion in Wimbledon's 120-year history and the first 13th seed to win the title. The Russian beat Serena Williams in the final. 24 June 2004. Tony O'Brien

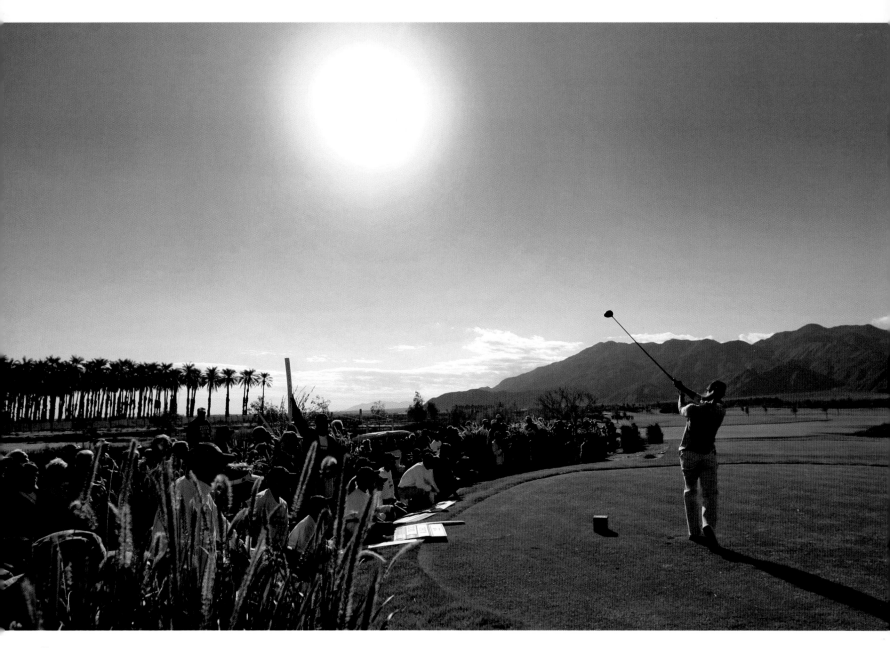

## SÖRENSTAM'S SWING

ABOVE Swede Annika Sörenstam tees off on the 13th hole during the second round of the 2004 LG Skins Game at La Quinta, California. Skins is a golf betting game with money placed on each hole. The winner of the hole takes the money; if it is halved the money is carried over to the next hole. A player winning a hole is said to have won a 'skin'. Fred Couples won this game for the fifth time, taking 11 skins and earning a total $640,000. 28 November 2004. Lucy Nicholson

## RYDER CUP TRIUMPH

OPPOSITE Spectators watch as Darren Clarke plays a practice drive before the 2006 Ryder Cup at the K Club in Ireland. The Northern Irishman made himself available for the biennial team golf match against the United States as a wildcard selection for captain Ian Woosnam just three weeks after his wife Heather died following a long battle against cancer. 'Every single one of us has dedicated this to Heather and Darren,' said Woosnam after Europe triumphed for a third consecutive time. 19 September 2006. Kieran Doherty

## BEACH SHOT

Fijian Vijay Singh is silhouetted against Carmel Bay as he hits his approach shot
on the ninth fairway at Pebble Beach golf links during the final round of 2004
of the AT&T National Pro-Am. The tournament was originally known as the
Bing Crosby Pro-Am after the American crooner and keen golf fan. Singh
went on to win the tournament with a four-round total of 272, 16 under par.
8 February 2004. Robert Galbraith

## ON COURSE

BELOW Adam Scott of Australia hits from a bunker on the third day of practice for the 88th PGA Championship in Medinah, Illinois. Scott was tipped as a future world number one after winning the 2004 Players Championship aged 24. 16 August 2006. John Gress

BOTTOM Lee Westwood and Sergio Garcia check their shoes at the 34th Ryder Cup at the Belfry. Europe beat the U.S. in a contest that had been postponed for a year because of the September 11, 2001, attacks on the United States. 28 September 2002. Win McNamee

BELOW Ernie Els hits a shot on the sixth hole at the Singapore Open. The South African lost to Adam Scott in a three-hole playoff for the title after a tropical downpour had reduced the tournament to 54 holes. 7 September 2006. Vivek Prakash

BOTTOM Padraig Harrington pitches out of the rough during his final round at the Tour Players' Championship at Gut Kaden near Hamburg. In 2006, Harrington became the first Irishman in 17 years to win the European Order of Merit. 18 May 2003. Kai Pfaffenbach

## BOWLED OVER

TOP  Pakistan's Shoaib Akhtar bowls on the opening day of the second test against India in Lahore. India went on to win their maiden test series in Pakistan. Akhtar, the first bowler to be measured bowling at 160 kph (100 mph), is nicknamed the 'Rawalpindi Express.' 5 April 2004. Arko Datta

ABOVE  Chris Gayle of the West Indies celebrates his century against South Africa during their ICC Champions Trophy semi-final in Jaipur. West Indies lost to Australia in the final. 2 November 2006. Arko Datta

TOP  Australia wicketkeeper Adam Gilchrist dives for a catch during a World Cup pool match against England in Port Elizabeth, South Africa. Australia went on to beat India in the final. 2 March 2003. David Gray

ABOVE  New Zealand's Andre Adams is bowled by Pakistan's Shoaib Akhtar for five in the fifth one-day game at the Westpac Stadium in Wellington. 17 January 2004. Anthony Phelps

## BOUNDARY BOUND

Australia captain Ricky Ponting crashes the ball under a leaping Ian Bell at silly point while England wicketkeeper Geraint Jones watches intently on the third day of the fourth test of the 2005 Ashes series at Trent Bridge in Nottingham. England won an exciting match in a consistently enthralling series to go 2–1 up in the five-match series. They then drew at The Oval in London to win a series against their oldest rivals for the first time in 18 years. 27 August 2005. Darren Staples

## ABOVE THE RIM

ABOVE Milwaukee Bucks forward Joe Smith (8) attempts a shot that fails with Philadelphia 76ers forward Chris Webber and centre Steven Hunter (45) providing a tight defence in the first quarter of NBA action at the Bradley Center in Milwaukee. 23 November 2005. Allen Fredrickson

ABOVE RIGHT Los Angeles Clippers Elton Brand (right) fights for a rebound with Denver Nuggets Marcus Camby during game 1 of the NBA Western Conference first round playoff series in Los Angeles. 22 April 2006. Lucy Nicholson

OPPOSITE ABOVE LEFT Jason Kidd of the New Jersey Nets defends against Phoenix Suns guard Steve Nash in the third quarter of their NBA game in East Rutherford, New Jersey. 27 March 2006. The Nets won 110–72. Jeff Zelevansky

OPPOSITE ABOVE RIGHT Phoenix Suns forward Quentin Richardson watches the ball hang on the rim during first-half action against San Antonio Spurs in Game 4 of the 2005 NBA Western Conference Finals in San Antonio, Texas. 30 May 2005. Lucy Nicholson

OPPOSITE BELOW LEFT LeBron James (centre) of the U.S. tries to grab a rebound past Greece's Dimitris Diamantidis (left) and Mihalis Kakiouzis in their semi-final at the world championships in Saitama, Japan. Greece upset the Americans 101–95 and finished with the silver medal, behind Spain. 1 September 2006. Lucy Nicholson

OPPOSITE BELOW RIGHT Angola's Joaquim Gomes goes for a reverse lay-up watched by New Zealand's Craig Bradshaw (left) and Pero Cameron during a world championship first-round game in Hiroshima. African champions Angola beat New Zealand, inevitably known as the Tall Blacks, 95–73. 21 August 2006. Adrees Latif

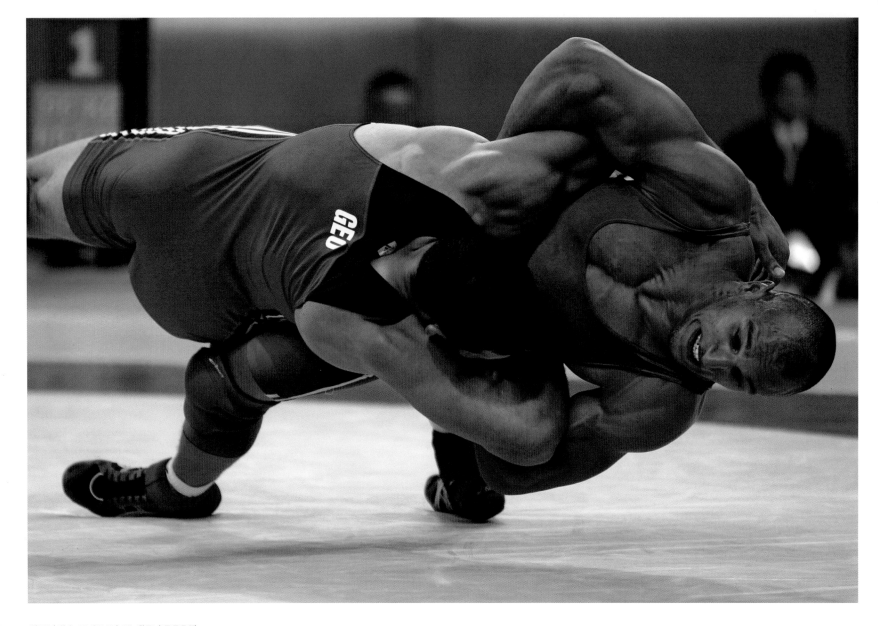

## GRECO-ROMAN GRAPPLE

Egypt's Karam Ibrahim (right) grapples with Georgia's Ramaz Nozadze on his way
to a gold medal in the men's Greco-Roman 96 kgs competition at the 2004 Athens
Olympics. The flamboyant Ibrahim, a women's underwear manufacturer from
Alexandria, won Egypt's first Olympic gold medal since 1948. He then raised a
finger in triumph, kissed the mat and flipped his exultant coach to the floor before
performing a perfect somersault. 26 August 2004. Yves Herman

## WRESTLEMANIA!

Canadian Chris Benoit looks to the referee as Chavo Guerrero pins him to the floor during a World Wrestling Entertainment show in Madrid. Professional wrestling, compared to its Olympic cousins Greco-Roman and freestyle, is pure spectacle with such rules as there are designed to be entirely secondary to entertainment. 6 December 2006. Susana Vera

## OUT FOR THE COUNT

Thailand bantamweight Saensak Singmanasak lies in the ring after he was knocked out by Australia's Emmett Gazzard in a World Boxing Foundation fight on the night that world championship boxing returned to Singapore after a 17-year absence. The WBF, a recent addition to the many boxing governing bodies who each have their own version of the world titles, was founded by Mick Croucher in Australia in 2003. Croucher, whose great-grandfather was a bare-knuckle fighter in England, is a former professional light-middleweight. 25 November 2006. Vivek Prakash

## PUNCH POWER

TOP  Oscar de la Hoya, one of the best and most glamorous boxers at the turn of the 21st century, is instructed by trainer Floyd Mayweather Snr during his title fight with Shane Mosley. De la Hoya, the son of Mexican immigrants who was brought up in Los Angeles, won a gold medal at the 1992 Barcelona Olympics and after turning professional won world titles in six different divisions. He met his match in Mosley, who outpointed him twice over 12 rounds, winning their Las Vegas fight for the World Boxing Council and World Boxing Association super-welterweight titles. 13 September 2003. R. Marsh Starks

ABOVE  Ricky Hatton (left) of England hits World Boxing Association welterweight champion Luis Collazo of the U.S. in the eleventh round in Boston. Hatton won on a unanimous decision. 13 May 2006. Brian Snyder

TOP  Dariusz 'Tiger' Michalczewski of Poland takes a punch from Fabrice Tiozzo of France during their World Boxing Association light heavyweight fight in Hamburg. Tiozzo retained his title with a sixth-round technical knockout. 26 February 2005. Christian Charisius

ABOVE  Vitali Klitschko of Ukraine stands over Britain's Danny Williams after knocking him down during his defence of the World Boxing Council heavyweight title in Las Vegas. 11 December 2004. Mike Blake

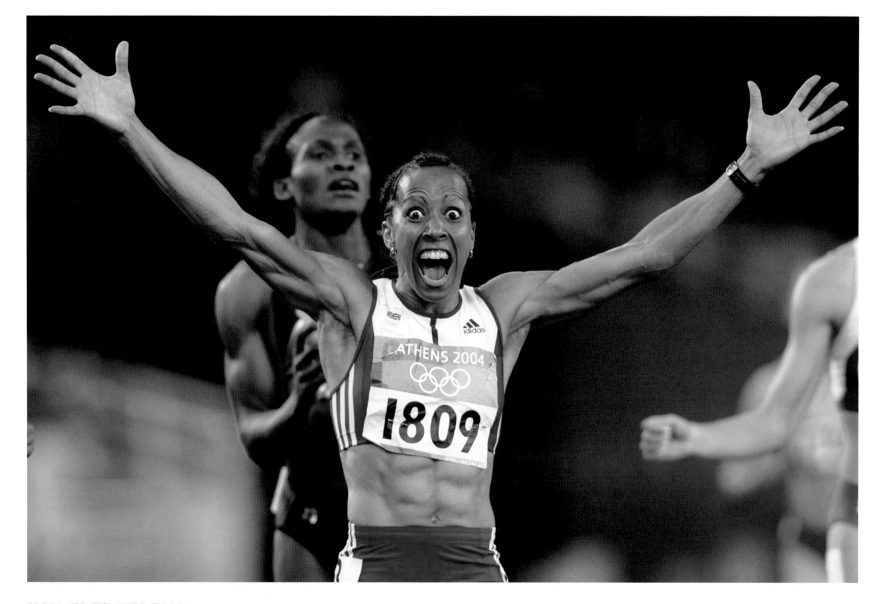

## HOLMES STRIKES GOLD

Years of disappointment and injury are forgotten as Britain's Kelly Holmes wins
the women's 800 metres final at the 2004 Athens Olympics. Holmes beat her
training partner Maria Mutola, who had dominated the event for a decade. She went
on to complete an 800–1,500 double, a feat which had previously been beyond any
Briton, including twice Olympic 1,500 metres champion Sebastian Coe who won
800 metres silver medals at the 1980 Moscow and 1984 Los Angeles Games.
23 August 2004. Gary Hershorn

## KNOCKOUT AT LAST

World Boxing Organization junior welterweight champion Miguel Cotto rejoices after repulsing an unexpectedly torrid challenge from Colombian Ricardo Torres in Atlantic City, New Jersey. Cotto felled the challenger four times but each time Torres came back to rock the champion, including a right hand to the chin which had the Puerto Rican reeling. In the seventh round, Cotto finally prevailed, pounding Torres around the head and body and scoring a knockout with a left hook to the Colombian's face. 24 September 2005. Tim Shaffer

## DOWN AND OUT

TOP U.S. sprinter Jon Drummond lies on the track in protest after he was disqualified in the second round of the 100 metres at the 2003 Paris world athletics championships. Competition was suspended for nearly an hour as officials tried to get Drummond to leave the track. The former U.S. champion, who alternately lay down, beat his chest and burst into tears, was finally persuaded to leave. He later withdrew from the 4x100 metres relay squad and said: 'I honestly believe I did not false start. My spirit is broken because it has always been my desire to provide entertainment for the fans.' 24 August 2003. Yannis Behrakis

ABOVE Portugal striker Hélder Postiga crouches on the pitch in dejection after his team lose 1–0 to France in a World Cup semi-final in Munich. 5 July 2006. Alessandro Bianchi

TOP Jesus Hernandez of Spain sits injured after a crash during the 16th stage of the Tour of Spain cycling race between Almería and Calar Alto. 12 September 2006. Victor Fraile

ABOVE Los Angeles Lakers' Derek Fisher lies on the floor after being knocked down during Game Two against the Minnesota Timberwolves in the Western Conference Finals in Minneapolis. 23 May 2004. John Gress

# THE LIMITS OF ENDURANCE

A runner bites his arm in pain as he receives first aid after collapsing at the finish line in the 2005 Nairobi marathon. The race was won by Samson Barmao in two hours 12 minutes 15 seconds. The Nairobi marathon, first held in 2003, is part of a four-stage race including the Hong Kong, Mumbai and Singapore marathons. In 2006, London, New York City, Boston, Chicago and Berlin combined to form a marathon majors grand slam circuit with the overall men's and women's winners gathering half a million dollars each. Runners score points in each race they contest over a two-year period. 23 October 2005. Radu Sigheti

## WAITING FOR THE OFF

TOP New Zealand's All Blacks gather before their rugby test against Italy in Rome. After a routine 59–10 defeat of Italy, the All Blacks had a record five-try 45–6 defeat of Six Nations champions France two weeks later. 13 November 2004. Alessandro Bianchi

ABOVE Riders are reflected in Francisco Mancebo's sunglasses before the start of the 16th stage of the 2004 Tour of Spain from Olivenza to Cáceres. The Tour of Spain is one of the world's big three cycling endurance races along with the Tour de France and the Giro d'Italia. 21 September 2004. Victor Fraile

TOP England sprinter Darren Campbell waits to start his men's 200 metres heat at the Commonwealth Games in Melbourne. He was later disqualified for running outside his lane. 22 March 2006. David Gray

ABOVE Athletes wait for the start of the 100 metres event of the men's decathlon at the European athletics championships in Gothenburg. 10 August 2006. Kai Pfaffenbach

OPPOSITE St Louis Cardinals pitcher Anthony Reyes listens to the playing of 'God Bless America' during Game One of Major League Baseball's World Series against the Detroit Tigers in Detroit. The Cardinals won the series 4–1. 21 October 2006. Brian Snyder

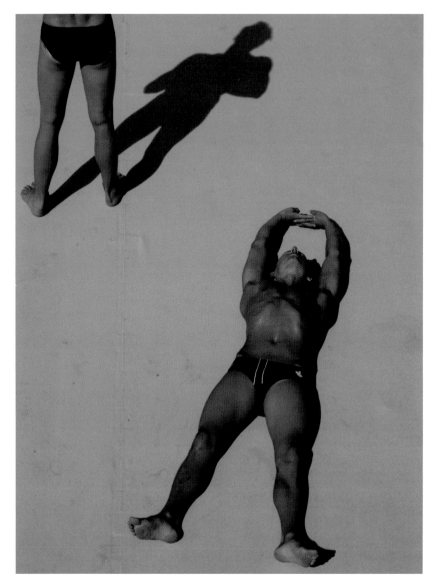

## LIMBERING UP

OPPOSITE TOP LEFT A surfer stretches before the qualifying series of the Pantin Classic Pro World championships at Pantin Beach in Ferrol, northern Spain. 7 September 2006. Miguel Vidal

OPPOSITE TOP RIGHT Spain's coach Luis Aragonés encourages players during a training session in Cádiz before their friendly soccer match against Romania. 14 November 2006. Marcelo del Pozo

OPPOSITE CENTRE LEFT Scotland's Dougie Hall (centre) and fellow players practise scrummaging in training at Murrayfield Stadium in Edinburgh, Scotland, before the test against Romania. 6 November 2006. David Moir

OPPOSITE CENTRE RIGHT Sarah Drury of the United States stretches during a practice session for the FIVB women's volleyball world championships in Kobe, western Japan. 2 November 2006. Toru Hanai

OPPOSITE BELOW LEFT An athlete trains for the discus by throwing bicycle tyres in Nauru, the world's smallest republic. 13 September 2001. Mark Baker

OPPOSITE BELOW RIGHT Australian cricketers warm up at a training session at the WACA Ground in Perth, three days before the third Ashes test against England. 11 December 2006. David Gray

THIS PAGE ABOVE Canadian swimmer Morgan Knabe rests on the swimming pool deck next to team mate Scott Dickens during a morning training session at the Olympic aquatic centre ahead of the 2004 Athens Games. 11 August 2004. David Gray

THIS PAGE BELOW France's short track speed skating team begin free practice for the Short Track World Cup and Olympic qualifying competition in Bormio, northern Italy. 10 November 2005. Max Rossi

## RETURN TO ATHENS

LEFT An athlete passes by a statue on the final lap of the men's marathon, the last event of the 2004 Olympic Games. Runners followed the approximate route covered by Spiridon Louis at the first modern Games in 1896. That in turn supposedly traced the course taken in 490 BC by Phidippides from the battlefield at Marathon to Athens, where he announced the Greek victory over Persia. The athletes finished in the Panathinaiko stadium, the ancient stadium that was fully rebuilt to stage the athletics in 1896. 29 August 2004. Damir Sagolj

BELOW Gianna Angelopoulos, president of the 2004 Athens Olympics organizing committee, holds a torch lit with the Olympic flame in the Panathinaiko stadium. The Olympic torch relay, carrying a flame lit by the rays of the sun at the site of Ancient Olympia, was introduced at the 1936 Berlin Olympics. The flame is borne by a series of relay runners to the host city where it is used to light the cauldron at the opening ceremony. 31 March 2004. Yannis Behrakis

## ON YOUR MARKS

Jamaican Asafa Powell bounds in the blocks before the start of the 2006
Commonwealth Games 100 metres final in Melbourne. Nigeria's Deji Aliu is in
lane eight with Jacey Harper of Trinidad and Tobago in seven. World record holder
Powell won his first major title since his disqualification in the second round at the
2003 Paris world championships and fifth place in the final of the 2004 Athens
Olympics. He missed the 2005 Helsinki world championships through injury.
20 March 2006. Andy Clark

## PULLING AHEAD

Ethiopian Kenenisa Bekele strides away from the field in a 3,000 metres race at the Zurich golden league meeting, the richest and most prestigious of the big European meetings. Bekele won the world long and short cross country titles five times before announcing in 2006 that he would concentrate on the track. He was already the world 5,000 and 10,000 metres record holder as well as the world and Olympic gold medallist in the longer event. 19 August 2005. Sebastian Derungs

## LUNGE FOR THE LINE

Chinese Liu Xiang equals the world 110 metres hurdles record of 12.91 seconds in the 2004 Athens Olympics final. In 2006 Lui broke the record he had held jointly with Britain's Colin Jackson when he clocked 12.88 at the Lausanne grand prix. 'I always thought it was impossible to get close to Jackson's world record,' he said. 'But I levelled it first and then broke it. Maybe it can stand until I become a grandfather.' 27 August 2004. Gary Hershorn

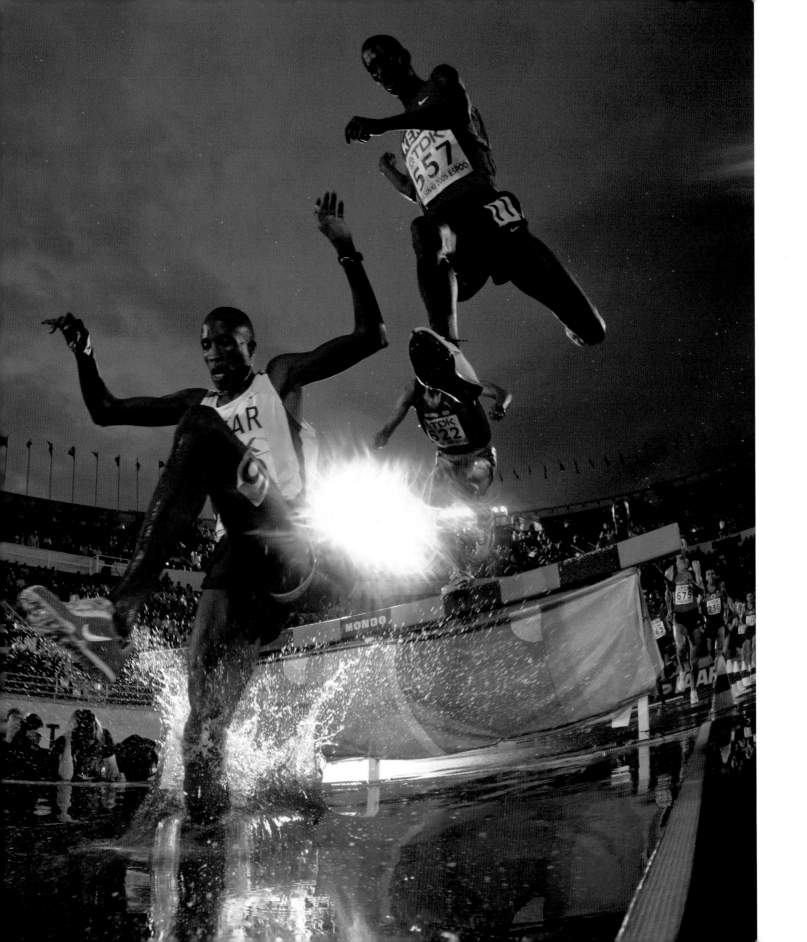

## MAKING A SPLASH

OPPOSITE Saif Saaeed Shaheen of Qatar splashes through the water barrier on his way to the gold medal ahead of Olympic champion Ezekiel Kemboi in the final of the 3,000 metres steeplechase at the 2005 Helsinki world championships. Shaheen, formerly known as Stephen Cherono in his native Kenya, is the highest profile track and field athlete to change nationality for economic reasons. He was granted Qatari citizenship in 2003 and nine days later set an Asian steeplechase record. He won Qatar's first world championships track and field medal in the same year when he finished first at the Paris world championships. Shaheen did not compete at the 2004 Athens Olympics after Kenya refused to agree for the International Olympic Committee's qualification rules to be waived. In his absence Kemboi led a Kenyan clean sweep. 9 August 2005. Kai Pfaffenbach

BELOW Austria's Günther Weidlinger lands in the water during the 3,000 metres steeplechase semi-final at the European athletics championships in Gothenburg. 9 August 2006. Ruben Sprich

## ATHLETE FROM HEAD TO TOE

ABOVE Bahrain's Ruqaya Al-Ghasara gives thanks after winning the 200 metres gold medal at the 2006 Asian Games in Doha. The 24-year-old wore a hijab, a scarf which covers the hair and neck, along with leggings and long sleeves. Only her face and hands were exposed. 'Wearing conservative clothes has encouraged me,' she said. 'Wearing a veil proves that Muslim women face no obstacles. This is a glory to all Muslim women.' 11 December 2006. Jerry Lampen

RIGHT South Africa's Dina Phakula risks injury as she runs barefoot in the women's 1,500 metres heats at the 2006 Melbourne Commonwealth Games. Ethiopia's Abebe Bikila is the most famous barefoot runner, winning the men's marathon at the 1960 Rome Olympics. He retained the title four years later in Tokyo wearing running shoes. South African Zola Budd, who was controversially granted British citizenship shortly before the 1984 Los Angeles Games, also ran barefoot. 20 March 2006. Andy Clark

## CITIUS, ALTIUS, FORTIUS

TOP Czech Roman Šebrle competes in the long jump on his way to winning the decathlon gold at the 2004 Athens Olympics. In 2001, Šebrle became the first man to break 9,000 points in the 10-event competition. 23 August 2004. Ruben Sprich

ABOVE Jan Železny wins javelin bronze at the 2006 Gothenburg European championships in his last international appearance before he announced his retirement. The Czech won three Olympic and three world titles and set five world records. 9 August 2006. Kai Pfaffenbach

TOP Shot putter Reese Hoffa throws during the U.S. Olympic trials in Sacramento. Hoffa placed second to earn a spot on the team for the Athens Olympics, where he failed to make the cut for the final. 10 July 2004. Jason Reed

ABOVE Lithuania's Virgilijus Alekna throws the discus to win the gold medal at the European athletics championships in Gothenburg. It was the double world and Olympic champion's 18th win in as many competitions in a year. 12 August 2006. Kai Pfaffenbach

Dwight Phillips soars through the air during the men's long jump competition at the 2004 U.S. Olympic trials in Sacramento. Phillips completed a rare treble at the Athens Olympics the following month. The man dubbed Spiderman at the 2003 Paris world championships because of his distinctive blue-and-white body suit won the Olympic long jump gold comfortably with a leap of 8.59 metres after winning both the world indoor and outdoor titles. 11 July 2004. Jason Reed

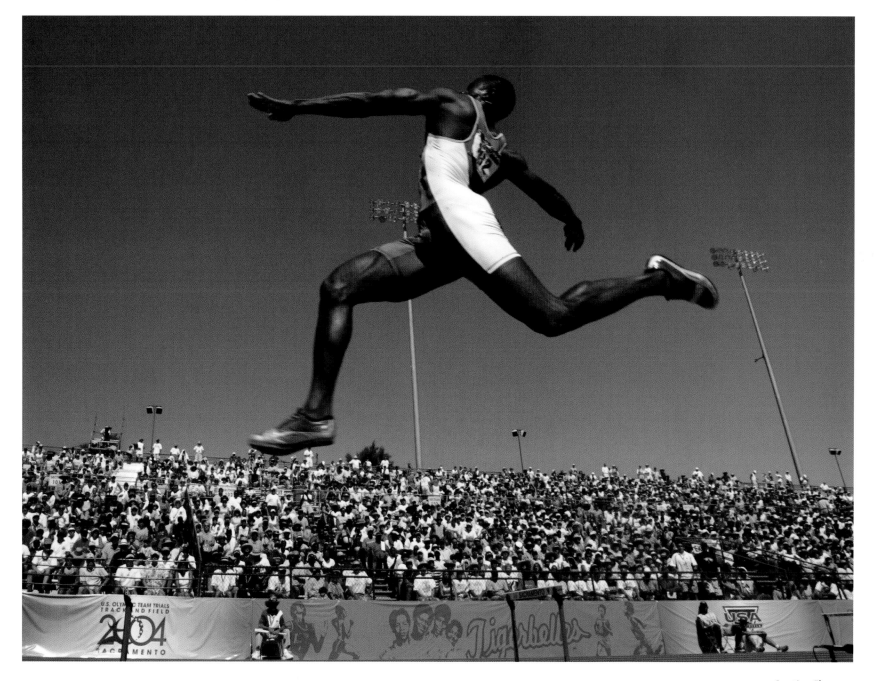

## RAISING THE BAR

Russian pole vaulter Yelena Isinbayeva sets her second world record in the space of a week, clearing 4.90 metres at London's Crystal Palace. A year later, at the same venue, she became the first woman to break the five-metres barrier. Isinbayeva has been in a class of her own since taking up pole vaulting after training as a gymnast. She set world records at the 2004 Athens Olympics and at the Helsinki world championships the following year. 30 July 2004. Brandon Malone

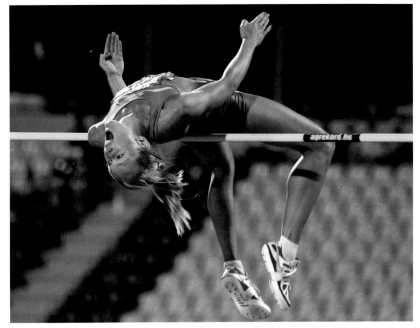

TOP Sweden's Olympic and world heptathlon champion Carolina Klüft (third from right), seen here in a 200 metres heat on the first day of her event, added a second European title on a day of high emotion in front of her home fans in Gothenburg. 7 August 2006. Phil Noble

ABOVE Russia's Tatyana Lebedeva, the Olympic long jump champion, switched to triple jump in Gothenburg to win a European gold medal. 9 August 2006. Kai Pfaffenbach

TOP World record holder Tatyana Lysenko of Russia competes in the women's hammer throw at the European athletics championships in Gothenburg, where she won gold with a throw of 76.67 metres. 8 August 2006. Kai Pfaffenbach

ABOVE Kajsa Bergqvist wins the women's high jump event at the IAAF Super Grand Prix in Doha. The Swede had become world outdoor champion the previous year after missing the Athens Olympics through injury. 12 May 2006. Fadi Alassaad

## HEADSTRONG

Japan's Hisashi Mizutori dismounts from the parallel bars at the 2005 world gymnastics championships in Melbourne. Mizutori finished second to team mate Hiroyuki Tomita, who became the first Japanese to win the all-around title since Shigeru Kasamatsu 31 years earlier. Japan is one of the traditional powerhouses of men's artistic gymnastics, winning every Olympic team title from 1960 through 1976. They won again at the 2004 Athens Games, with both Tomita and Mizutori on the team. 24 November 2005. Tim Wimborne

## FEET FIRST

Venezuela's Keisa Monterola wins bronze in the women's pole vault at the 2006 Central American and Caribbean Games in Caragena, Colombia. The women's pole vault was not introduced into major competition until 1997, when American Stacy Dragila won the world indoor title in Paris. Dragila was again successful when the first outdoor world competition was staged in Seville in 1999 and completed an historic treble with gold in the inaugural Olympic event at the 2000 Sydney Games. 25 July 2006. Daniel Munoz

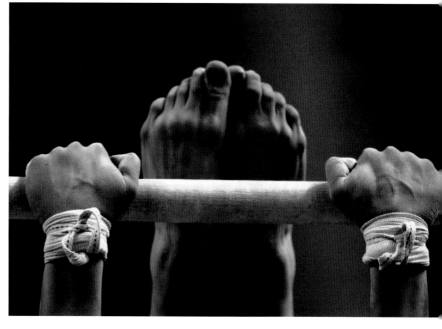

## A FIRM GRIP

TOP Daniel Popescu of Romania goes through his horizontal bar routine during an artistic gymnastics test event for the Olympic Games in Athens. Popescu went on to win a team bronze at the Olympics. 18 March 2004. Yannis Behrakis

ABOVE Romanian Marius Urzică presents his pommel horse routine at the 25th European artistic gymnastics championships in the Greek town of Patras. Urzică won the gold medal in the floor competition. 28 April 2002. Yannis Behrakis

TOP Sasha Artemev of the U.S. performs on the rings at the Athens Olympic test event. His compatriot Paul Hamm won the Olympic all-round gold in Athens in controversial circumstances after a mix-up over the scoring. 18 March 2004. Yannis Behrakis

ABOVE Soultana Kosaxi of host nation Greece hangs from the uneven bars during the test event for the 2004 Olympics in the Athens indoor arena. The arena hosted trampoline and basketball as well as gymnastics at the Games. 17 March 2004. Yannis Behrakis

TOP Canadian Melanie Banville performs on the asymmetric bars during the test event in the Athens Olympic indoor arena. 18 March 2004. Yannis Behrakis

ABOVE An Argentine gymnast chalks her hands before starting her asymmetric bars routine in the team final at the 14th Pan American Games in Santo Domingo in the Dominican Republic. Argentina failed to win a medal in the event, with the U.S. taking gold. 2 August 2003. Jason Reed

TOP Argentina's Maria Sol Poliandri competes in the asymmetric bars final at the South American Games in Buenos Aires. Argentina topped the medals table at the Games with 107 golds. 13 November 2006. Enrique Marcarian

ABOVE A gymnast balances on the beam in practice for the world championships in Aarhus, Denmark. Surprise winner Irina Krasnianska gave Ukraine their first gold medal in 11 years after an ankle injury ruled out Chinese favourite Zhang Nan. 12 October 2006. Max Rossi

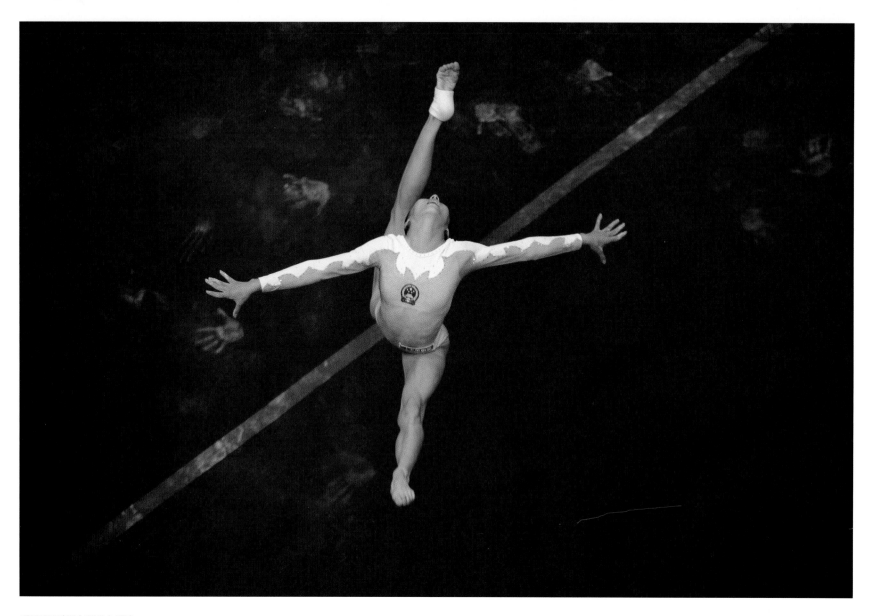

## CHINESE GRACE

China's Pang Panpan competes in the women's floor final at the 2006 Shanghai
World Cup. Pang won the beam title at the event and three months later helped
China to win the women's world team title in Aarhus, Denmark. It was one of a
record eight world gold medals for China, boosting the team's hopes of outclassing
all comers at the 2008 Beijing Olympics. 16 July 2006. Aly Song

## DUTCH STRENGTH

Dutchman Yuri van Gelder dismounts from the rings en route to winning the bronze medal at the 2006 world championships in Aarhus. Van Gelder went into the event as the defending champion but lost out to world championship debutant Chen Yibing of China. Van Gelder's sculpted biceps reveal the strength required to perform on this demanding apparatus. 20 October 2006. Max Rossi

## PARALLEL PERSPECTIVE

OPPOSITE Romania's Dorin Razvan Selariu competes on the rings at the same time as Switzerland's Niki Böschenstein performs on the floor during the 2006 world gymnastics championships in Aarhus, Denmark. After a judging fiasco at the 2004 Olympic Games, when noisy protests from the crowd forced judges to increase Russian Alexei Nemov's mark in the horizontal bar, the old 10 scale was scrapped and a new, open-ended scoring system made its global debut in Aarhus, though it puzzled many fans. 14 October 2006. Max Rossi

## BOUNCE BACK

ABOVE Olympic champion Yuri Nikitin from Ukraine (left) and bronze medallist Henrik Stehlik of Germany perform on the trampoline during a gymnastics exhibition at the 2004 Athens Olympics. The first Olympic men's trampoline champion was 30-year-old Russian Alexandre Moskalenko who decided to come out of retirement when the sport was introduced at the 2000 Sydney Olympics. The former world champion had to lose 24 kg (53 lb) to get back into shape but won easily. 24 August 2004. Kim Kyung-Hoon

## TOUCHÉ

ABOVE Russia (left) take on Germany in the women's team epee final at the 2004 Athens Olympics on their way to retaining the title. Olympic fencing evolved from 16th-century duelling with the epee derived from the rapier. The other two weapons are the foil and the sabre. The epee is the heaviest of the three implements and the entire body is a target. Contacts with the opponent are recorded electronically with lights appearing on a scoring box after a touch. 20 August 2004. Kieran Doherty

## SPEED BLUR

OPPOSITE Athletes start a 1,500 metres semi-final at the short track World Cup and Olympic speed skating qualifying competition in Bormio, Italy. Apolo Anton Ohno of the U.S. took first place ahead of South Korea's Ho-Suk Lee. Ohno gained unwelcome fame at the 2002 Salt Lake City Games when Kim Dong-sung was disqualified in the 1,500, giving the American the gold medal and attracting the wrath of thousands of South Koreans who sent hate mail and threatened to boycott U.S. goods. 11 November 2005. Max Rossi

## TO THE WATER

Some of the 1,800 contestants at the start of the swimming leg of the 2004 Nice triathlon. Competitors swim 4 km (2.5 miles), cycle 120 km (74.5 miles) then finish with a 30-km (18.6-mile) running race. The triathlon originated in France with a report in the French newspaper *L'Auto* in 1920 describing a competition featuring a 3-km race, a 12-km bike ride and a swim across a channel. It was introduced at the 2000 Sydney Olympics where local fans claimed the first champion, Canadian Simon Whitfield, as their own on the grounds that he had an Australian father. 26 September 2004. Eric Gaillard

## TO THE COURSE

Cross-country skiers at the start of the 2006 Engadin ski marathon in Maloja, Switzerland. About 12,000 competitors took part in the race over the Olympic marathon distance of 42.2 km (26.2 miles) between Maloja and S-chanf in the Engadin valley via the ski resort of St Moritz. The course includes 'Mattress Hill', a steep drop through a forest where organizers tie mattresses to tree trunks to protect skiers who crash. The annual race has been staged since 1969. 12 March 2006.
Sebastian Derungs

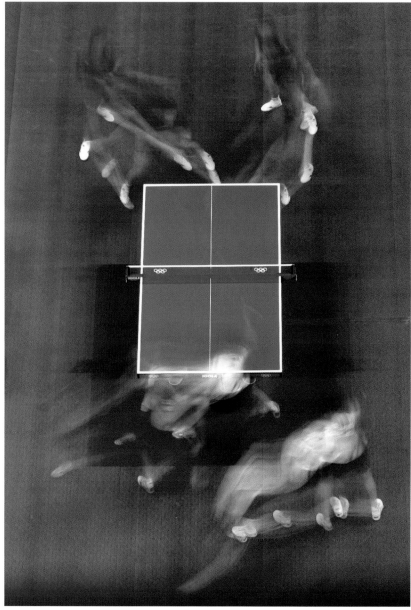

## TURNING THE TABLES

ABOVE Paey Fern Tan of Singapore serves to U.S. doubles pair Whitney Ping and Jasna Reed during the second round of the 2004 Athens Olympics table tennis tournament. Doubles is the most exciting form of table tennis, a sport originally devised as an indoor, miniaturized version of lawn tennis. It is immensely popular in east Asia, particularly in China, where the game was instrumental in bringing a rapprochement with the United States. In 1971 a U.S. team in Japan for the world championships was invited by the Chinese team to visit the republic. They were the first Americans to visit Beijing for 22 years, clearing the way for President Nixon's historic visit in the following year. 15 August 2004. Mike Hutchings

ABOVE China's Qi Chen and Lin Ma (top) play Hong Kong's Lai Chak Ko and Ching Li to win the men's doubles table tennis gold medal at the Athens Olympics. China won three of the four table tennis titles in Athens. 21 August 2004. Kieran Doherty

## SHUTTLECOCK SMASH

France's Hongyan Pi, the world number three and leading European badminton player, lines up a smash against Elena Nozdran of Ukraine during the second round of the 2005 world badminton championships in Anaheim, California. China has become the dominant force in world badminton. In 2006, Chinese players won four of the five golds at the Madrid world championships, the Thomas Cup men's team event for the sixth time and their fifth successive women's Uber Cup. 17 August 2005. Lucy Nicholson

## HANDS UP FOR VOLLEYBALL

Cuba team members' hands pictured above the net during the women's volleyball quarter-final against Italy at the 2004 Athens Olympics. Volleyball, a combination of basketball skills and tennis scoring, was given full Olympic status at the 1964 Tokyo Games. Cuba have dominated the women's game but after winning the Olympic gold three times in a row they lost to China in the semi-finals in Athens, gaining some consolation by beating Brazil in the third-place playoff. 24 August 2004.

Jorge Silva

BELOW Brazilian Jacqueline Carvalho on the attack as Caroline Wensink (right) and Alice Blom of the Netherlands attempt to block during a first-round match at the 2006 world championships in Kobe, Japan. Brazil were hot favourites but were surprisingly beaten 3–2 in the final by Russia, who won their first title since 1990. The Brazilian men fared better the following month, overwhelming Poland 3–0 to retain their world title. 3 November 2006. Toru Hanai

## PERFECTLY POISED

ABOVE  Beatrice Adelizzi of Italy captured during the preliminary of the free
solo routine at the 2006 European synchronized swimming championships in
Budapest. Synchronized swimming began in Canada in the 1920s then became
popular in the United States during the following decade. It was brought to the
screen by a former national swimming champion Esther Williams, whose 1944
film *Bathing Beauty* was the first of several musicals to include elaborate swimming
routines. 26 July 2006. Peter Andrews

RIGHT  Members of the Riverside Acquettes take the plunge for their programme at
the 2005 U.S. Open synchronized swimming championships in Poway, California.
Synchronized swimming was introduced at the 1984 Los Angeles Olympics and
although its detractors claim it is nothing more than water ballet, its original
description, it has always been popular. Contestants complete a technical and
free programme with points awarded for technical merit and artistic impression.
15 July 2005. Mike Blake

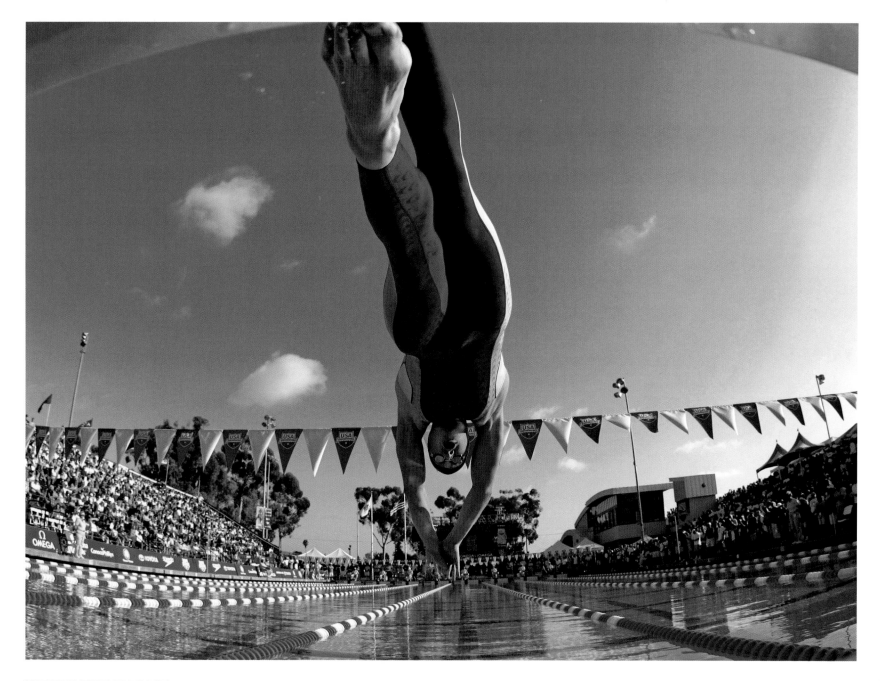

## TAKING THE PLUNGE

Peter Vanderkaay dives into the pool at the start of the men's 400 metres freestyle final at the 2006 U.S. swimming championships in Irvine, California. Vanderkaay was a member of the U.S. 4x200 metres relay team, with Michael Phelps, Ryan Lochte and Klete Keller, who upset the Australian quartet of Ian Thorpe, Grant Hackett, Michael Klim and Nicholas Springer at the 2004 Athens Olympics. He won a world gold medal in the relay the following year. 1 August 2006. Lucy Nicholson

## CHAMPIONS OF THE POOL

ABOVE Cullen Jones competes in the men's 50 metres freestyle heats at the U.S. national championships in Irvine. A fortnight later, Jones helped the American 4x100 freestyle relay team to break the world record at the Pan Pacific championships in Victoria, Canada. They set a blistering time of three minutes 12.46 seconds, more than seven-tenths of a second faster than the previous record set by surprise gold medallists South Africa at the 2004 Olympics. 3 August 2006. Lucy Nicholson

TOP Laure Manaudou of France swims the butterfly leg of the women's 200 metres individual medley final on her way to winning one of four gold medals she collected at the European Aquatic Championships in Budapest. 3 August 2006. Laszlo Balogh

ABOVE Dániel Gyurta of Hungary, who won an Olympic silver medal at the age of just 15 in Athens, rises out of the water during a 200 metres breaststroke heat at the Budapest European championships. 2 August 2006. Laszlo Balogh

## POWER AND GRACE

ABOVE Alexandre Despatie from Canada sprays water as he dives during a practice session before the preliminary competition in the three-metre springboard at the 17th Commonwealth Games in Manchester. At the age of 17, Despatie won two golds and a bronze at the Games. His haul over the following years included two world titles in 2005 and three more Commonwealth Games golds in 2006 in Melbourne, as well as an Olympic silver in Athens. 26 July 2002. David Gray

TOP The feet of South African diver Jenna Dreyer push away from the three-metre springboard during the Commonwealth Games in Melbourne. Dreyer placed 10th. 25 March 2006. Andy Clark

ABOVE Bermuda's Commonwealth Games team member Katura Horton-Perinchief floats to the surface during a diving practice session in Melbourne. 14 March 2006. Tim Wimborne

ABOVE Yulia Pakhalina of Russia holds her position as she dives on her way to winning the bronze medal in the three-metre springboard final at the Athens Olympic Games behind China's Guo Jinjing and Wu Minxia. Pakhalina also won silver in the synchronized event. 26 August 2004. Damir Sagolj

ABOVE Kwon Kyung-min and Cho Kwan-hoon of South Korea plunge into the water in the men's three-metre springboard synchronized event at the 14th Diving World Cup in the Athens Olympic Aquatic Centre. 18 February 2004. Yannis Behrakis

## A SHOT AT GLORY

India's Rajyavardhan Singh Rathore unloads spent shells during the men's double trap shooting final at the Asian Games in Doha. Rathore, a Commonwealth Games champion and Athens Olympics silver medallist, helped India to win the team silver medal behind China. 5 December 2006. Caren Firouz

ABOVE Australian Lauryn Ogilvie scores a hit on a target clay on her way to winning the gold medal in the women's skeet singles in Bisley, England, which hosted shooting events at the 2002 Commonwealth Games. Ogilvie, who previously competed for the U.S., also won pairs gold. 2 August 2002. Ian Waldie

RIGHT Annette Woodward, Australia's oldest Olympian in 28 years at the age of 57, trains in Melbourne after being selected for the Athens Olympic team in the 25-metre pistol. Woodward, a radiographer, came out of retirement to make the team after nursing her dying husband. She finished 18th. 26 July 2004. Stuart Milligan

## A SHOT IN THE DARK

ABOVE A skier is silhouetted as she passes a lamp during the women's 7.5-km (4.6-mile) sprint at a biathlon World Cup event in Khanty-Mansiysk in western Siberia. German Katrin Apel, a relay gold medallist from the 2002 Salt Lake City Olympics, won the race for her first victory in three years. 16 March 2005. Sergei Karpukhin

## COURSING ACROSS COUNTRY

RIGHT Seen from the air, some of the 11,000 cross-country skiers in the Engadin ski marathon cross a frozen lake near Sils in Switzerland. The race has been an annual event on the second Sunday in March since 1969. A separate women's race, a week earlier, began in 2000. During a typical race, course-side volunteers hand out 21,500 chocolate bars, 20,000 energy tablets and 10,000 bananas to participants. 13 March 2005. Pascal Lauener

## COOL RUNNINGS

Jamaicans Winston Watt and Wayne Blackwood shoot downhill during the 2005 men's bobsleigh World Cup in Cesana Pariol, Italy, the venue for the Turin Winter Olympics competition in the following year. A bobsleigh team from the Caribbean island provoked intense interest at the 1988 Calgary Winter Olympics where they crashed violently on the final run. Their exploits were later made into a Disney movie called *Cool Runnings*. 22 January 2005. Max Rossi

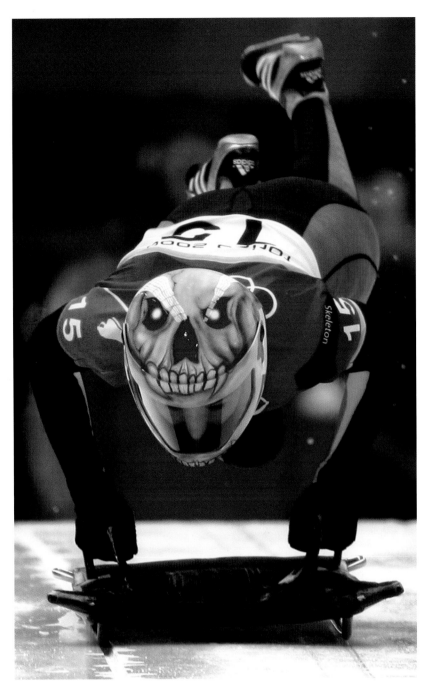

## LUGE LOOP

Spectators' shadows are cast on the track as American Courtney Zablocki competes in the first run of the women's luge at the 2006 Turin Olympics. Zablocki missed a medal by just 0.004 seconds, finishing fourth behind a trio of Germans led by defending champion Sylke Otto, but still produced the best performance by an American woman in luge history. The final was marred by three crashes and Zablocki's team mate Samantha Retrosi was taken to hospital with concussion. 13 February 2006. Pawel Kopczynski

## SKELETON START

Poland's Monika Wołowiec starts her run in the women's skeleton at the Turin Winter Olympics. The race was won by Maya Pedersen, who gave Switzerland their first gold of the Games. Britain's Shelley Rudman collected a surprise silver in her first full season of competition and former world champion Diana Sartor was fourth despite being nine weeks pregnant, a fact she kept from her coach until after the race. 16 February 2006. Jean-Paul Pelissier

## SKATER IN FLIGHT

ABOVE Tong Jian of China waits to catch Pang Qing in the pairs free skating at the Salt Lake City Winter Olympics. The competition ended in scandal when French judge Marie-Reine Le Gougne admitted she had been pressured by her federation president to mark down Canadians Jamie Salé and David Pelletier in order to ensure the title went to Russia's Yelena Berezhnaya and Anton Sikharulidze. After days of arguments, the Canadians were awarded duplicate gold medals and figure skating officials set about devising a new scoring system. 11 February 2002. David Gray

## AIRBORNE ELEGANCE

RIGHT Canada's Deidra Dionne practises for the aerials freestyle competition at the Turin Winter Olympic site in Sauze d'Oulx, Italy. Dionne, a bronze medallist at the 2002 Olympics, broke her neck in September 2005 when she crashed while training in Australia. After seven hours of surgery she battled through rehabilitation to return to competition for the Turin Games five months later, though she failed to reach her event final. 19 February 2006. Dylan Martinez

## AIMING FOR A MEDAL

ABOVE Norway's silver medallist Ole Einar Bjørndalen shoots during the men's 12.5-km biathlon pursuit at the 2006 Turin Olympics. Bjørndalen, who had won a gold and two silvers at the 1998 Nagano Olympics, was a sensation at the 2002 Salt Lake City Games when he captured all four titles in the space of nine days. But he was hampered by a sinus problem in Turin and had to settle for two silvers and a bronze. 18 February 2006. Jean-Paul Pelissier

## SUPER-G ON MONO-SKI

LEFT Tyler Walker of the U.S. skis during his men's super-G at the ninth Paralympic Games in Sestriere, Italy, where he finished sixth. Walker, who had both legs amputated below the knee as a child because of a congenital disorder, became the first mono-ski champion at the World X Games in January 2007, when his event made its debut at the annual extreme sports event in Colorado. 14 March 2006. Tony Gentile

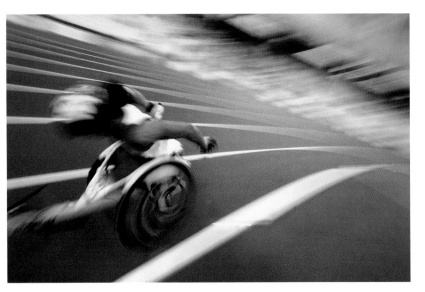

## THE PARALYMPIC GAMES

The Paralympic Games is the elite multi-sport event for athletes with physical disabilities, visual disabilities, cerebral palsy and for amputees. Governed by the International Paralympic Committee, the Games take place every four years following the Olympic Games. The name comes from the Greek word 'para' (meaning 'alongside' or 'beside'), referring to the event running parallel to the Olympic Games. The modern Paralympics evolved from a 1948 sports competition for injured British war veterans, organized by Sir Ludwig Guttmann. Four years later, competitors from the Netherlands were invited. By 1960, an Olympic-style event was established. Nearly 4,000 athletes competed at the 2004 Games in Athens. China topped the medals table ahead of Britain and Canada. Events held for the first time at Athens included five-a-side blind football and women's sitting volleyball.

OPPOSITE LEFT ABOVE  New Zealand's Gerry Tinker in the wheelchair rugby semi-final at the Athens Paralympics. 24 September 2004. Yiorgos Karahalis

OPPOSITE LEFT CENTRE  An athlete competes in the Athens Paralympics. 21 September 2004. Yannis Behrakis

OPPOSITE LEFT BELOW  A woman athlete competes in the final of the 5,000 metres at the Athens Paralympics. 21 September 2004. Yannis Behrakis

OPPOSITE RIGHT  A guide adjusts the hands of a blind athlete before the men's 100 metres final at the Athens Paralympics. 22 September 2004. Yannis Behrakis

ABOVE  Colombian swimmer Robinson Martinez (bottom) trains in California for the Athens Paralympics. 21 May 2004. Eduardo Munoz

## ICEBREAKERS

LEFT Pittsburgh Penguins' Sidney Crosby skates past an adoring fan during the first period of the NHL game against the Toronto Maple Leafs in Toronto. Hailed as ice hockey's next big player by 'The Great One' himself, Wayne Gretzky, Crosby lived up to the hype, becoming, at 19 years and five months, the youngest player voted to start the All-Star Game since fan balloting began in 1986. 18 April 2006. Mike Cassese

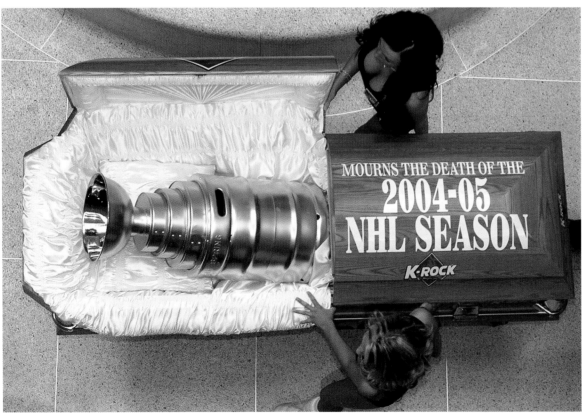

LEFT A mock Stanley Cup is wheeled into a shopping mall during a staged funeral procession for the cancelled NHL season in Edmonton. In a dispute over salary caps, the league locked out its players in September 2004. Five months later, still unable to reach an agreement with players, the NHL cancelled the remaining schedule and became the first North American professional sports league to lose an entire season to a labour dispute. 5 February 2005. Dan Riedlhuber

RIGHT Celebrating Edmonton Oilers fans cast shadows on the ice behind Carolina Hurricanes' goaltender Cam Ward after the Oilers' Ryan Smyth scored during the third period of Game 6 in the NHL Stanley Cup finals in Edmonton, Alberta. Two days later the Hurricanes beat the Oilers in Game 7 to win their first cup and rookie Ward was named Most Valuable Player of the playoffs. 17 June 2006. Andy Clark

RIGHT Pittsburgh Penguins defenceman Noah Welch hits Anaheim Ducks forward Travis Moen into the boards during an NHL game in Anaheim, California, which the home team won 3–2. The Ducks opened the 2006–7 season with an NHL record of 16 games without a loss in regulation time before falling to the Calgary Flames. But the California team regained their momentum and advanced to the playoffs for the second straight season. 6 November 2006. Mike Blake

## TAKE OFF

ABOVE Russia's Dmitry Ipatov soars from the ski jumping hill as a watching official huddles under an umbrella to protect herself from heavy rain during practice for the second stop of the Four-Hills tournament in Garmisch-Partenkirchen, Germany. The event was shortened to one jump because of strong winds and poor conditions. Unseasonably warm weather and rain disrupted winter sports events across Europe in 2006–7, prompting ski federations to turn their thoughts to the prospect of global warming. 1 January 2007. Kai Pfaffenbach

## REFLECTIONS ON ICE

LEFT An athlete warms up at the 2006 Olympic speed skating venue, the Oval Lingotto, during practice for a World Cup event in Turin. The colours on the ice are reflections from a giant television screen. At the Turin Olympics, the hall rang to the cheers of Italians as Enrico Fabris pushed the home team to a gold medal in the team pursuit before winning another gold in the 1,500 metres. 'Enrico, you are part of Italian sports history now,' Prime Minister Silvio Berlusconi told Fabris, who also collected a 5,000 metres bronze. 8 December 2005. Max Rossi

## TREADING WATER

ABOVE  Triathletes gather in the water before swimming in the 2006 Ironman Triathlon in Kailua-Kona, Hawaii. Introduced in 1978, the Hawaii Ironman event comprises a 4-km (2.4-mile) swim, a 180-km (112-mile) bike ride and a 42.2 km (26.2-mile) run. Today it is the world's premier triathlon with 1,500 athletes enlisted on the 25th anniversary in 2003. 21 October 2006. Hugh Gentry

## POWERING AHEAD

RIGHT  High-speed raceboats leave a wake at the start of the 2002 Dubai grand prix world offshore championship race. Victory 7, driven by Ali Nasser and Ali Al Qamar of the United Arab Emirates, won the race, followed by Spirit of Norway driven by Bjorn Gjelsten and Steve Curtis. Powerboat racing is immensely popular in the United Arab Emirates, with the Dubai grand prix staged at the International Marine Club every December. 18 October 2002. Chris Helgren

## SAILING TO VICTORY

Danish skipper Jesper Bank of the German America's Cup crew 'United Internet Team Germany' steers the yacht GER-72 during a practice session in the Kiel Fjord near the Baltic coastal town of Kiel. The challenge was Germany's first in the history of the Cup, the world's oldest sporting trophy which dates back to 1851. Newcomers from China and South Africa joined the battle to win the right to challenge Swiss defenders Alinghi in the 2007 Cup, opening up a sport often seen as elitist. 6 August 2005. Christian Charisius

RIGHT A crew member of America's Cup holders Alinghi climbs the ropes to change the sail on the day of an official welcome ceremony in Valencia, Spain. The trophy returned to Europe for the first time in 152 years when Swiss-backed Alinghi scored an historic victory over Team New Zealand in 2003. Alinghi, bankrolled by Swiss billionaire Ernesto Bertarelli, were defending the cup in Valencia in 2007. 12 April 2005. Sebastian Derungs

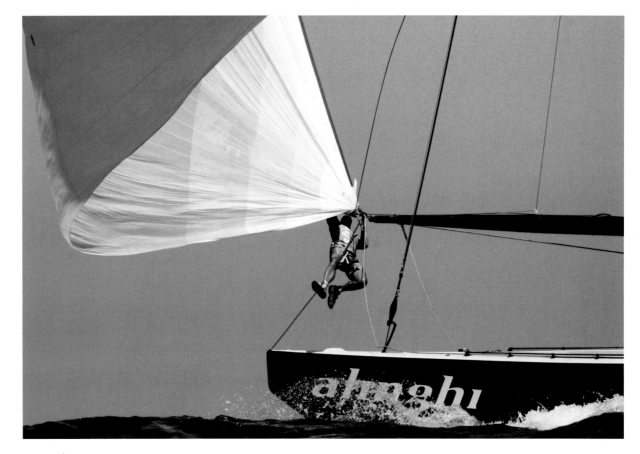

RIGHT Nicorette and Skandia jostle for position in large swells outside Sydney Heads after the start of the 2004 Sydney-to-Hobart yacht race. Sweden's Nicorette won line honours in the 60th annual 628-nautical-mile race, after the starting fleet of 116 yachts had been devastated by gale-force winds and huge seas. Skandia capsized in the Tasman sea after losing her keel. In 1998 six sailors died and five boats sank on one of the world's roughest stretches of water. 26 December 2004. David Gray

## INDOOR ENDURO

Motorbike riders Samuli Aro from Finland and Spaniard Ivan Cervantes in action
at the VI Enduro Indoor International of Barcelona at the city's Sant Jordi stadium.
Both men helped manufacturer KTM to win a host of world titles. As its name
indicates, enduro racing is a test of riders' stamina and is staged off road in rugged
natural terrain, often through forests. Indoor racing artificially replicates those
conditions. 14 November 2004. Albert Gea

## WILD WATER

Athletes warm up during the first day of World Cup canoe and kayak racing at the Athens Helliniko complex. The wild water facility for the 2004 Olympics, where German Birgit Fischer won her eighth gold at the age of 42, was hailed as one of the world's best competition venues. Athens, however, struggled to find long-term uses for many of its Olympic venues and in 2007 the Helliniko site was leased to a consortium who planned to turn it into a fun park. 8 July 2005. Yiorgos Karahalis

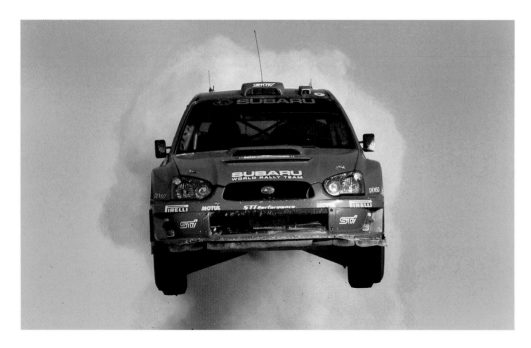

## SOLBERG SOARS

ABOVE Subaru Impreza driver Petter Solberg of Norway goes airborne in the Tandalo stage on the second day of the Rally of Italy in Sardinia. Frenchman Sébastien Loeb took the championship lead with victory in Sardinia. The Citroën driver went on to take the world title for the second successive year after winning a record 10 rallies, hitting a bull in Argentina and postponing his honeymoon at a crucial stage of the season. 30 April 2005. Giampiero Sposito

## DEFYING THE DESERT

RIGHT Bleached animal bones highlight the hostile terrain of the United Arab Emirates Desert Challenge as Stéphane Peterhansel of France steers his Mitsubishi on the fourth leg in Moreed. Peterhansel won the event in 2002 and 2003. The former skateboarding champion has won a record nine titles in the Dakar Rally, considered the toughest and most dangerous challenge in world motor sports. In 2007 he won for a third time in the car category, after six victories on two wheels. 13 November 2005. Eric Gaillard

## THE TRAVELLING CIRCUS

ABOVE Michael Schumacher and his crew in Ferrari red are reflected in the glass of the stands as he makes a pit stop during the Spanish Formula One Grand Prix. The German driver won the Barcelona race for the fifth time in his career and the third year in a row. He retired at the end of 2006 as the most successful driver in Formula One history with a record seven titles and 91 race wins. 4 May 2003. Albert Gea

OPPOSITE ABOVE Renault's Fernando Alonso of Spain celebrates winning his second successive Formula One world championship after finishing runner-up to local hero Felipe Massa of Ferrari in the Brazilian Grand Prix. Schumacher was fourth in his farewell race. 22 October 2006. Bruno Domingos

OPPOSITE BELOW Abdel Rouf, a member of the Bahrain Royal Arab Stud, watches Minardi driver Patrick Friesacher of Austria during Formula One practice. Bahrain hosted the first Grand Prix in the Middle East in 2004 at a new, $150-million circuit. 2 April 2005. Wolfgang Rattay

## ACCLAIM FOR ALONSO

Spaniard Fernando Alonso cruises into the pits after his victory in the 2006
Canadian Grand Prix in Montreal. At the age of 25 Alonso became Formula One's
youngest double world champion when he won the 2006 title with a second-place
finish in the season-ending Brazilian Grand Prix and helped Renault to take
the constructors' title. In a move agreed a year earlier, Alonso then switched to
success-starved former champions McLaren, also home to Briton Lewis Hamilton,
who took the sport by storm with his run of success in 2007, becoming, at the age
of 22, the first black driver to win a Grand Prix with his debut victory in Canada.
25 June 2006. Chris Wattie

## TYRE CHECK

A Renault team mechanic marks a Michelin tyre before the 2006 U.S. Grand Prix at Indianapolis. The 2005 race descended into chaos when only six cars started after Michelin discovered its tyres were unsafe and could not be used through the final high-speed banked corner. Fans booed and jeered and some threw objects on to the track as the 14 cars with Michelin tyres peeled off into the pit lane rather than take up their starting positions after the parade lap. 29 June 2006. John Gress

## REFLECTIONS ON A RACE

Spaniard Fernando Alonso is reflected in a fireman's helmet during free practice for the 2006 French Grand Prix at Magny-Cours. Alonso, in a Renault, finished second behind seven-times champion Michael Schumacher, driving a Ferrari, who made history by becoming the first driver to win the same Grand Prix eight times, lapping all but the top seven drivers. It was the 100th French Grand Prix since Renault won the first race at Le Mans. 14 July 2006. Jean-Paul Pelissier

## FAST TRACK

BELOW American Jimmie Johnson celebrates his victory at the 48th Daytona 500 on the roof of his confetti-covered Chevrolet at Daytona Beach, Florida. The race was marred by a record 11 cautions for accidents which eliminated several of the front-runners. NASCAR's biggest race has a prize purse of more than $18 million. In 2007, former Formula One driver Juan Pablo Montoya of Colombia finished 19th in the race after switching to a career in U.S. stock car racing. 19 February 2006. Mark Wallheiser

OPPOSITE Tony Stewart spins his car in celebration after winning the 2006 NASCAR race at the Atlanta Motor Speedway in Hampton, Georgia. Stewart set himself up as the favourite to win the 2007 Daytona 500 with good results in the build-up but crashed out of the race on lap 152 after a collision with fellow leader Kurt Busch. Instead, Kevin Harvick took victory by just 0.02 seconds after overtaking Mark Martin on the final lap. 29 October 2006. Steve Schaefer

## TWO-WHEEL SPEED

RIGHT Honda MotoGP rider Marco Melandri of Italy glances backwards during the second practice session of the Italian motorcycling grand prix at the Mugello race track. The race was won by another Italian, Valentino Rossi, who lost his opportunity to win a sixth successive championship when he crashed during the final race in Valencia. As a result American Nicky Hayden claimed his first world championship on a Honda. 2 June 2006. Max Rossi

BELOW Italy's Honda rider Max Biaggi heads into Goddards' bend during practice at the 2004 British MotoGP at Donington Park in central England. Biaggi, four times world 250cc champion but long overshadowed by his flamboyant compatriot Valentino Rossi in the premier class, finished 12th as his arch-rival won and romped to the season's world title, his fourth in a row. Rossi won again in 2005. 24 July 2004. Darren Staples

OPPOSITE Spain's Alvaro Bautista leads the field during qualifying for the Dutch TT 125cc motorcycling race in Assen. The race, always held on the last Saturday of June, is the biggest sports event of the year in the Netherlands. Motorcycling fans, who flock to the race from around Europe, have dubbed the venue 'The Cathedral'. 23 June 2006. Paul Vreeker

## SUPERCROSS STUNT

U.S. competitor Andy Cole performs a backflip during the freestyle competition
at the International Supercross event in the Buesa Arena in Vitoria, northern Spain.
3 April 2004. Victor Fraile

## DESERT RIDERS

RIGHT Grant Robertson (left) from Australia, Stefano Candida (centre) from Italy and Ali al Shanfari from the United Arab Emirates ride the Ruba al Khali stage on the third day of the UAE Desert Challenge, near Lewa, south of Abu Dhabi. The race is regarded as the traditional warm-up for the tough Dakar Rally. 1 November 2002. Anwar Mirza

## STORM IN THE SAND

BELOW Some of the 1,000 racers in the annual Le Touquet beach race in northern France jostle for position on the 15.5-km (9.6-mile) circuit. Frenchman Arnaud Demeester, dubbed Sand-Man, became the first competitor to win the event six times with his 2007 victory, which was watched by an estimated 250,000 spectators. 18 February 2001. Bob Martin

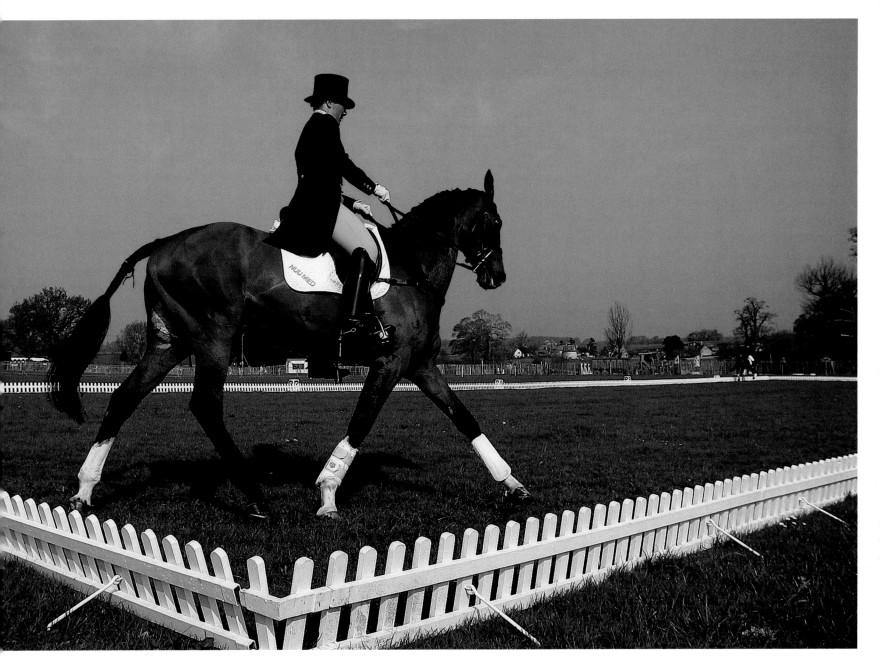

## LEAP OF FAITH

OPPOSITE Canadian John Anderson, on Gestine 36, jumps over the water during
the CN International Open Cup at the 2006 Spruce Meadows Masters in Calgary,
Alberta. Spruce Meadows, located in the foothills of the Canadian Rockies, hosts an
annual showjumping event in the autumn. Equestrian is the only Olympic event
teaming men and women with animals. It includes three disciplines: dressage,
jumping and the three-day event. 10 September 2006. Todd Korol

## BADMINTON'S ELITE

ABOVE England's Lucy Wiegersma, riding In the Purple, practises before the
dressage section at the 2006 Badminton horse trials. Dressage is conducted over
three rounds with horse and rider performing set routines in a walk, trot and
canter during the first two rounds. The third round is freestyle with individually
choreographed routines performed to music. Badminton, in Gloucestershire,
England, is one of five international elite three-day events. 4 May 2006. Eddie Keogh

## RECORD RACE

OPPOSITE A record crowd of 112,668 watches Smarty Jones, ridden by Stewart Elliott, gallop to an historic victory in the 2004 Preakness Stakes in Baltimore. Smarty Jones won by 11½ lengths, bettering the previous biggest winning margin of 10 lengths set by Survivor in the 1873 inaugural race. The three-year-old had already won the Kentucky Derby, first leg of the coveted Triple Crown, but his bid ended when he finished second at the Belmont Stakes to 36–1 outsider Birdstone. 15 May 2004. Gary Hershorn

## FINAL FENCE

BELOW Competitors clear the last fence of the Jewson Novices Handicap steeplechase on the final day of the 2006 Cheltenham festival in Gloucestershire, England. Cheltenham is the climax of the National Hunt season, featuring the Champion Hurdle, the Queen Mother Champion Chase and the Cheltenham Gold Cup on successive days. It is particularly popular with Irish trainers and in 2007, for the first time, there were more entrants from Ireland than Britain in the Champion Hurdle. 16 March 2006. Toby Melville

## THE FLYING TOMATO

A multiple exposure shows Shaun White taking the final jump to win the men's snowboard slopestyle event at the ninth Winter X Games in Aspen, Colorado. The American, nicknamed 'The Flying Tomato' for his unkempt red hair, won the 2006 Turin Olympics gold medal in halfpipe, an event in which riders rise up over the rim of a half-cylinder and perform aerial tricks. The win brought White celebrity status at home. 29 January 2005. Rick Wilking

## IN PURSUIT

Members of the French team during qualifying for the men's team pursuit at the 2004 track cycling world championships in Melbourne. The event features two teams of four riders who start on opposite sides of the velodrome. Team members follow each other closely to minimize air resistance with the object of catching and overhauling the other team. The winner is the team whose third rider crosses the line first. 28 May 2004. David Gray

## CYCLING ON TOUR

LEFT Cyclists cross a bridge on the fourth stage of the Tour of Spain cycling race from Águilas to the Mediterranean resort of Roquetas de Mar. Unheralded Spaniard Aitor González, predictably nicknamed 'Speedy', won the three-week race, which ended in Real Madrid's Bernabéu stadium. The Vuelta, as it is known in Spain, is one of cycling's three big annual stage races, along with the Tour de France and the Giro d'Italia. 10 September 2002. Marcelo del Pozo

LEFT The leading pack tackle a climb during the 163-km (101-mile) 16th stage of the 2002 Giro d'Italia from Conegliano to Corvara. Mexican Julio Perez Cuapio won the stage while Australian Cadel Evans took the leader's pink jersey. The Giro was inspired by the Tour de France and designed, like the French classic, to increase a newspaper's circulation, in this case *La Gazzetta dello Sport* which is printed on pink paper. 29 May 2002. Stefano Rellandini

RIGHT Riders pass in front of a chemical plant during the 150.5-km (93.5-mile) first stage of the 2004 Tour of Qatar cycle race in Doha. Saunier Duval team rider Francisco Ventoso of Spain won the stage and took the gold leader's jersey. The Tour, across a flat desert around the hinterlands of Qatar, is one of the many sports transplanted from Europe to the Middle East, where there is no tradition of cycling. Doha hosted the 2006 Asian Games and plans to bid for the 2016 Olympics. 2 February 2004. Jacky Naegelen

RIGHT A man watches the pack go by on the fifth stage of the Tour of Spain, from Alcázar de San Juan to Cuenca. Spanish climbing specialist Roberto Heras won what would have been a record fourth victory when the Vuelta ended in Madrid, but was later stripped of the title and banned for two years after testing positive for the banned blood booster erythropoietin (EPO) and Russian Denis Menchov was crowned champion instead. 31 August 2005. Dani Cardona

ABOVE Barcelona's Samuel Eto'o celebrates scoring against Real Sociedad in a Primera Liga game in San Sebastián. Barca went on to win a second successive league title. 18 March 2006. Felix Ordonez

ABOVE LEFT Goalkeeper Oliver Kahn advises his Bayern Munich team mates in the German cup final against Eintracht Frankfurt in Berlin. Bayern won the cup for the 13th time. 29 April 2006. Kai Pfaffenbach

LEFT Italian international Alessandro Del Piero watches the action as his Juventus draw 3–3 with Empoli in a Serie A match at the 'Castellani' Stadium in Empoli. 25 January 2004. Alessandro Bianchi

BELOW LEFT Fabio Cannavaro heads the ball during nine-times European champions Real Madrid's 1–0 win over Steaua Bucharest in the Champions League group stage in Madrid. 1 November 2006. Ricardo Ordonez

BELOW European footballer of the year Pavel Nedvěd wheels away after scoring Juventus's late winner over Bayern Munich in a Champions League group match in Turin. 19 October 2004. Stefano Rellandini

ABOVE Raúl is delighted to end an 11-month scoring drought with two goals in Real Madrid's 5–1 Champions League group stage win over Dynamo Kiev in Madrid. 26 September 2006. Felix Ordonez

ABOVE RIGHT Inter Milan's Luis Figo gestures during a Serie A match against Fiorentina in Milan. The club ended the season third but were named champions after a match-fixing investigation. 25 September 2005. Alessandro Bianchi

RIGHT Thierry Henry looks over his shoulder during France's Euro 2008 qualifying match against Scotland at Hampden Park in Glasgow. Scotland won 1–0. 7 October 2006. Dylan Martinez

RIGHT BELOW Chelsea's Michael Ballack blows a kiss as he celebrates scoring against Sheffield United during their English Premier League soccer match at Stamford Bridge in London. 17 March 2007. Alessia Pierdomenico

BELOW Liverpool's Michael Owen is ecstatic after scoring his club's second goal in their 2–0 win over arch-rivals Manchester United in England's League Cup final in Cardiff. 2 March 2003. Jeff J Mitchell

## THE FALL GUY

ABOVE Portugal's Cristiano Ronaldo sits on the pitch while France coach Raymond Domenech gesticulates during their 2006 World Cup semi-final in Munich. Ronaldo was jeered during the match by fans convinced he persistently dived in an attempt to fool referees that he had been fouled. They booed again shortly after Zinedine Zidane had converted the winning penalty when Ronaldo fell theatrically to the pitch in a blatant dive which was ignored by referee Jorge Larrionda. 5 July 2006. Alex Grimm

## DROGBA TAKES FLIGHT

OPPOSITE Chelsea's Didier Drogba soars over Levski Sofia goalkeeper Bozhidar Mitrev after a challenge during their Champions League group match at Stamford Bridge in London which ended 2–0 for the home side. Ivory Coast international Drogba provoked a media storm in March 2006 when he told a television interviewer: 'Sometimes I dive.' He later said his imperfect English had given the wrong impression and denied diving. European governing body UEFA vowed to crack down on the practice, saying players found guilty would be banned for at least two games. 5 December 2006. Dylan Martinez

## ENGLAND'S ASHES

ABOVE  The end of an unforgettable day at The Oval in London as the England
captain Michael Vaughan holds the tiny urn containing the Ashes, the symbol of
cricket supremacy between the old country and its former colony Australia. England
lost the Ashes in 1989 and never looked like winning them back until 2005, when
the nation was transfixed by one of the great sporting contests. In the following
year, Australia took emphatic revenge with a 5–0 series whitewash at home.
12 September 2005. Russell Boyce

## LIVERPOOL'S COMEBACK

RIGHT  Liverpool soccer captain Steve Gerrard is surrounded by a sea of red after
his team's astonishing comeback in the 2005 European Champions League final
against AC Milan in Istanbul. The English team were seemingly dead and buried at
halftime when they trailed the Italian giants 3–0. Midfielder Gerrard gave his side a
sliver of hope with a headed goal then Vladimír Šmicer and Xabi Alonso levelled the
scores. Jerzy Dudek saved from Andrea Pirlo and Andriy Shevchenko in the penalty
shootout to clinch victory. 25 May 2005. Dylan Martinez

## GOALKEEPERS' DESPAIR

OPPOSITE Valencia goalkeeper Santiago Cañizares slumps in despair after a goal from Olympiakos's Michalis Konstantinou in a Champions League group match in Athens against a background of fog created by flares lit by the Greek side's fans. In common with some other European clubs, Olympiakos fans have repeatedly breached regulations forbidding the use of flares from the European governing body UEFA. Supporters at the San Siro stadium in Milan are also frequent offenders. 12 September 2006. Yannis Behrakis

BELOW Celtic goalkeeper Artur Boric reacts with horror after missing a penalty from Rangers' Spanish striker Nacho Novo during a Scottish Premier League match. Rangers won 3–1. Rangers, the club of Glasgow's Protestant community, have a long-standing rivalry with Celtic, who were founded in the late 19th century after a wave of Roman Catholic immigration from Ireland. The Old Firm, as the two clubs are known, have dominated Scottish football. 20 August 2005. Jeff J Mitchell

ABOVE Alouettes players shower head coach Don Matthews with a bucket of ice after their team's win in the Canadian Football League Eastern Final at Olympic Stadium in Montreal. 9 November 2003. Shaun Best

ABOVE LEFT Russia's Davis Cup tennis players throw team mate Igor Andreev into the air as they celebrate a 3–2 victory over France in their quarter-final in Moscow. 17 July 2005. Grigory Dukor

LEFT European captain Ian Woosnam kisses the Ryder Cup at The K Club in County Kildare, Ireland, after his team of golfers defeat the U.S. to retain the trophy. 24 September 2006. Kieran Doherty

LEFT BELOW Sweden's Anja Pärson performs her trademark belly slide across the snow to celebrate winning super-G gold at the Alpine skiing world championships in Åre, Sweden. 6 February 2007. Wolfgang Rattay

BELOW The San Antonio Spurs celebrate with the Larry O'Brien trophy after their win against the Detroit Pistons in Game Seven of the NBA Finals in San Antonio, Texas. 23 June 2005. Mike Blake

ABOVE  Italy's Ivan Basso sprays champagne from the podium to celebrate winning the 20th stage of the Giro d'Italia cycling race from Trento to Aprica. 27 May 2006. Stefano Rellandini

ABOVE RIGHT  Italian fencer Aldo Montano is thrown in the air by supporters after winning the gold medal in the men's sabre final at the Athens Olympic Games. 14 August 2004. Tony Gentile

RIGHT  Carolina Hurricanes captain Rod Brind'Amour kisses the NHL's Stanley Cup after winning the ice hockey series against the Edmonton Oilers in Raleigh, North Carolina. 19 June 2006. Mike Blake

RIGHT BELOW  Honda's Nicky Hayden of the U.S. takes a victory lap after winning the MotoGP world championship during the Spanish grand prix at the Cheste track near Valencia. 29 October 2006. Heino Kalis

BELOW  Greece players led by Traianos Dellas raise the cup after beating hosts Portugal to win the Euro 2004 soccer championship final in Lisbon. 4 July 2004. Kai Pfaffenbach

## TO THE VICTOR THE SPOILS

ABOVE Captain Cafu bows his head and holds the soccer World Cup aloft after Brazil win the trophy for a record fifth time in the 2002 final against Germany. After a difficult qualifying campaign, Brazil played like liberated men in the tournament jointly hosted by Japan and South Korea. A rejuvenated Ronaldo scored both goals in the final while Ronaldinho and Rivaldo dazzled in midfield and Cafu, playing with Roberto Carlos at the back, was the rock on which opposition attacks foundered. 30 June 2002. Dylan Martinez

RIGHT Fabio Cannavaro acknowledges the applause after leading Italy to a penalty shootout victory in the 2006 World Cup final over France in Berlin. The teams had been tied 1–1 after extra time. The steadfast Italian defender won FIFA's World Player of the Year ahead of French captain Zinedine Zidane, who was sent off in the final, and Brazilian playmaker Ronaldinho. 9 July 2006. Dylan Martinez

# Heroes and Zeroes
Champions / Celebrities / Fallen Idols

A mourner watches George Best's funeral cortege pass through the streets of Belfast. Widely regarded as the best soccer player ever to emerge from the British Isles, Best relished but was eventually consumed by the pop star lifestyle, alcohol addiction leading to his premature death in 2005 at the age of 59. 3 December 2005. Fran Veale.

## DAVID BECKHAM

Soccer and show business formed the ultimate alliance in January 2007 when David Beckham announced he had signed for the Los Angeles Galaxy at a weekly wage of one million dollars. It was a marriage made in a Hollywood heaven for the marketing men and a coup for Major League Soccer in its perennial battle to sustain a sport which barely registers with the average American sports fan. Cynics might argue that Los Angeles is the ideal resting point for the former England captain and his ambitious wife, the one time pop idol Victoria who has never replicated the success she briefly enjoyed with the Spice Girls in the late 1990s.

At the age of 31, Beckham was the best-known and most photogenic footballer in the world. But he had passed his sell-by date with Real Madrid, where his commercial value had overshadowed his contribution on the field, and he had also been dropped by England in 2006 after relinquishing the captaincy following another disappointing World Cup campaign.

In his prime with Manchester United and England, Beckham's defining skill was his ability to strike a sumptuous pass, free-kick or penalty with his right foot. Despite periodic appearances in central midfield, he always looked more comfortable on the right, where his crossing could be fully effective and his modest speed and ability on the ball less exposed.

Although Beckham's fame far exceeded his ability he remained a model professional, his commitment to his sport commendably unaffected by the glare of publicity he commanded throughout the world and the jet set life he so obviously enjoyed. Given the latter, his ultimate career choice was impeccable.

OPPOSITE, ABOVE LEFT A fan watches Beckham on a giant screen at the Euro 2004 qualifier against Slovakia in Middlesbrough. 11 June 2003.
Jeff J. Mitchell

OPPOSITE, ABOVE RIGHT David and Victoria Beckham arrive in Rome for the wedding of actors Tom Cruise and Katie Holmes. 17 November 2006.
Tony Gentile

OPPOSITE, BELOW LEFT Thai fans hold pictures of Beckham as they await his arrival with Real Madrid in Bangkok. 28 July 2005. Sukree Sukplang

OPPOSITE, BELOW RIGHT Beckham gestures after Real's Primera Liga match against Deportivo la Coruña at Coruña's Riazor stadium. 7 January 2007. Miguel Vidal

RIGHT Beckham leaves after a promotional event in Tokyo. 29 December 2006. Toru Hanai

LEFT Beckham kicks the ball during England's second-round World Cup match against Ecuador in Stuttgart. 25 June 2006. Alex Grimm

TOP Beckham celebrates scoring against Azerbaijan in England's World Cup qualifier at St James' Park, Newcastle. 30 March 2005. Darren Staples

ABOVE A dejected Beckham after England's 2–1 quarter-final loss to Brazil in the 2002 World Cup in Shizuoka. 21 June 2002. Andrew Budd

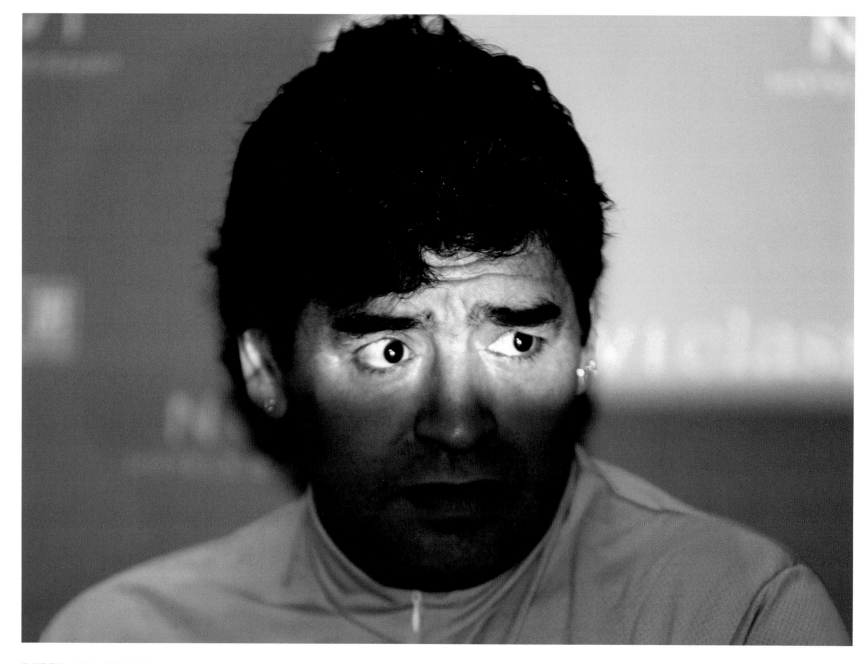

## DIEGO MARADONA

Thousands kept a silent vigil in the streets of Buenos Aires in 2004 as Diego Maradona fought a lonely and apparently losing battle in a private hospital. Grotesquely overweight, with a heart weakened by years of cocaine abuse, the little Argentine who had dazzled and delighted throughout the 1980s was close to death.

Desperate times demanded desperate measures. After his discharge, Maradona underwent a stomach-stapling operation in a Colombian hospital and, against all the odds, was present in Germany to cheer on his old team in the 2006 World Cup.

Maradona had emerged from a Buenos Aires slum to conquer the world. Stocky and powerful with a low centre of gravity and the ability to accelerate suddenly from a standing start, he made his professional debut with Argentinos Juniors shortly before his 16th birthday. After the 1982 World Cup he moved to Europe, playing first for Barcelona and then Napoli. He enjoyed both his most notorious and his finest moments at the 1986 World Cup, where he scored illegally against England with his left hand then added a second legitimate goal after an astonishing run through his bewildered opponents with the ball seemingly attached to his left foot.

Argentina won the Cup but Maradona's life was already spinning out of control and he was banned for 15 months in 1991 after a positive test for cocaine. He returned seemingly restored to full vigour at the 1994 World Cup but tested positive for a cocktail of stimulants and never represented his country again.

Maradona launched a successful TV talk show in Argentina in 2005 that lasted for one season, but in 2007 he was back in hospital being treated for the effects of excessive drinking, eating and cigar smoking.

OPPOSITE Maradona listens to reporters' questions after arriving in Novi Vinodolski, Croatia, to play a charity match. 15 June 2005. Nikola Solic

ABOVE Maradona waves an Olympiakos shirt bearing his name during a league game against Iraklis in Athens. 16 January 2005. John Kolesidis

RIGHT, TOP TO BOTTOM A cigar-smoking Maradona at an Argentine first division match in Buenos Aires. 19 February 2006. Marcos Brindicci. Maradona, wearing a Boca Juniors shirt, thanks fans at his farewell match in Buenos Aires. 10 November 2001. Enrique Marcarian. A fan outside the Buenos Aires clinic treating Maradona for heart and breathing problems. 21 April 2004. Marcos Brindicci

FAR LEFT Zidane chases the ball past two Greek players during France's Euro 2004 quarter-final in Lisbon. 25 June 2004. Jean-Paul Pelissier

LEFT Referee Horacio Elizondo shows Zidane a red card during France's 2006 World Cup final against Italy in Berlin. 9 July 2006. Jerry Lampen

## ZINEDINE ZIDANE

Tough, resilient, supremely skilled and fiercely devoted to family and friends, Zinedine Zidane was the world's pre-eminent midfielder for the best part of a decade with Juventus, Real Madrid and France. But he never forgot his working-class roots in Marseille where his Algerian immigrant father Smail toiled in a warehouse to bring up his family. After spells with Cannes and Bordeaux, Zidane moved to Juventus, then Real Madrid. A once-in-a-lifetime player with mesmerizing footwork and an explosive shot, he was equally adept in the air. He also had an occasionally violent temper and was sent off for stamping in the first round of the 1998 World Cup. But he returned to help France win, scoring from two headers in the final against Brazil, and was part of the 2000 European championship-winning side.

Past his best but still able to turn a match on its head, Zidane made his final appearance for France at the 2006 World Cup. In the final against Italy he converted a penalty and narrowly missed with a header when, with time running out, his temper flared and he was sent off for head-butting Marco Materazzi.

OPPOSITE ABOVE  Zidane celebrates after scoring during a Euro 2004 group match against Switzerland in Coimbra, Portugal. 21 June 2004. Pascal Lauener

OPPOSITE BELOW LEFT  'Zidane will score' says the slogan painted on a fan at the World Cup final in Berlin. 9 July 2006. Charles Platiau

OPPOSITE BELOW RIGHT  Zidane traps the ball during France's second-round World Cup match against Spain in Hanover. 27 June 2006. Shaun Best

TOP  Zidane plays soccer with children in Corso on a charity visit to Algeria. 12 December 2006. Louafi Larbi

ABOVE  French President Jacques Chirac receives Zidane at the Élysée Palace in Paris, the day after the World Cup final. 10 July 2006. Philippe Wojazer

RIGHT  Zidane leaves the pitch after receiving a red card during the World Cup final against Italy in Berlin. 9 July 2006. Dylan Martinez

## RONALDO

At the turn of the century Ronaldo's still unfulfilled career hung in the balance. A striker of breathtaking ability worthy of mention in the same breath as Pele, he was World Player of the Year in 1996 and 1997 and a sensation at the 1998 World Cup as Brazil strode imperiously to the final against hosts France. Yet on the morning of the match he suffered a mysterious fit and during the game he was a listless ghost at the French feast during a 3–0 defeat.

Following a knee injury in 1999, the prognosis was bleak. But after an 18-month convalescence Ronaldo returned to football, moved to Real Madrid and was selected for the 2002 World Cup. The tournament was a triumph for Ronaldo and Brazil. He scored eight goals in seven games, including both goals in the 2–0 final win over Germany, to equal Pele's record of 12 World Cup goals.

Four years later Ronaldo became the all-time World Cup goal-scoring record holder, with his 15th goal against Ghana, beating German Gerd Müller's previous mark. But the fires were now burning low, he was clearly overweight and there were only intermittent flashes of his old, irresistible dynamism.

OPPOSITE, CLOCKWISE FROM TOP Turkish players watch Ronaldo score during a World Cup semi-final in Saitama. 26 June 2002. Ruben Sprich. Ronaldo celebrates after a goal against Germany in the World Cup final in Yokohama. 30 June 2002. Dan Chung. Ronaldo tries to beat Costa Rica goalkeeper Erick Lonnis in a World Cup game in Suwon. 13 June 2002. Petar Kujundzic. Ronaldo fights for the ball in a World Cup qualifier against Chile in Santiago. 6 June 2004. Sergio Moraes

BELOW Dejection for Ronaldo after Brazil lose to France in a World Cup quarter-final in Frankfurt. 1 July 2006. Alex Grimm

## WAYNE ROONEY

Precociously talented and possessing a physical maturity beyond his years, Wayne Rooney is the most exciting player to emerge in the English game since Paul Gascoigne in the early 1990s.

Rooney was brought up in Liverpool and initially played for Everton, the team he worshipped as a boy, before transferring to Manchester United in 2004. He became the youngest goal scorer in the Premier League when he scored against Arsenal at the age of 16, then set another record when he represented England against Australia aged 17. Selected for the 2004 European championship, Rooney brought the confidence and flair he showed at club level to the international game.

Two years later at the World Cup in Germany, following a swift recovery after breaking the fourth metatarsal in his right foot, he came on as a replacement against Trinidad and Tobago. He started against Sweden and Ecuador and was clearly going to be a key player in a lacklustre team in the quarter-final against Portugal. But a short-fused temper let him down: he was sent off for stamping on Portugal defender Ricardo Carvalho's groin. In his absence, England were again eliminated on penalties.

ABOVE Rooney celebrates his goal against Birmingham City during their English Premier League match in Birmingham. 28 December 2005. Darren Staples

## RONALDINHO

Like so many Brazilians before him, Ronaldinho learned his skills in beach football. He quickly made his name at the Porto Alegre club Gremio. His ball skills and a flair for scoring spectacular goals attracted worldwide attention after he made his national debut in 1999 and he decided to try his luck in Europe with Paris Saint-Germain.

After top-scoring at the 1999 Confederations Cup, Ronaldinho joined Ronaldo and Rivaldo at the 2002 World Cup in Japan and South Korea, where he played a leading part in Brazil's successful campaign. He also provided one of the tournament's enduring images with an audacious free kick which drifted over a frantically back-pedalling England goalkeeper David Seaman in the quarter-finals.

Ronaldinho joined Barcelona in 2003 and in his first season inspired the Catalan club to 17 consecutive matches without defeat and to second place in the league. The following season they went one better and in December 2004 Ronaldinho was named FIFA player of the year, an award he won again in 2005.

Barcelona claimed European club football's greatest prize in 2006 when they beat Arsenal 2–1 in the Champions League final. But in the World Cup later that year Ronaldinho, in common with his team mates, was uncharacteristically subdued and although he started all of Brazil's five matches he failed to score a goal.

BELOW A jubilant Ronaldinho after scoring for Barcelona against Werder Bremen in a Champions League group match in Barcelona. 5 December 2006. Albert Gea

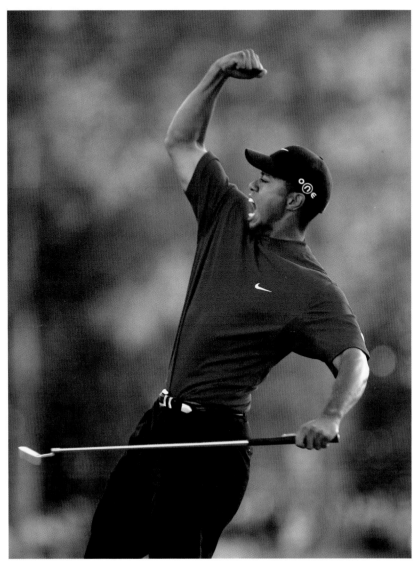

## TIGER WOODS

Once in a generation an athlete arrives with skills and charisma abundant enough to transcend their sport. Baseball produced Babe Ruth, cricket Don Bradman and golf Jack Nicklaus. People with little interest in sport knew their names, much as they knew Pablo Picasso was a painter. Today golf has Tiger Woods, the most famous athlete in the world, and on course to overtake Nicklaus's record of 18 major titles.

The son of a black American Vietnam war veteran and a Thai mother, Woods paraded his skills at the age of three on the Mike Douglas television show. His late father Earl had no doubts of his son's genius. Tiger, he proclaimed, could become a new messiah. Sensibly, Tiger concentrated on golf. By 2007, after 10 years on the circuit, he was the best in the world in all facets of the game – the longest driver, the most accurate iron player, commanding the best approach shots and deadly with the putter. In a sport where players such as the generously proportioned Phil Mickelson can still flourish, he was also the fittest. 'He has raised the bar to a level only he can jump,' said Nicklaus's one-time rival Tom Watson. 'He is something supernatural.'

## MICHAEL SCHUMACHER

'Flawed' and 'genius': as the chequered flag went down on Michael Schumacher for the final time at the Brazilian Grand Prix in 2006 and the assessments began, these were the words most freely used. There was no doubting the magnitude of Schumacher's achievements. He was Formula One champion a record seven times and set other records that may never be beaten, including most race victories, fastest laps, pole positions and races won in a single season. According to *EuroBusiness* magazine, he became the world's first billionaire athlete in 2005.

But Schumacher's methods have sometimes aroused disquiet and even anger since he made a sensational debut for Jordan in the 1991 season. In 1994, he became the first German to win the championship after a controversial collision with Briton Damon Hill in the final race in Australia. He took a one-point lead over Jacques Villeneuve into the final race of the 1997 season at Jerez, where there was another collision as the Canadian tried to overtake. Schumacher, who retired from the race, giving Villeneuve the title, was deemed to be at fault and disqualified from the championship. At the 2006 Monaco Grand Prix, enraged rivals accused the German of cheating when he stopped his car at the penultimate corner in qualifying in a blatant attempt to block them.

On the plus side, Schumacher was a supremely dedicated professional who poured his talents and energy into making the Ferrari team as good as it could possibly be. Before his arrival no Ferrari driver had won the championship since Jody Scheckter in 1979 and the Italians were widely derided by their rivals. He is also a devoted family man who treasures his privacy, and has given generously to charity.

OPPOSITE Schumacher looks in his Ferrari's rearview mirror in the pit lane during practice for the Monaco Grand Prix. 31 May 2003. Pascal Deschamps

BELOW The Ferrari crew practise their pit stop manoeuvres at the Sepang circuit in Malaysia. 20 March 2003. Bazuki Muhammad

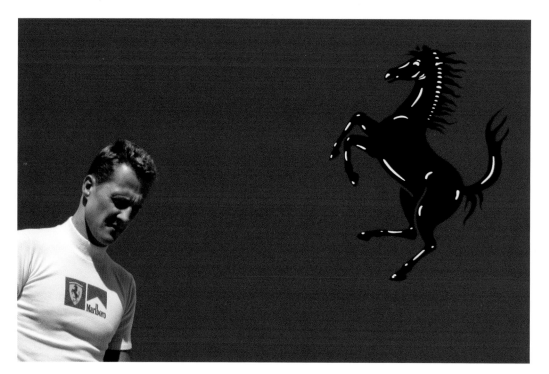

LEFT Schumacher walks in the paddock during a free practice session at the Jerez race track. 17 September 2004. Marcelo Del Pozo

BELOW LEFT Schumacher sprays champagne on cheering fans as he celebrates winning the Italian Grand Prix at Monza. 14 September 2003. Dylan Martinez

BELOW Schumacher jumps for joy on the podium after winning the Malaysian Grand Prix at Sepang. 21 March 2004. Zainal Abd Halim

OPPOSITE ABOVE Schumacher drives in free practice for the Italian Grand Prix at Monza. 3 September 2005. Chris Helgren

OPPOSITE BELOW Schumacher shakes hands with Renault's Fernando Alonso before his final race in Brazil. 22 October 2006. Sergio Moraes

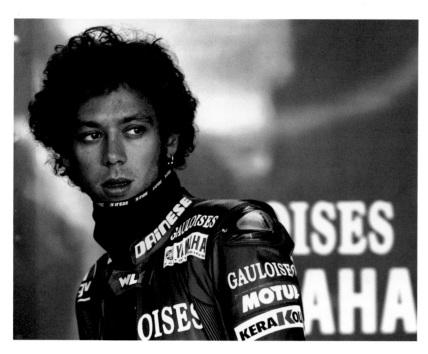

## VALENTINO ROSSI

The son of former 250cc grand prix winner Graziano, flamboyant Italian Valentino Rossi has been almost single-handedly responsible for raising the profile of his sport with titles in all four classes.

In addition he embraced the challenge of moving from the powerful Honda team to under-performing Yamaha in 2004, when he demonstrated emphatically that man, not the machine, was the key factor by taking his fourth top-category world title with nine victories and five pole positions.

After coming up through the ranks with go-karts and mini-bikes, Rossi finished ninth in the 125cc series with Aprilia in his first grand prix series in 1996 at the age of 17. In the following year he won the title with 11 wins from 15 races. Rossi moved up to the 250cc in 1998 and won the title in 1999.

The process was repeated when he raced a works-supported Honda 500cc bike in 2000, finishing second to American Kenny Roberts on a Suzuki, then winning in 2001 before the 500cc championship was replaced by the MotoGP. Rossi swept to victories in the next two seasons on a full factory machine engineered by Jerry Burgess, finishing in the top three in each of the 16 races in 2003 before making his momentous decision to move to Yamaha.

After winning five titles in a row, Rossi – nicknamed 'The Doctor' for his calculated, clinical approach to racing – was dethroned by Honda's American Nicky Hayden in 2006. Although the charismatic Rossi signed a contract with Yamaha through the 2008 season, test drives with Ferrari and victory in the 2006 Monza Rally exhibition event suggested he was considering a future on four wheels. He discounted a move to Formula One but has talked about a possible switch to the World Rally Championship.

ABOVE Rossi prepares for a free practice session at the Masaryk circuit in Brno. 20 August 2004. David W. Cerny

RIGHT Rossi rides down the final straight on his way to British Grand Prix victory at Donington Park. 24 July 2005. Toby Melville

LEFT Yao stands for the national anthems before a world basketball championship game against Slovenia in Sapporo. 24 August 2006. Toru Hanai

BELOW LEFT Phoenix Suns' Kurt Thomas guards Yao during NBA action in Phoenix, Arizona. 29 November 2006. Jeff Topping

BELOW RIGHT Yao lifts a shot over New York Knicks centre Nazr Mohammed in an NBA game in New York. 21 January 2005. Ray Stubblebine

OPPOSITE Yao (second from right) fights for a rebound during a Houston Rockets game against the Lakers in Los Angeles. 7 January 2005. Lucy Nicholson

## YAO MING

Yao Ming has become a celebrity in two countries with his own fan club and a personal website devoted to his life and exploits in the U.S. National Basketball Association. One of the tallest players in the world at 2.27 metres (7 feet 5½ inches), Yao is a popular figure in the United States with his unaffected good humour and on-court prowess. In China he is revered as an example of the country's growing significance in the international sporting community.

Born in the vibrant, bustling city of Shanghai, Yao played for China at the 2000 Sydney Olympics, joining Wang Zhizhi and Mengke Bateer in a trio dubbed 'The Walking Great Wall'. He debuted in the Chinese league at the age of 17 and was the Most Valuable Player in the Chinese league in 2000–1, averaging 27 points and 19 rebounds a game. Yao became eligible for the 2002 NBA draft, showed awesome form at a training camp and was the number one overall draft pick for the Houston Rockets. He was the first international player without U.S. college experience to be selected first overall.

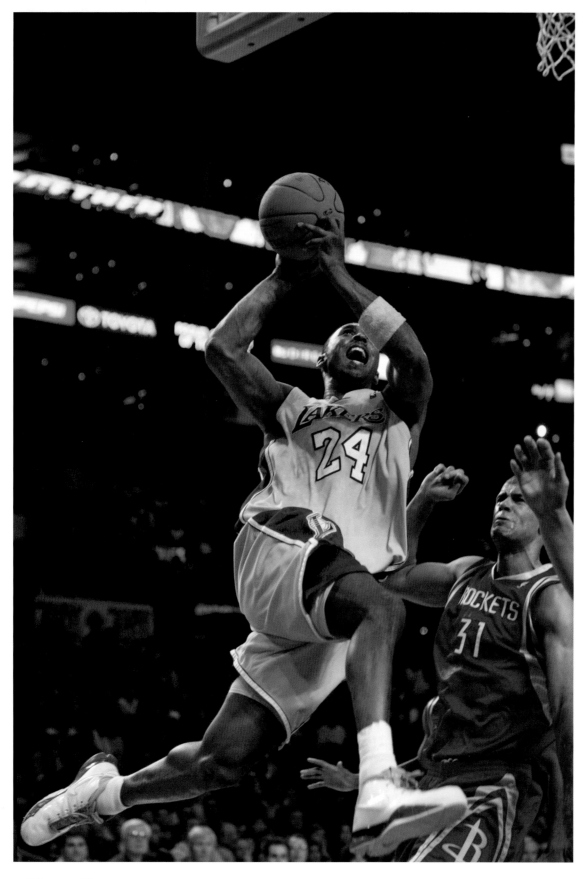

LEFT Bryant outjumps his opponents in an NBA game against the Houston Rockets in Los Angeles. 16 December 2006. Lucy Nicholson

OPPOSITE ABOVE Bryant, watched by his wife Vanessa, weeps at a news conference in Los Angeles as he admits to adultery. 18 July 2003. Lucy Nicholson

OPPOSITE BELOW Bryant, wearing a jersey with his new number, is interviewed during media day in Los Angeles. 2 October 2006. Lucy Nicholson

## KOBE BRYANT

Charges of raping a teenaged Colorado hotel employee in 2003 seemed to spell certain ruin for Kobe Bryant, an outstanding shooting guard in the Los Angeles Lakers although forced to live in the immense shadow of Shaquille O'Neal until the latter was traded to the Miami Heat.

Bryant denied rape but admitted adultery at an emotional news conference. Vanessa Laine, his wife of two years and mother of his daughter, stood by her man and he was supported by his team mates. But women's groups were outraged and sponsors, including McDonalds and Coca Cola, fled. After a late decision to drop charges, Bryant paid his accuser an undisclosed sum in a civil suit.

Bryant's on-court reputation had also been tarnished in a book by coach Phil Jackson outlining the Lakers' 2003–4 season, in which he said Bryant was uncoachable. But Bryant fought back. He captivated the fans when he scored 81 points in one game in January 2006, second only to Wilt Chamberlain's 100-point record. After his infamous feuds with O'Neal he also became more of a team player, taking the leader's role by concentrating on assists as much as shots. Off court he stayed out of trouble and the endorsements started to trickle back, including a commercial for Nike.

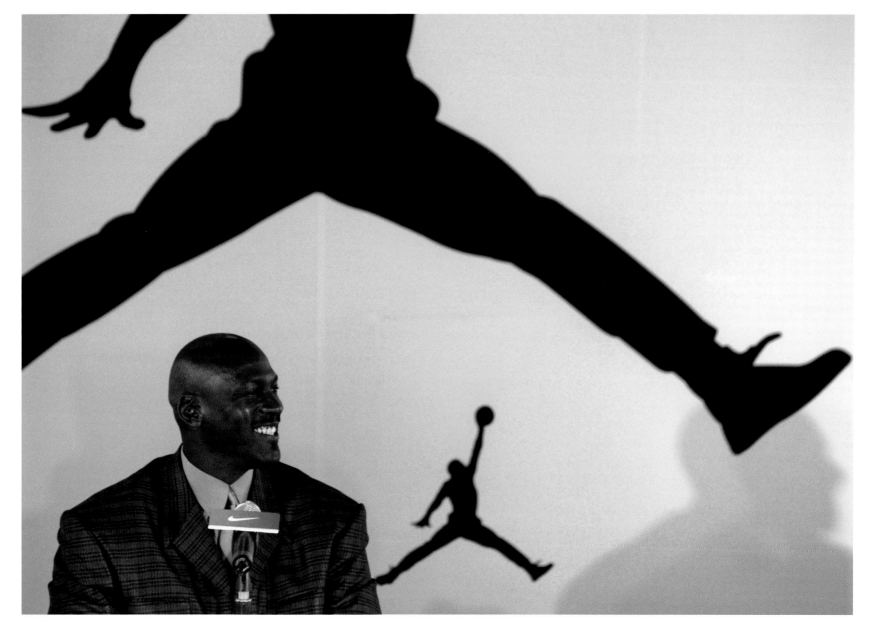

## MICHAEL JORDAN

Arguably the best player ever to step on to a basketball court, Michael Jordan is indisputably the most famous. During his peak with the Chicago Bulls in the mid-1980s and early 1990s Jordan appeared to defy gravity, earning him the sobriquets 'Air Jordan' and 'His Airness'. Inspired by Jordan's athleticism, non-stop hustling and extraordinary scoring feats, the Bulls won three NBA championships in a row, before Jordan unexpectedly retired after the murder of his father in 1993 to enjoy a brief, undistinguished flirtation with professional baseball.

He returned to the Bulls, recaptured his old form and produced the play of the century in game six of the 1998 finals when he stole the ball from Karl Malone, dribbled upcourt and scored the goal that gave the Bulls another hat-trick of championships.

Jordan was a marketing phenomenon, and a spokesman for such major brands as Nike and Coca Cola. He was on the cover of *Sports Illustrated* a record 49 times

and named the greatest sportsman of the 20th century by the sports channel ESPN. He retired as a player after the 2003 season with a lifetime average of 30 points a game. His extensive business and endorsement contracts had made him one of the wealthiest athletes in the world. *Forbes* magazine put his personal income from Nike at $25 million a year in 2004, adding that his brand generated an estimated $500 million per annum for the shoe company.

ABOVE Jordan smiles during a news conference in Hong Kong on his first Asian tour. 21 May 2004. Bobby Yip

## SHAQUILLE O'NEAL

Shaquille O'Neal, the pre-eminent centre of his time, was a man made in the city of dreams. After moving from Orlando to the Los Angeles Lakers for $120 million in 1996, he took up an acting and music career that he pursued with the same application he gave to his sport, cutting rap albums and featuring in movies. In the same year he was a member of the U.S. gold medal-winning team at the Atlanta Olympics.

Although O'Neal teamed up with teenager Kobe Bryant, the Lakers continued to promise more than they produced until Phil Jackson took charge in 1999. Jackson's triangle offence featuring O'Neal and Bryant took the Lakers to consecutive NBA titles in 2000, 2001 and 2002. After frequent attempts to get the salary increases he felt his abilities deserved, O'Neal was traded to the Miami Heat in 2004. He raised his game at the right moments to help the Heat deliver an NBA championship two years later, his fourth title in seven seasons.

RIGHT O'Neal (right) and Philadelphia 76ers' Dikembe Mutombo reach for the ball during the NBA Finals in Philadelphia. 10 June 2001. Mike Blake

## BARRY BONDS

Barry Bonds's statistics are as impressive as his bodybuilder's physique. Record for most home runs in a season (73 in 2001), second in the all-time list for home runs (734 at the end of the 2006 season), record for most walks in a career (2,426) and a seven-times Most Valuable Player in the National league.

A left-handed slugger and thrower combining speed and power, Bonds was born to play professional baseball. His father Bobby was a major league player from 1968 to 1981 and his godfather was the famous Giants player Willie Mays. So far, so commendable. But controversy has swirled around Bonds since the turn of the century when he began to consistently hit homers in unprecedented numbers. In 2000 he struck a career-best 49, in the next year he gathered 73 to break Mark McGwire's single-season record by three. Three 45-home run seasons followed.

The change in Bonds's physique was just as striking. Muscles bulged from chest and biceps, the result he said of intensive off-season weight training. Persistent rumours of steroid use gathered force when a federal raid on Victor Conte's BALCO laboratory, a manufacturer of previously undetectable steroids, turned up the name of Bonds on a list of clients. Bonds admitted taking substances supplied by Conte but denied he had ever knowingly taken banned performance-enhancing drugs. Despite the scandal, Bonds signed a one-year contract with the San Francisco Giants in February 2007, at the age of 42, and began racking up the 22 home runs he needed to break Hank Aaron's career record.

LEFT A spectator taunts Bonds during the Giants' National League game against the Phillies in Philadelphia. 7 May 2006. Gary Hershorn

ABOVE St Louis Cardinals' slugger Mark McGwire extends his hitless streak to 29 at bats in Milwaukee. McGwire, who has never tested positive for steroids, refused under oath to answer questions about steroid use during a U.S. Congressional hearing on the subject and was snubbed by Hall of Fame voters in 2007 despite having hit 583 home runs during his career. 4 July 2001. Allen Fredrickson

## ROGER FEDERER

Beautifully balanced, fluid, and possessed of an infinite variety of shots, Roger Federer's game is probably already the most aesthetically pleasing in the history of tennis. At his peak there is no one to touch him on hard surfaces and he is now coming to terms with the slower bounce and prolonged rallies on clay courts. By the time he finishes the Swiss may be the greatest male player of all time.

The Australian Open provided a turning point in Federer's career when he lost in five sets to the unpredictable Russian Marat Safin in 2005. After talking to his coach Tony Roche, Federer decided he needed to work harder on his endurance.

Two years later, Federer's utter dominance of the men's game was highlighted in the 2007 Australian Open final when he became only the fourth man to win a grand slam tournament without dropping a set. It was his 10th grand slam title, matching the tally of American Bill Tilden in the 1920s and bringing Pete Sampras's record of 14 well in reach.

Just how good is Federer? And how good can he become? Like most Australians, Rod Laver, who won the grand slam in 1962 and again in 1969, does not bestow praise lightly. 'Roger Federer is a genius but he is only in the middle of his career,' Laver said. 'If he keeps going the way he is, then he will be the best player ever.'

OPPOSITE Federer serves to Lleyton Hewitt in their semi-final at the U.S. Open in New York. 10 September 2005.
Lucy Nicholson

TOP LEFT Federer is applauded by court attendants after winning a point against Mark Philippoussis in the Wimbledon final in London. 6 July 2003. Ian Hodgson

ABOVE LEFT Federer keeps his eye on the ball during the Australian Open in Melbourne. 14 January 2003. David Gray

TOP RIGHT Federer kisses the men's U.S. Open trophy after beating Andy Roddick in the final in New York. 10 September 2006. Shaun Best

ABOVE RIGHT Federer shakes hands with Spain's Rafael Nadal after winning their Wimbledon final in London. 9 July 2006. Darren Staples

PREVIOUS PAGES, LEFT Federer plays a shot to Colombia's Alejandro Falla during the French Open in Paris. 31 May 2006. Philippe Wojazer

PREVIOUS PAGES, RIGHT Federer drops to his knees as he celebrates his win over Andy Roddick in the Wimbledon final in London. 4 July 2004. Kevin Lamarque

## WILLIAMS SISTERS

Compton, California, with its gang violence and drug-related murders, was the bleak environment in which Richard Williams vowed his daughters Venus and Serena would learn and conquer the game of the white middle classes. Williams coached his daughters from text books and videos. He instilled mental toughness and played the media game for all it was worth. Venus and Serena, he said, were the next two female Michael Jordans.

The family moved to Florida and into the tutelage of professional coaches. The sisters' power and athleticism were exceptional for teenagers and after entering the professional ranks Serena won the family's first grand slam at the age of 17 with victory in the U.S. Open. Venus made a sensational start to the new century. She won the U.S. and Wimbledon singles, the singles gold at the Sydney Olympics and teamed with Serena to win the Olympic doubles title as well. The following year was equally successful. Venus won the U.S. and Wimbledon titles again. She did not drop a set in the U.S. tournament, defeating Serena 6–2 6–4 in the final. Then it was Serena's turn. Starting with the French Open in 2002, the sisters met in five grand slam finals, all won by Serena.

Then in 2003 their elder sister Yetunde Price was murdered in California. The emotional turmoil and a series of injuries led to a prolonged form slump, relieved in 2005 when Venus beat Lindsay Davenport in the longest Wimbledon women's final.

Both sisters have used their celebrity status to pursue long-standing interests in fashion. They have had problems with motivation and fitness but – as Serena demonstrated in the 2007 Australian Open final, when she made Russian Maria Sharapova look like a nervous schoolchild – at their best they are still untouchable.

PREVIOUS PAGES, ABOVE LEFT Serena (left) and Venus Williams confer during a doubles match against Elena Dementieva and Vera Zvonareva in Hong Kong. 6 January 2005. Bobby Yip

PREVIOUS PAGES, BELOW LEFT Serena Williams celebrates winning a point against Svetlana Kuznetsova in the China Open final in Beijing. 26 September 2004. Andrew Wong

PREVIOUS PAGES, RIGHT Venus Williams jumps for joy after beating Lindsay Davenport to win the Wimbledon title in London. 2 July 2005. Kieran Doherty

OPPOSITE Serena Williams serves to compatriot Ashley Harkleroad during the JP Morgan Chase tournament in Carson, California. 9 August 2006. Lucy Nicholson

RIGHT Venus Williams plays a shot to compatriot Bethanie Mattek during the Wimbledon championships in London. 28 June 2006. Darren Staples

BELOW Venus (left) and Serena Williams answer questions from children on a visit to a Washington tennis centre. 8 December 2005. Jason Reed

BELOW RIGHT Serena Williams wears tennis 'boots' before her quarter-final against Amélie Mauresmo at the Australian Open in Melbourne. 25 January 2005. Stuart Milligan

# ANDRE AGASSI

A driven parent, a talented offspring and a childhood dominated by remorseless practice: it is a familiar story and one not always followed by a happy ending.

A tennis racket was the young Andre Agassi's constant companion as his father Mike, an Olympic boxer for Iran, transferred his dreams to his son's shoulders. Andre hit thousands of balls in practice and at the age of 13 was sent to Nick Bollettieri's famed academy. Bollettieri recognized an outstanding talent but, predictably, Agassi rebelled, adopted the American punk fashion styles of the early 1990s and seriously considered giving up the game.

But with the innate good sense that characterized his career, Agassi realized he had a unique gift and turned professional aged 16. He still wore his hair long but on the court he was totally focused, displaying the extraordinary reflexes and counter-punching skills honed by his endless years of practice.

Agassi's natural affinity with clay courts took him to the French Open finals in 1990 and 1991. He initially shunned the grass of Wimbledon, saying that he did not intend to adhere to the All England Club's dress regulations requiring all-white clothing. The year after his 1991 debut, though, Agassi won his first grand slam title at Wimbledon. By the end of his career, which finished with an emotional farewell at the 2006 U.S. Open, he had become only the fifth male player to win the grand slam singles titles in Australia, Paris, London and New York.

At his peak, after a slump in the late 1990s and before chronic back problems forced him to quit, Agassi was the total professional and a splendid ambassador for the game. After a failed marriage with the movie actress Brooke Shields he also found personal happiness by marrying the German grand slam champion Steffi Graf.

OPPOSITE ABOVE LEFT Agassi blows
kisses to the crowd after losing to
Benjamin Becker at the U.S. Open
in New York. 3 September 2006.
Kevin Lamarque

OPPOSITE ABOVE RIGHT Agassi signs
autographs after his quarter-final
win over Sébastien Grosjean at the
Australian Open in Melbourne.
27 January 2004. David Gray

OPPOSITE BELOW LEFT Agassi bows
to the crowd after his final U.S. Open
match, a loss to Benjamin Becker,
in New York. 3 September 2006.
Brendan McDermid

OPPOSITE BELOW RIGHT Agassi talks
to the media after arriving at his
charitable foundation's benefit concert
in Las Vegas. 7 October 2006.
Tiffany Brown

RIGHT Agassi serves to Tomas Berdych
in the third round of the U.S. Open in
New York. 3 September 2005. Shaun Best

## PETE SAMPRAS

Tennis fans who prefer erratic brilliance to sustained excellence found Pete Sampras boring. But that was not a criticism that much bothered the American serve-and-volley expert who won a record 14 grand slam tournaments before he retired in August 2003.

Tall and athletic, Sampras had a classical first serve which inspired the nickname 'Pistol Pete'. His second serve could be just as devastating, earning him frequent aces, and he followed up with the best overhead and forehand in the game. His game was ideally suited to Wimbledon's grass courts, where he won a record-equalling seven titles. He shared the U.S. Open record of five titles with Jimmy Connors.

Great players flourish most when they encounter great rivals and Sampras was fortunate to play in the same era as Andre Agassi. The pair met in Sampras's first grand slam final and 12 years later Agassi was again on the opposite side of the net when Sampras won his final grand slam title in the U.S. Open.

## MARTINA NAVRATILOVA

Czech emigrant Martina Navratilova transformed herself from a chubby teenager into a finely-honed athlete who dominated the women's game in the 1980s. She won her 18th and final grand slam singles title in 1990, a triumph that proved only a prelude to an astonishing second act in a remarkable career.

In 2000, aged 44, Navratilova returned to competitive doubles. Partnering Leander Paes, she won the 2003 Australian and Wimbledon mixed doubles titles. At the of 46 years and eight months she was the oldest ever grand slam champion. In the following year, she was controversially given a wild card for the Wimbledon singles but responded by winning her first-round match in straight sets, becoming the oldest player to win a singles match in the open era. Finally, in 2006, even the tireless Navratilova had had enough and announced her impending retirement. She lost her last match at Wimbledon, playing in the mixed doubles, but ended her career in triumph when she partnered Bob Bryan to the U.S. Open title.

OPPOSITE Sampras runs for a return during
his second round match with Juan Ignacio Chela
at the Australian Open in Melbourne. 17 January 2002.
Mark Baker

BELOW Navratilova serves during a mixed doubles
match at the U.S. Open in New York. 5 September 2005.
Ray Stubblebine

## LANCE ARMSTRONG

Three years before the first of his record seven Tour de France wins, Lance Armstrong was given less than a 50 percent chance of recovering from testicular cancer which had spread to his brain and lungs. Privately, the doctors were even more pessimistic. But Armstrong endured surgery and harrowing chemotherapy with defiance and stoicism. He afterwards described his ordeal as 'the best thing that ever happened to me'.

Nothing had ever come easy to the tough, fiercely determined Texan whose father had walked out on his mother Linda when Armstrong was only two. He took the surname of his stepfather while Linda devoted her life to caring for her talented son. Armstrong made his name as a triathlete then joined the U.S. Olympic cycling development programme. He became the national amateur champion in 1991, world champion in 1993 and achieved his first Tour stage win in the same year.

After making a full recovery from cancer, Armstrong transferred his burning will to live to his sport and prepared with an unsparing rigour for the Tour de France. Unlike most of his rivals, he devoted himself exclusively to the Tour and was rewarded with seven wins from 1999 to 2005 before retiring.

Inevitably in a sport plagued by a series of drugs scandals, Armstrong has been accused of taking performance-enhancing substances. He denied reports that he had used the blood-booster erythropoietin (EPO) during his career after retroactive testing of samples taken during the 1999 Tour was conducted.

LEFT Armstrong and the pack cycle past the Pyrenees on the Tour's 16th stage from Mourenx to Pau. 19 July 2005. Eric Gaillard

ABOVE Armstrong passes the Arc de Triomphe in Paris after winning his seventh Tour de France. 24 July 2005. Philippe Wojazer

TOP Armstrong cycles in the pack on the final stage of the Tour de France from Corbeil-Essonnes to Paris. 24 July 2005. Thierry Roge

ABOVE Armstrong wins the 17th stage of the Tour from Bourg-d'Oisans to Le Grand Bornand. 22 July 2004. Wolfgang Rattay

TOP RIGHT A fan waves to Tour riders during the eighth stage between Sallanches and L'Alpe d'Huez. 13 July 2003. Eric Gaillard

ABOVE RIGHT Armstrong leads his team to victory in the time trial fourth stage from Tours to Blois. 5 July 2005. Jacky Naegelen

BELOW Six-year-old William Douglas encourages Armstrong during the Tour of Georgia in Rome, Georgia. 21 April 2005. Tami Chappell

## FLOYD LANDIS

Just as he had seemed out of contention for the 2006 Tour de France, a dazzling win in the final mountain stage elevated Floyd Landis from 11th place to third. On 23 July Landis acknowledged the applause on the Champs Élysées as he rode home to succeed Lance Armstrong as champion. He was the third American to win the world's greatest endurance race after Armstrong and Greg LeMond.

Landis had grown up in Pennsylvania as a member of the socially conservative Mennonite sect. His father was opposed to his eldest son's passion for cycling but eventually relented when it became clear that nothing was going to deter young Floyd. His persistence was rewarded when he was recruited by Armstrong to race in his U.S. Postal team in three Tours, and 2006 appeared to be the ultimate reward when he defied the odds to win after his earlier collapse in the mountains.

Then the rumours started, Landis pulled out of a Danish race, and the news subsequently emerged that he had tested positive for excessive amounts of the male sex hormone testosterone. After the second urine sample confirmed the result Landis was sacked by his Phonak team and faced becoming the first man in the 103-year history of the race to lose his title for doping. Phonak later disbanded. The race had begun without nine riders, including the 1997 winner Jan Ullrich and Giro d'Italia champion Ivan Basso, who were withdrawn by their teams because they had been implicated in a Spanish doping investigation. Landis, who has denied ever knowingly taking a performance-enhancing drug, was left in limbo as his case went through the official channels with the ultimate verdict likely to come from sport's final authority, the Lausanne-based Court of Arbitration for Sport.

LEFT Fans applaud Landis on the Tour de France 17th stage from Saint-Jean-De-Maurienne to Morzine. 20 July 2006. Eric Gaillard

ABOVE LEFT Landis cycles the 19th time trial stage of the 93rd Tour between Le Creusot and Montceau-Les-Mines. 22 July 2006. Stefano Rellandini

ABOVE RIGHT Landis walks to the start podium before the 13th stage of the Tour in Béziers. 15 July 2006. Stefano Rellandini

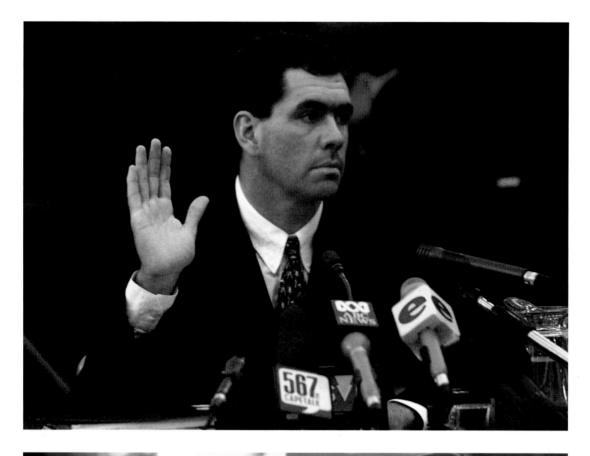

## HANSIE CRONJE

The immediate reaction was disbelief, summed up by the headline 'RUBBISH!' in a South African newspaper. According to Delhi police transcripts, South Africa cricket captain Hansie Cronje had held conversations with an Indian bookmaker which clearly indicated he had been involved in match-fixing.

Scepticism extended well beyond South Africa's shores. Cronje, captain of the multi-racial team representing the new rainbow republic, had a fixed public image as an upright, principled character who wore a wrist band inscribed with the letters WWJD (What Would Jesus Do?).

It quickly transpired that not all was as it seemed, not only with Cronje but also with the game of cricket, in which gambling was rife during its formative years before the game was appropriated by the Victorians to help extend their brand of muscular Christianity throughout the world.

After emphatic initial denials, Cronje confessed that he had discussed fixing the results of matches, including the rain-affected fifth test against England at Centurion in 2000, won by the tourists after both teams forfeited an innings on the final day in order to ensure a result.

A South African government commission established that Cronje was obsessed by money. He was banned for life and after worldwide investigations two other test captains, India's Mohammad Azharuddin and Pakistan's Salim Malik, were also given lifetime bans for involvement in match-fixing.

Despite international opprobrium, Cronje evoked mixed emotions in South Africa. In 2004 he was voted the 11th greatest South African, two years after his death at the age of 32 when the aircraft he was flying in crashed into a mountain.

LEFT ABOVE Cronje prepares to testify at the inquiry into allegations of match-fixing in South African cricket. 15 June 2000. Mike Hutchings

LEFT Flowers left in memory of Cronje sit outside Newlands Cricket Ground before the 2003 World Cup in Cape Town. 8 February 2003. David Gray

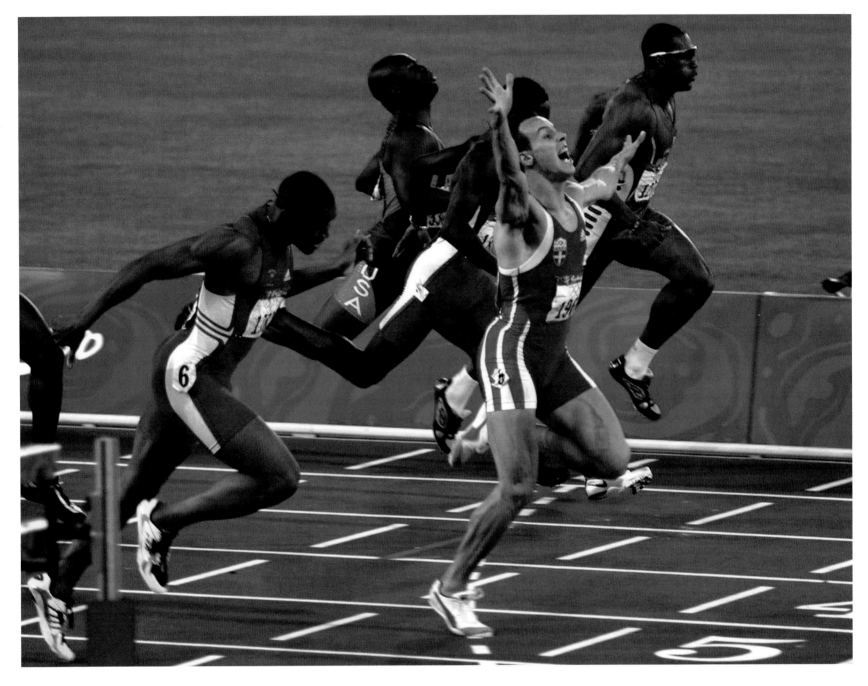

## COSTAS KENTERIS

An outlandish farce unfolded on the eve of the opening ceremony of the 2004 Athens Olympics as word spread that Greece's leading sprint hopes Costas Kenteris and Katerina Thanou had failed to turn up for a dope test. Kenteris, who exploded from nowhere to win the 2000 Sydney Olympic 200 metres title, had been expected to light the Olympic flame. Thanou was the 100 metres silver medallist behind Marion Jones in Sydney. Reports on Greek television throughout the night outlined an increasingly incredible tale in which the pair had taken off into the suburbs on a motorcycle before they crashed and ended up in hospital.

Kenteris and Thanou were withdrawn from the Games and suspended by the International Association of Athletics Federations (IAAF) for missing three scheduled out-of-competition dope tests in a year. Two alleged eye-witnesses to the crash were later charged with perjury and a group of doctors who examined them were charged with making false medical statements. In a low-key finale, proceedings were dropped in 2006 when Kenteris and Thanou admitted violating doping laws. Although neither athlete ever failed a dope test, suspicions had been aroused after the Sydney Games by their absence from the European athletics circuit, the meetings which athletes use to make their money and tune up for major championships.

ABOVE Kenteris crosses the line to win the 200 metres final at the Sydney Olympics. 28 September 2000. Zainal Abd Halim

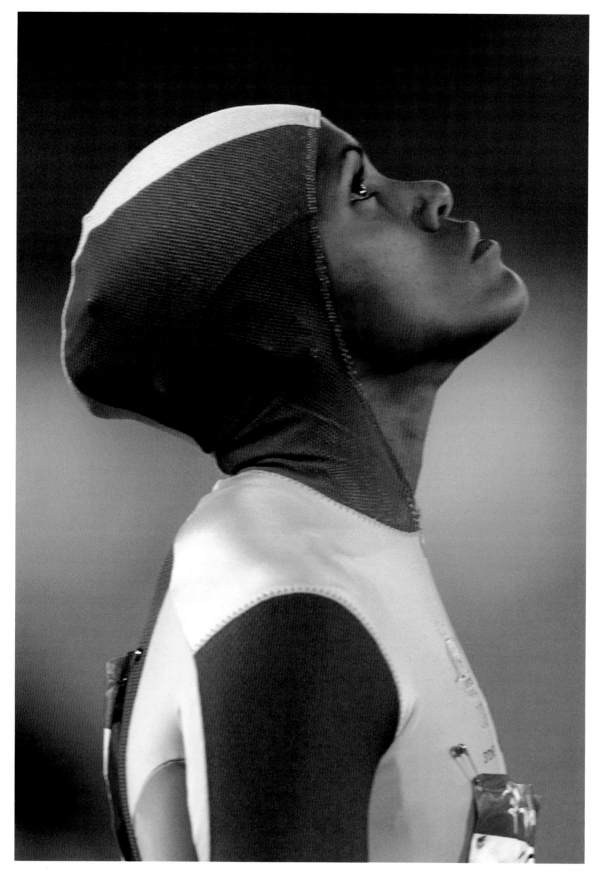

## CATHY FREEMAN

The identity of the person chosen to light the Olympic flame is traditionally a closely guarded secret. The appearance of Muhammad Ali at the 1996 Atlanta Games was met with initially hesitant and disbelieving applause followed by an exultant roar when, with left arm shaking uncontrollably as a result of Parkinson's syndrome, he raised the torch with both hands. Four years on at the Sydney Games there was a similarly explosive reaction when Cathy Freeman emerged to ignite the cauldron.

Like Ali, Freeman is a member of an oppressed race, the Aboriginal Australians who were hunted and killed for sport by 19th-century European settlers. Growing up in the late 20th century, that legacy remained formative. 'When we walked into new places, we were totally intimidated because we felt that, being black, we had no right to be there,' she recalled. At the 1994 Commonwealth Games in Edmonton, Freeman courted controversy by carrying the Aboriginal flag as well as the Australian flag during her victory lap after winning the 400 metres gold medal. But her defiance made her a symbol of hope and reconciliation for indigenous and non-indigenous Australians alike.

Freeman won the world title in 1997 and again two years later. But in Atlanta she had finished second to the deceptively languid but undeniably gifted Frenchwoman Marie-José Perec, and a battle royal was in prospect on home territory.

The pressure was immense. Australia's once proud track record had receded into distant memory and Freeman was the only realistic hope to win her country's 100th athletics gold medal.

In the event, it was Perec who succumbed to the pressure, fleeing Sydney with a series of unlikely excuses, including an unidentified intruder in her hotel room. Freeman duly delivered gold on a tumultuous night at the Olympic stadium. Mission completed, she continued to compete after the Games but never recaptured her original passion and dedication and opted to retire in 2003.

LEFT Freeman prepares to run the 400 metres final at the Sydney Olympic Games. 25 September 2000. Mark Baker

## JUSTIN GATLIN

Those brave souls striving against the odds to retain faith in the credibility of track and field thought they had found their man when Justin Gatlin emerged as the latest American track sensation.

Gatlin was serious and modest, the latter quality especially prized in the ego-ridden world of international sprinting. He also spoke eloquently about his opposition to drugs, after a positive test for an amphetamine was excused on the grounds it was medication for attention deficit disorder.

At the 2004 Athens Olympics Gatlin clocked 9.85 seconds, the second fastest time in Games' history, to win the 100 metres. The following year he won the world title in Helsinki by the widest margin in the history of the championships and added the 200 metres to follow compatriot Maurice Greene into the record books as the only man to win both titles at a world championships.

Then, in July 2006, Gatlin's image was sullied when he announced that he had tested positive for unusually high levels of the male sex hormone testosterone after a relay race in Kansas in April, a charge which U.S. officials said could carry an eight-year ban.

RIGHT Gatlin celebrates winning the 100 metres final at the Athens 2004 Olympic Games. 22 August 2004. Richard Heathcote

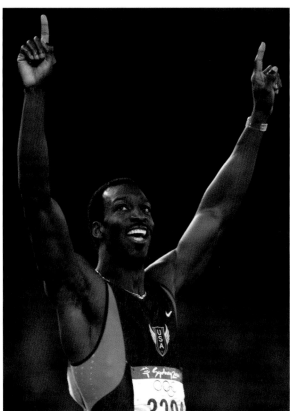

## MICHAEL JOHNSON

Michael Johnson was the best sprinter in the world for a decade, untouchable over 200 and 400 metres in major championships. His 19.32 second win in the 1996 Atlanta Olympics 200 metres final, taking nearly a third of a second off his previous world record, remains one of the truly epic track and field performances. He had already won the 400 metres, the first stage of an ambitious and unprecedented Olympic programme involving eight races in seven days.

Johnson concluded his career by winning the 400 metres gold at the 2000 Sydney Olympics. He had already added the 400 metres world record to his collection at the 1999 Seville world championships and when he decided to retire after Sydney there was nothing left to achieve.

OPPOSITE, CLOCKWISE FROM TOP LEFT Johnson watches a replay of his heat at the U.S. Olympic trials in Sacramento. 15 July 2000. Gary Hershorn. Johnson wins his 400 metres heat at the Sydney Olympics. 22 September 2000. Jerry Lampen. Johnson celebrates after winning the 400 metres final at the Sydney Olympics. 25 September 2000. Ian Waldie

## MARION JONES

In 1999 Marion Jones announced she would attempt to win the 100, 200, 4x100, 4x400 and long jump at the 2000 Sydney Olympics, bettering the four gold medals Carl Lewis won at the 1984 Los Angeles Games. In the end she had to settle for three gold and two bronze medals and, ominously, during the Games it was announced that her husband C.J. Hunter had tested positive for the steroid nandrolone. She herself was subsequently investigated in connection with the BALCO laboratory doping scandal, but no formal charges were pressed. In 2006 she tested positive for the blood booster EPO but was cleared when the second urine sample did not match the first. Jones qualified for the 2004 Athens Olympics but failed to win a medal.

CLOCKWISE FROM ABOVE Jones competes in the long jump final at the Athens Olympics. 27 August 2004. Kai Pfaffenbach. Jones kneels after winning the 200 metres final at the Sydney Olympics. 28 September 2000. Gary Hershorn. Jones runs in the 4x100 relay at the Team Challenge in Munich. 8 August 2004. Alexandra Beier

## PAULA RADCLIFFE

For more years than she would care to remember, Paula Radcliffe epitomized the gallant British loser, leading for lap after lap in major championship 10,000 metres finals only to be overtaken in the final 400 metres by a posse of light-footed Africans. In fact until 2002, when she transferred to the marathon, all Radcliffe had to show for her efforts on the track was a silver medal at the 1999 Seville world championships.

Her life was to change dramatically in 2002 when she won the London marathon in two hours 18 minutes 56 seconds, the fastest debut by a woman. She went on to win world cross country, Commonwealth and European track gold medals, then captured the marathon record with 2:17:18 in Chicago. In 2003 she reduced the record to 2:15:25 with a brilliant solo run in London. All seemed set fair for the 2004 Athens Olympics.

Radcliffe carried a heavy burden of expectation as the fastest woman in the field and one of Britain's few gold medal hopes. But despite running from the front as

always, she never looked happy in the stifling heat and humidity, and after slipping to fourth she suddenly pulled out with about four kilometres (2½ miles) remaining.

She sat weeping by the roadside and was eventually accompanied by her parents and trainer-husband Gary Lough to the finish line. Distressed that she had let down her country and friends, Radcliffe competed in the 10,000 metres but again failed to finish.

Showing the grit and determination which had characterized her career, she was soon back in training and won the New York marathon later in the year. Vindication came in 2005, when Radcliffe won the world championships gold medal in Helsinki. In the following year she announced she was having a baby in early 2007 but planned to return to her full-time running career.

## HERMANN MAIER

Downhill racer Hermann Maier has all the attributes necessary for success in a sport as dangerous as it is exciting. Aggressive, strong and fearless, Maier possesses an admirable work ethic and complete dedication. He has also coped with reverses which would have daunted a less resilient spirit. Sent home from the Austrian ski academy in Schladming because he was deemed too frail to succeed, Maier took up bricklaying in the summer and worked as a ski instructor in the winter.

After a series of successes in regional races he finally made the powerful Austrian ski team and won his first World Cup race, a super-G in Garmisch-Partenkirchen in Germany. A spectacular crash in the downhill at the 1998 Nagano Olympics did not prevent Maier winning the giant slalom and super-G titles and he ended the season by winning the overall World Cup title. He won the overall World Cup again in 2000, 2001 and 2004.

Maier's career had appeared over when he narrowly escaped death in a motorcycle accident in August 2001. A compound fracture of his right leg

was serious enough for doctors to consider amputation. Instead Maier underwent reconstructive surgery and hours of physiotherapy, and although the 2002 Salt Lake City Olympics were out of the question, he returned to competition in January 2003.

ABOVE Maier removes his race bib after finishing second in a World Cup super-G in Val Gardena, Italy. 17 December 2004. Dylan Martinez

# JANICA KOSTELIĆ

Pain and Janica Kostelić are lifetime companions. The only woman to win four Olympic Alpine skiing gold medals broke her leg at the age of 11. Two years later she broke an ankle. Then, aged 17, she damaged her right knee in a career-threatening injury which required five hours' reconstructive surgery. By the time she won her fourth gold medal at the 2006 Turin Olympics, Kostelić had survived 11 operations on her fragile knees and the loss of her thyroid gland.

The Croatian's exceptional resilience was forged in extraordinary times. As Yugoslavia disintegrated into civil war, Kostelić's father Ante, a former skier and handball exponent, drove Janica and her older brother Ivica hard – literally. Ante ferried his children around European ski resorts in his car, which doubled at night as the family's sleeping quarters. Janica and Ivica, with little else to distract them, practised endlessly.

The rewards came during eight days at the 2002 Salt Lake City Olympics when Janica won gold medals in the combined, slalom and giant slalom and finished second in the super-G.

Fate had one further test for Kostelić. In 2003 she found herself increasingly struggling for breath. Eventually she collapsed and was air-lifted to hospital, where an over-active thyroid gland was diagnosed (coincidentally the same complaint suffered by twice Olympic 100 metres champion Gail Devers, still competing in 2007 at the age of 40). After surgery Kostelić returned to dominate her sport and in Turin she became the first woman to win the combined title for a second time.

BELOW Kostelić embarks on a practice run for a World Cup downhill race in St Moritz. 19 January 2006. Wolfgang Rattay

## YEVGENY PLUSHENKO

Yevgeny Plushenko has pushed back the barriers in figure skating since he became the youngest male skater to receive a perfect score of 6.0, a landmark achieved at the age of 16. He was the first man to perform a quadruple toe loop-triple toe loop-triple loop jump in competition and has landed quadruple lutz jumps in practice.

After starting his career at the age of four he won the 1997 junior world championship at the age of 15. In the following year he was third in the senior championship.

Plushenko was coached by Alexei Mishin, who coincidentally trained his great rival Alexei Yagudin, the 1998 world champion. The pair came head-to-head at the 2002 Salt Lake City Olympics, where it was Yagudin who prevailed after finishing first in the short programme. Plushenko, fourth in the short programme, rallied with a dazzling display in the free programme to the music from 'Carmen' but could not overhaul Yagudin for the gold. Yagudin's retirement paved the way for Plushenko's triumph at the 2006 Turin Olympics.

OPPOSITE Plushenko performs in the short programme at the European championships in Turin. 26 January 2005. Tony Gentile

## CINDY KLASSEN

Medals flocked Cindy Klassen's way at the 2006 Turin Games, albeit in speed-skating with its proliferation of events over various distances. Winning bronze medals in the 3,000 and 5,000 metres, silvers in the 1,000 and team pursuit, and a gold in the 1,500, she equalled American Eric Heiden's 1980 record of five Olympic speed-skating medals and became the first Canadian to collect six Olympic medals after her bronze at the 2002 Salt Lake City Olympics. Unsurprisingly Klassen was named 'woman of the Games' by International Olympic Committee president Jacques Rogge.

A descendant of Mennonite immigrants to Manitoba, Klassen was a member of the Canadian youth ice hockey team but turned her attention to speed-skating when she was not selected for the 1998 Nagano Olympics.

She sustained a potentially career-ending injury at the start of the 2003–4 season when her right forearm was sliced to the bone, cutting through 12 tendons, a nerve and an artery. But despite losing the feeling in two fingers, Klassen's skating was unaffected.

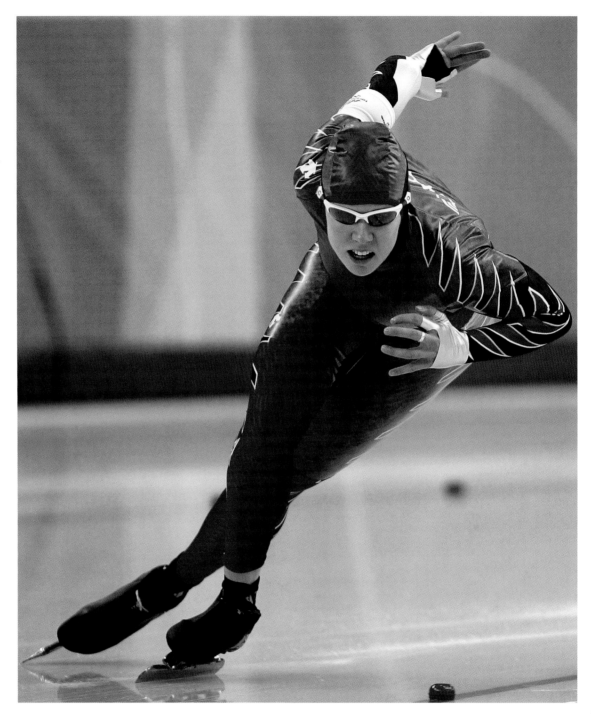

ABOVE Klassen races in the 1,000 metres at the Turin Winter Olympics. 19 February 2006. Jerry Lampen

## MICHAEL PHELPS

Swimming offers the chance for multiple gold medals. American Mark Spitz won a record seven at the 1972 Munich Games. In 2004, his compatriot Michael Phelps announced he would attempt eight gold medals at the Games in Athens: the 200 metres freestyle, the 100 and 200 butterfly, the 200 and 400 individual medleys, the 4x100 and 4x200 freestyle relays and the 4x100 medley relay.

Phelps had his critics within the U.S. team. Gary Hall and Jason Lezak publicly criticized the decision to allow him to swim in the 100 metres relay team because he had not swum in individual events at the trials. In the event Phelps fell short of his target by two, managing only bronze in the 200 metres freestyle while the U.S. team finished third in the 4x100 relay. Nonetheless, his overall tally of eight medals equalled the previous record set by gymnast Alexander Dityatin at the 1980 Moscow Olympics.

In 2007, Phelps won an unprecedented seven gold medals at the world championships in Melbourne, including four individual world records.

## IAN THORPE

Swimmers typically mature and retire early, soon wearying of the grind of endless training laps. It was still a shock, though, when Australia's greatest Olympian Ian Thorpe announced he was quitting in 2006 at the age of 24.

Thorpe, at only 17, was the focus of obsessive Australian media attention at the 2000 Sydney Olympics, where he set a world record in the 400 metres freestyle, then anchored the 4x100 quartet to a second world record. His Dutch rival Pieter van den Hoogenband then stunned the noisy crowd at the Olympic pool into silence when he prevailed in the 200 metres freestyle final. But Thorpe won his third and final gold medal when he led the 4x200 freestyle relay squad to victory.

He added two more at the 2004 Athens Games then took a year off to recharge for an anticipated tilt at the 2008 Beijing Olympics. A comeback at the 2006 Commonwealth Games was aborted when he was struck down by glandular fever and a move from Sydney to Los Angeles failed to revive his flagging enthusiasm.

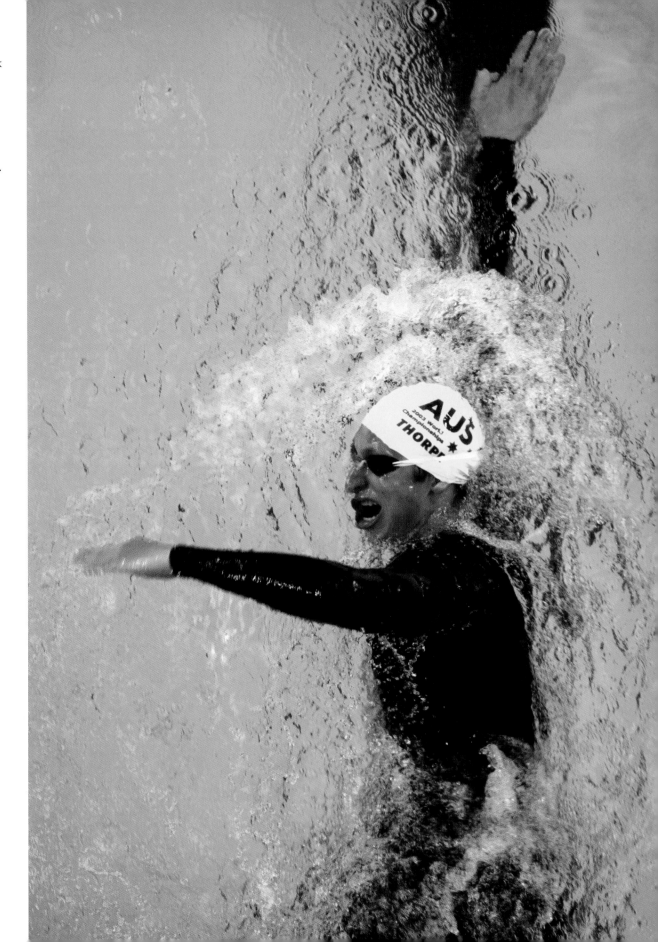

OPPOSITE  Phelps touches the starting block before a training session at the Athens Olympic Aquatic Centre. 12 August 2004.
David Gray

RIGHT  Thorpe in action during his 400 metres freestyle final at the world championships in Barcelona. 20 July 2003.
Albert Gea

## FRANKIE DETTORI

The effervescent, Italian-born jockey Frankie Dettori – a crowd favourite with his flamboyant leaping dismount – hails from exotic stock. His mother was a trapeze artist and his uncle a circus clown. More relevantly, his father Gianfranco was Italy's leading jockey. He was given a palomino pony at the age of eight and left school at the age of 13 to pursue a racing career, moving to Britain and joining trainer Luca Cumani at Newmarket two years later.

Dettori made racing history and a bookmaker's nightmare on 28 September 1996 by winning all seven races on the card at Ascot. He had no inkling himself that he was going to achieve the unthinkable. 'I could have an each-way chance in the first and I may win the third,' he said on the morning of the meeting. Instead he rode Wall Street, Diffident, Mark of Esteem, Decorated Hero, Fatefully, Lochangel and Fujiyama Crest to consecutive victories which were later dubbed the 'Magnificent Seven'.

In 2006, Dettori again sent the bookmakers into a spin by riding five winners at Goodwood for cumulative odds of 779–1.

LEFT  Dettori leaps from Papineau after winning the Gold Cup race at Royal Ascot in England. 17 June 2004.
Peter MacDiarmid

## STEVE REDGRAVE

'Anyone who sees me go anywhere near a boat again, ever, you've got my permission to shoot me.' Memorable words from an exhausted Steve Redgrave when asked if he would be rowing at the 2000 Sydney Olympics after winning his fourth Olympic gold at the 1996 Atlanta Games. But, as history records, Redgrave reconsidered at leisure and went on to win a fifth gold medal in Sydney before finally retiring.

Briton Redgrave, a large man 1.96 metres (6 feet 5 inches) tall, won his first Olympic gold at the 1984 Olympics in the coxed four. With Andy Holmes he won the coxless pairs in 1988, teamed with Matthew Pinsent to win the same title in Barcelona and Atlanta and made his farewell in the coxless four with Pinsent, Tim Foster and James Cracknell in Sydney.

Redgrave, who was diagnosed with diabetes in 1997, had a ferocious work ethic. He competed for Britain in bobsleigh and ran three London marathons for charity, but was more than happy to give up the never-ending grind of training. 'I hated training,' he said. 'It was a means to an end.'

ABOVE Tim Foster, Matthew Pinsent, Steve Redgrave and James Cracknell (left to right) celebrate winning Olympic gold in the coxless four in Sydney. 23 September 2000. Andy Clark

## ELLEN MACARTHUR

Born in the land-locked British county of Derbyshire in a nation of famous seafarers, Ellen MacArthur was fascinated by the ocean as a child and sailed her own dinghy at the age of eight. She pursued her vocation with a single-minded passion even when the battle to find a sponsor seemed hopeless. The retail group Kingfisher came to her rescue in 1998 and were immediately rewarded for their investment when MacArthur won her class in the solo Route du Rhum race that year. MacArthur, a fluent French speaker, became a heroine in France and then an international celebrity when she finished second in the 2000–1 Vendée Globe round-the-world solo race aged 24. In 2005 she sailed into the record books when she completed a solo round-the-world voyage, often in atrocious weather, in record-breaking time.

ABOVE MacArthur sails into Falmouth, Cornwall, after breaking the solo round-the-world record. 8 February 2005. Stephen Hird

## MICHELLE WIE

Michelle Wie, the willowy American with the whiplash drive, is determined to explore territories where no other women apart from Babe Didrikson, Annika Sörenstam and Suzy Whaley have ventured.

At the age of 12 she was the youngest person to qualify for an LPGA event. At 13 she was the youngest person, man or woman, to win an adult championship. Still only 13, she was the youngest player to make the cut at an LPGA tournament. By the end of 2006 she still had to win an LPGA event although was consistently among the leaders. But Wie has now also attempted to make her mark in the men's game by emulating Didrikson and Sörenstam and entering PGA tournaments. 'I belong on the LPGA, I belong on the PGA. I think I belong on both,' she said.

OPPOSITE Wie hits her tee shot on the fifth hole in the Sony Open second round in Honolulu. 16 January 2004. Lucy Pemoni

ABOVE Tyson flexes his biceps after the weigh-in for his title fight against Lennox Lewis in Memphis. 6 June 2002. Jeff J. Mitchell

OPPOSITE ABOVE Tyson playfully bites his son during a news conference in Tunica, Mississippi. 20 February 2003. Peter Jones

OPPOSITE BELOW Tyson sits on the canvas after being knocked out by Briton Danny Williams in their heavyweight fight in Louisville. 30 July 2004. Peter Jones

## MIKE TYSON

By the start of the new century, Mike Tyson was no longer the feared and respected fighter of his prime but had become little more than a travelling freak show. After his life unravelled following a rape conviction he had demonstrated similar lack of discipline in the ring, biting Evander Holyfield's ear and trying to break South African Francois Botha's arms. Still there was no doubting Tyson's crowd-pulling potential, and he was greeted by large crowds when he walked the streets of London in 2000 on a brief visit during which he recorded knockouts against mediocre opposition.

Lennox Lewis was a different proposition. A fight scheduled for Nevada was cancelled when the state boxing commission refused to grant Tyson a licence. The fight finally went ahead in Memphis on 8 June 2002, when Lewis exposed Tyson with a commanding victory in eight rounds. The American was never to be taken seriously as a fighter again.

Tyson filed for bankruptcy in 2003 after squandering the millions he had earned. He was knocked out by a journeyman Briton Danny Williams in 2004 and in the following year he quit during a fight with the equally unheralded Kevin McBride.

## LENNOX LEWIS

Lennox Lewis fought hard and long for the respect he craved and ultimately deserved when he retired in 2004 as one of only three men after Gene Tunney and Rocky Marciano to retire as world heavyweight champion. The Briton had lost only two of 44 professional fights in 14 years as a professional after winning the 1988 Seoul Olympic super-heavyweight title for Canada.

Born in east London, he moved to Canada with his mother Violet at the age of nine and his soft but distinctive Canadian accent was one reason he failed to win popular acclaim when he returned to Britain. Instead the people's choice was the muscular but limited Frank Bruno, whose career had been carefully stage-managed. Lewis also failed to impress the Americans, who found him too passive for their liking, preferring to craft points victories rather than excite the crowds with a flurry of punches.

Despite the reservations on both sides of the Atlantic, Lewis gradually accumulated an impressive record. After signing with a British promoter, Lewis became the World Boxing Council champion by default when American Riddick Bowe threw the belt into a dustbin. He lost the title two years later to Olivier McCall in the second round of their fight at Wembley.

In 1999 Lewis became the undisputed world champion when he outpointed the fading Evander Holyfield and in 2002 he confirmed he was the best heavyweight of his era by stopping Mike Tyson in the eighth round of a one-sided fight in Memphis. Having disposed of the old generation he then beat the best of the new by stopping Ukrainian Vitali Klitschko before deciding to retire at the age of 38. 'One of the reasons I am retiring is because I respect boxing so much,' he said. 'It's time for the younger generation to have their chance.'

OPPOSITE Lewis shadow boxes during a workout in Tunica, Mississippi, ahead of his fight against Tyson. 5 June 2002. Jeff J. Mitchell

RIGHT Lewis has his hands taped before a workout at a Mississippi casino. 5 June 2002. Jeff J. Mitchell

BELOW Vitali Klitschko takes a hit from Lewis during their title fight in Los Angeles. 21 June 2003. Fred Greaves

## MUTTIAH MURALITHARAN

The son of a confectioner from Kandy, Muttiah Muralitharan is one of the most successful yet controversial cricketers to play the game.

At first glance, Muralitharan appears to consistently break the fundamental rule of bowling, namely the requirement to deliver the ball with a straight arm. From a front-on action, with eyes bulging, the Sri Lankan flicks the ball from a supple wrist. His stock delivery is the off-spinner, whipping into the batsman's body. He has also mastered the doosra, the ball which spins away from the batsman without a discernible change in action.

Muralitharan's relationship with the Australians has been particularly fraught. They were openly unhappy with his action after their first encounter in 1993 and in the 1995 Boxing Day test at Melbourne he was no-balled by Australian umpire Darrell Hair. The home crowds were also openly hostile and at one stage Muralitharan announced he would no longer tour the continent, a decision he later rescinded.

Muralitharan's career was rescued by the International Cricket Council (ICC), the game's ruling body. After extensive tests, photographs and analysis the ICC concluded that Muralitharan did not bend and straighten his arm illegally at the point of delivery. It concluded, instead, that his action created 'the optical illusion of throwing'.

Throughout the furore, Muralitharan has continued to accumulate a prodigious amount of wickets. He followed Shane Warne in reaching the 600 landmark and, provided a fragile shoulder stands the strain, there is a possibility he could become the first player to capture 1,000 victims.

ABOVE Muralitharan practises in the nets at Old Trafford, Manchester, before the third test against England. 11 June 2002. Ian Hodgson

# SHANE WARNE

A bleached blond with a well-chronicled fondness for the good things of life, Shane Warne turned leg-spin bowling into pure theatre. His delivery from outside leg stump to beat and bowl former England captain Mike Gatting in 1993 was rated the ball of the century. At the end of the decade he was the only current player ranked by the Wisden cricket almanac as one of the five greatest players of the 20th century.

From a relaxed amble to the crease, Warne would spin the ball prodigiously from a vigorous body action. He bowled with unremitting accuracy, infinite variety and high intelligence. Before he retired in 2006 after Australia had regained the Ashes from England with a 5–0 series whitewash, Warne had become the first bowler to reach 700 test wickets. He took a test hat-trick, was man-of-the-match in a World Cup final, and was almost single-handedly responsible for the revival of the subtle art of spin bowling when it appeared fast bowlers were destined to rule forever.

Like all great athletes, Warne's true calibre was revealed at its best in adversity. When England won the Ashes in 2005 in a series rated by common accord as the best ever, Warne at times seemed to be playing the home side on his own. Up to the final passages of play in the final test at The Oval, Warne still commanded centre stage and still looked as if he could wrest the game back for Australia with a master class of spin bowling.

Warne's exploits also hit the news pages. He was banned for a year after testing positive for a weight-reducing drug, which could also be used to mask steroid use, and his marriage broke up after a series of affairs. Because of his indiscretions he was never a serious contender as Australia test captain, a job in which he would surely have excelled.

BELOW Warne tosses a ball during training in Mumbai ahead of a warm-up match for Australia's test tour. 28 September 2004. Arko Datta

## ROBERT HOYZER

In January 2005, 25-year-old German referee Robert Hoyzer admitted fixing soccer matches for financial gain. In a scandal that severely embarrassed the 2006 World Cup hosts, Hoyzer said he had taken bribes from a Croatian mafia circle based in Berlin. The betting fraud amounted to two million euros. Hoyzer was sentenced to two years five months in jail while another former referee, Dominik Marks, was given an 18-month suspended sentence. Berlin-based Croatian Ante Sapina was found guilty of running the operation and sentenced to two years 11 months.

ABOVE Hoyzer referees a German Cup match between Paderborn and Hamburg whose result he was subsequently proven to have influenced for his own financial gain. 21 August 2004. Marc Koeppelmann

## PIERLUIGI COLLINA

With his distinctive bald head and prominent eyes, Italian referee Pierluigi Collina was instantly recognizable and universally respected as he patrolled the pitch. He refereed the 1996 Olympic Games final between Nigeria and Argentina and was chosen at the 1998 World Cup to officiate in the highly charged fixture between the Netherlands and neighbours Belgium. The multi-lingual Collina was then entrusted with the dramatic Champions League final between Bayern Munich and Manchester United in 1999 and the Euro 2000 qualification playoff between old rivals England and Scotland.

He crowned his career when he refereed the 2002 World Cup final between Germany and Brazil. His commanding display, at the end of a tournament which had produced plenty of controversy over refereeing standards, showed exactly why he was so widely respected among players as well as officials.

LEFT Collina reacts as Barcelona players complain about Chelsea's fourth goal during a Champions League match in London. 8 March 2005. Dylan Martinez

## GUUS HIDDINK

Guus Hiddink, the prototype of the modern professional soccer manager with his constant changes of address, learned his trade with PSV Eindhoven before taking a talented but erratic Netherlands side to fourth place in the 1998 World Cup. After a brief spell with Real Madrid, Hiddink demonstrated his ability to maximize slim resources by taking South Korea to the same spot four years later at the first Asian World Cup. His achievements with South Korea, who had not won a match in four previous tournaments, were recognized by a grateful nation when he was given honorary South Korean citizenship, while the World Cup stadium in Gwangju was renamed the Guus Hiddink stadium.

By 2006 Hiddink had transferred his allegiance to Australia, where he guided the Socceroos to the second round in their first World Cup appearance for 32 years.

Still seeking new challenges, Hiddink accepted the job of Russia head coach in 2006.

LEFT Hiddink gestures during a friendly soccer match between Australia and the Netherlands in Rotterdam. 4 June 2006. Jerry Lampen

## JOSÉ MOURINHO

A brooding, handsome Portuguese habitually dressed in an expensive coat, José Mourinho looks the perfect representative of the new Chelsea built from the wealth of Russian billionaire Roman Abramovich.

After spells at Benfica and União de Leiria, Mourinho moved to Porto and quickly established himself as the most successful soccer club coach in Europe, winning the championship in 2003 and 2004, the Portuguese and UEFA Cups in 2003, and the European Cup in 2004.

The latter was enough to convince Abramovich and Chelsea that he was the man to lead them into a new era and he was confirmed as manager in June 2004. Mourinho commands a higher profile than most of his players but has fully justified his sobriquet as 'the chosen one' after taking the under-achieving west London club to successive Premier League titles in 2005, their first for 50 years, and in 2006.

LEFT Mourinho awaits the start of Chelsea's Premier League match against Wigan Athletic in Wigan. 14 August 2005. Mike Finn-Kelsey

## ALEX FERGUSON

On 6 November 2006, Alex Ferguson marked 20 years in charge of Manchester United, the club he has led to a record 18 major trophies. Knighted for his services to soccer, Ferguson was born and raised in Glasgow, where he was a toolmaker in the Clyde shipyards before a successful professional soccer career. He forged his reputation as a manager at Aberdeen. In 1986 he took over at United, where he dealt with a drinking culture that had got out of hand and reconstructed the youth team. Success was slow but the arrival of volatile Frenchman Eric Cantona in 1992 and the emergence from the youth team of David Beckham and the Neville brothers transformed the club's fortunes. In 1999 Ferguson achieved what no other British manager had managed – the domestic league and Cup titles plus the European Cup.

ABOVE Ferguson (right) complains after Wayne Rooney is sent off during a game against Porto in an Amsterdam tournament. 4 August 2006. Toussaint Kluiters

## LUIZ FELIPE SCOLARI

Luiz Felipe Scolari not only bears a disconcerting resemblance to the American film actor Gene Hackman but also projects the same tough, uncompromising image. In Scolari's case it is no act. A pragmatist in a nation of soccer romantics, Scolari took charge of the national team in 2001 when Brazil were in danger of missing qualification for the World Cup the following year. Brazil ground out the results and travelled to Japan and South Korea without Romario, after Scolari rejected calls to select a striker he regarded as past his best. His judgment was vindicated when Rivaldo, Ronaldinho and a rejuvenated Ronaldo took Brazil to their fifth World Cup victory. Scolari then decamped to Portugal where he coached his new charges to the Euro 2004 final, where they lost to Greece.

ABOVE Scolari celebrates after Portugal's second round World Cup win over the Netherlands in Nuremberg. 25 June 2006. Jose Manuel Ribeiro

## TONY LA RUSSA

A dogged baseball player of limited talent, Tony La Russa earned a law degree from Florida State University but never practised. Instead he brought his intensity and drive to management.

La Russa's analytical approach to the game has led him to be dubbed 'the thinking man's manager'. He has managed the Chicago White Sox, the Oakland Athletics and, since 1996, the St Louis Cardinals. In 2004 he became the sixth manager to win pennants with both American and National League teams. Two years later he became the first manager to win multiple pennants in both leagues and one of only two to win the World Series with teams in both leagues. He is also one of only three managers to be named Manager of the Year in both of baseball's major leagues.

LEFT La Russa attends a Cardinals workout for the series playoffs against the New York Mets in New York. 10 October 2006. Mike Segar

## PHIL JACKSON

As an American coming of age in the 1960s, Phil Jackson naturally gravitated to the counter-culture, taking as his guidebook the hippie bible *Zen and the Art of Motorcycle Maintenance*. Partly as a result he became known as 'The Zen Master' after becoming the most successful basketball coach of his time.

Jackson graduated from playing to coaching in the NBA. He was head coach of the Chicago Bulls from 1989 to 1998 and the Los Angeles Lakers from 1999 to 2004, returning in 2005. With the peerless Michael Jordan at their heart, the Bulls won six NBA championships under Jackson in nine years. At the Lakers he drew the best out of Shaquille O'Neal and Kobe Bryant, who took the Lakers to three successive championships.

LEFT Jackson questions the referee during the Lakers' NBA game against the Portland Trail Blazers in Portland. 13 December 2003. Steve Dipaola

## JOHN BUCHANAN

Cerebral, bespectacled, with a fondness for the literary works of the Chinese warlord Sun Tzu, it is difficult to imagine anybody further removed from the stereotypical image of an Australian sports coach than John Buchanan.

The former university lecturer had a modest playing record but he took Queensland to their first Sheffield Shield triumph after decades of disappointment and duly succeeded Bob Simpson and Geoff Marsh in charge of the world's most successful national cricket side.

Buchanan's holistic approach, including off-field activities such as boot camps and poetry readings, did not win universal approval; Shane Warne remarked that he thought a coach was something to transport a team to and from training. However, Buchanan's overall record stands up to close scrutiny. At one stage his team had won 15 out of 15 tests and after losing the Ashes to England in 2005, Australia crushed their oldest opponents 5–0 in the following year.

RIGHT Buchanan (right) juggles the ball with Steve Waugh during a workout in Port of Spain, Trinidad. 15 April 2003. Andy Clark

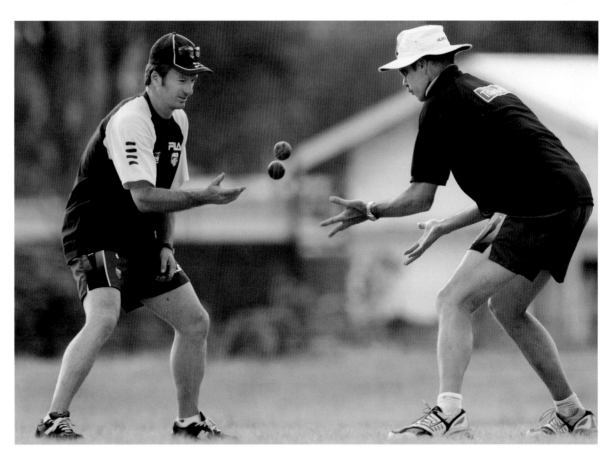

## CLIVE WOODWARD

Clive Woodward's place in English rugby folklore is secure. For Woodward's singular achievement was to coach the England side that overcame decades of southern hemisphere superiority to win the 2003 World Cup through a last-minute drop kick by Jonny Wilkinson.

As a player Woodward represented England and the Lions during the 1980s. After retirement he entered business, where he realized he wanted to bring the lessons he had learned from the commercial environment to the world of sport.

Woodward learned his trade as a club rugby coach and took over the national side in 1997. He immediately set about transforming the culture of English rugby, insisting on a fully professional environment for his players. The finest England XV yet assembled responded by beating New Zealand and Australia on their home territory in 2003 then winning the World Cup.

RIGHT Woodward holds rugby balls during a World Cup training session in Melbourne. 21 October 2003. Kieran Doherty

# The Spirit of Sport

## Dreams / Passion / Offbeat and Global Sports

A silhouette of a soccer player is projected on to a wall decorated with graffiti by World Cup fans in Dortmund, Germany. 13 June 2006. Andrea Comas

## SPORTS EDUCATION IN CHINA

Hungry for success, China has 300,000 children training rigorously in sports academies across the country. Future winners are plucked from kindergarten by scouts and drilled in gymnastics, table tennis, swimming, volleyball, badminton, weight-lifting and soccer. Beijing's famed Shishahai sports school has moulded dozens of international champions, including martial arts movie star Jet Li. Work starts at 6.30 a.m. and ends around 9 p.m. after a full day of practice and studying. Critics denounce the system as cruel, but the centres, modelled on Soviet sports schools, have helped the 2008 Olympic hosts to secure some 1,600 medals at Olympics, world championships and world cups since 1949. All photos by Reinhard Krause

BELOW Young Chinese gymnasts perform handstands at the Shishahai academy, the biggest sports boarding school in Beijing.

OPPOSITE ABOVE LEFT A boy grimaces as he exercises in the gymnastics hall of the Shishahai academy.

OPPOSITE ABOVE RIGHT Concentration is etched on the face of a young gymnast as he practises on the rings.

OPPOSITE BELOW Children hoping to continue China's Olympic success beyond the 2008 Beijing Games practise in the Shishahai gymnasium. All photos 21 December 2004.

## WELCOME TO BEIJING

Students exercise during a welcome ceremony for the British Culture, Media and Sport Secretary Tessa Jowell in Beijing. China, concerned at ignorance about the Olympics ahead of 2008, started up a programme in 530,000 schools to teach children the history of the Games and 'international manners'. 4 September 2006.

Jason Lee

## CHINESE OLYMPIC HOPEFULS

RIGHT Girls play in a swimming pool at a school in Shanghai where they are training as divers in the hope of continuing China's long domination of the sport at Olympic level. China took 24 of the 36 diving golds in the five Olympic Games before Beijing. 31 August 2006. Aly Song

BELOW Children swim while their parents wait at a pool in Wuxi, in eastern China's Jiangsu province. Despite the system of specialized training for youngsters, the country's Olympic chief Liu Peng complained in the run-up to the Beijing Games that Chinese swimmers had not improved enough. 3 August 2006. Huan Wei

## STREET CRICKET IN INDIA

TOP  Indian children play cricket in front of a temple in Mumbai. Youngsters in cricket-mad India, the world's second most populous nation, can be found playing improvised matches in almost every street of every city and town. 23 May 2005. David Gray

## SOUTH AFRICAN SOCCER DREAMERS

ABOVE  Aspiring soccer heroes train in Johannesburg. For the teenagers at the African Stars Soccer Academy, and thousands more across the country, the dream is to be part of the 'Bafana Bafana' national team at the 2010 World Cup on home soil. 30 April 2004. Mike Hutchings

## CUBAN BOXER IN TRAINING

A 13-year-old Cuban boy lifts a 15-kg (33-lb) weight during his boxing training session at an Old Havana neighbourhood gym. Cuba's state system has produced a steady stream of Olympic boxing champions. 12 August 2003. Claudia Daut

## BASKETBALL IN DIVIDED KOSOVO

BELOW  Kosovo Albanian boys play basketball in the snow near the ethnically divided town of Mitrovica. When all-Serb team Bambi joined the Kosovo league, playing against the Albanian majority, their coach's car was blown up. 8 February 2005.
Hazir Reka

## KABUL PALACE KICKABOUT

BOTTOM  In front of an old palace in Kabul, damaged during the civil war, Afghans gather for a kickabout. Soccer is hugely popular in Afghanistan but suffered under the Taliban, which imposed a litany of restrictions on games. 29 August 2006.
Ahmad Masood

## SOCCER IN AN ENGLISH HEATWAVE

BELOW  Two young men play soccer on a patch of dried-up ground in Gerrards Cross, Buckinghamshire, during a summer heatwave of record temperatures and lack of rain in England. 26 July 2006. Toby Melville

## COURTYARD SOCCER IN ABIDJAN

BOTTOM  Barefoot Ivorian boys play soccer in a courtyard in Abidjan with a makeshift goalmouth painted on the wall. The world's most popular sport needs nothing more than a ball and an open space. 26 October 2005. Thierry Gouegnon

## CHINESE GOLF BOOM

TOP A young Chinese golf player practises at Chaoyang Kosaido Golf Club in Beijing. The Chinese people have embraced golf with gusto and courses are springing up all over the country. 20 July 2006. Claro Cortes IV

## BOXING IN UGANDA

ABOVE American athlete Michael Johnson, winner of five Olympic gold medals, watches boys box at the Community Based Aids Programme boxing club in Kampala, Uganda. Johnson visited the project to celebrate five years of support from the Laureus Sport for Good Foundation. 26 October 2006. Euan Denholm

## CUBAN BASEBALL PASSION

TOP A Cuban boy plays baseball near the light tower at the entrance to Havana's bay. Baseball was introduced to Cuba 150 years ago by U.S. sailors loading sugar and has become a national passion on the Caribbean island. 25 November 2005. Claudia Daut

## FOOTBALL IN NEW YORK

ABOVE Children play football in Stuyvesant Square while enjoying record winter temperatures in New York. Though soccer is played by many American children, the homegrown game of football, along with baseball and basketball, remain the most popular spectator sports in the U.S. 6 January 2007. Lucas Jackson

## CAVE BASKETBALL IN CHINA

Two ethnic Miao children play basketball in a school playground inside a huge cave in a remote village in Ziyun county in southwest China. The village of Zhongdong, which means 'middle cave', is built in an enormous, natural cave, carved out of a mountain over thousands of years by wind, water and seismic shifts.
12 February 2007. Jason Lee

## SOCCER BEHIND THE BARRIER

Though there is officially no Palestinian state, FIFA recognizes the national team as Palestine and offered to pay for the refurbishment of the main soccer stadium in the Gaza Strip after the pitch was hit by an Israeli warhead in 2006. The conflict with Israel has hindered the development of the Palestinian professional game. The Palestinians use stadiums in Syria, Jordan and Egypt for matches for security reasons but have sometimes found their players unable to get to games abroad because of travel restrictions. The team labour in the lower reaches of FIFA's world rankings and have touted for recruits in Latin America, where many countries have communities of Palestinian and other Arab descent.

LEFT Palestinian players warm up for a friendly match beside a stretch of Israel's separation barrier which divides the West Bank village of Abu Dis. 9 June 2006.
Yannis Behrakis

ABOVE A Palestinian fan watches the friendly game in Abu Dis just a few hours before the World Cup kickoff in Germany. 9 June 2006. Yannis Behrakis

# THE DREAMS OF A TEENAGED BULLFIGHTER

Miguel Angel Delgado has the face of a choirboy and the build of a child yet he moves in the bullring with a calm assurance that belies his 16 years. Delgado started training at the age of eight at the Écija bullfighting school in southern Spain, one of a growing number of schools catering to boys and girls who dream of wearing the sequined 'suit of lights' in the country's bullrings. Some aficionados complain the schools churn out little bullfighting clones, ill-prepared for the cut-and-thrust of the circuit, but Delgado has attracted praise for his maturity and calmness. If he rises to the top of the pile, he could charge 100,000 euros ($125,400) for each appearance in the bullring. All photos by Marcelo del Pozo

BELOW LEFT Delgado dresses in his hotel room before going to Pinilla bullring to fight in Écija, southern Spain.

BOTTOM LEFT Beside an improvised shrine in his hotel room, Delgado adjusts his outfit before the bullfight.

BELOW Delgado (left) stands in the arena next to other apprentices.

BOTTOM After killing a bull and being given its ear as a trophy, Delgado is carried out of the ring in triumph.

OPPOSITE The teenager drives a sword into a bull at Pinilla bullring. All photos 17 June 2006.

## PASSION AND CONTROVERSY IN THE BULLRING

Bullfighting is a national symbol in Spain and arouses deep emotions both for and against. The cachet enjoyed by matadors endures and leading fighters command huge fees: El Juli (opposite above left) was said to have turned down 150,000 euros for one appearance in Seville. Yet there is also a vocal and increasingly militant anti-bullfighting camp, and the sport has come under pressure in forums such as the European Parliament for infringing animal rights regulations.

OPPOSITE  Spanish matador Fernando Cepeda prepares to drive his sword into a bull during a bullfight in Las Ventas bullring in Madrid. 19 May 2005. Victor Fraile

BELOW  El Juli, one of Spain's top young matadors, gets ready to perform a pass during a bullfight in Seville's Maestranza bullring. 11 April 2004. Marcelo del Pozo

BOTTOM  Francisco Marco manoeuvres in front of a fighting bull in Pamplona during the San Fermín Festival, when thousands of people run through the winding streets to the bullring early each morning, dodging six bulls which have been let loose. Fifteen people have been killed since 1924. 8 July 2003. Damir Sagolj

BELOW  Salvador Cortés holds his prize, the ears of a bull he has just fought and killed during a bullfight in Seville, as he is acclaimed by fans. 28 April 2006. Marcelo del Pozo

BOTTOM  Matador Miguel Abellán performs a pass as a bull does a somersault after getting its horn stuck in the ground during a bullfight in Seville. 29 April 2006. Marcelo del Pozo

## FESTIVE BULL-TAMING IN INDIA

OPPOSITE  Indian villagers try to catch a bull during the Jallikattu bull-taming festival in the village of Palamedu, 500 km (310 miles) southwest of the city of Chennai. Injuries are common in the annual event, which is held as part of southern India's harvest festival of Pongal. Daredevil participants try to catch a bull and run with it for 50 metres (160 feet) to win prizes including television sets, bicycles and cash. Breath tests are conducted and anyone found to have been drinking alcohol is barred from running. 15 January 2006. Babu

## BRAZILIAN RODEO

BELOW  A cowboy loses his hat as he competes in the bulldogging event at the Barretos Rodeo in Brazil. Barretos, in western São Paulo state, hosts one of the largest rodeos in the world. It has swollen from a get-together of bachelor cowboys into a mega-event drawing U.S. riders, country music stars and 1.2 million visitors during 10 hot and dusty days of raucous competition. Brazil's 1,300 rodeo festivals pull in more than 25 million visitors per year – five times the attendance at soccer games – and are spurring an economic bonanza. The region of Barretos now earns $150 million a year, or around three times the revenue of Rio de Janeiro's world-famous Carnival. 25 August 2006. Paulo Whitaker

## THE MANLY SPORTS OF MONGOLIA

The Naadam festival, Mongolia's national games, took on special significance in 2006 as the country marked 800 years since Genghis Khan united disparate tribes to form the Mongol Empire. In district centres across the vast nation, nomadic herders who make up nearly half of Mongolia's 2.7 million people congregated into stadiums for the annual pageant featuring what are known as the country's 'three manly sports': archery, bareback horse racing and wrestling. Mongolians say Naadam, the biggest event in the national calendar, is also about pride in the country's independence after centuries of rule under the Manchus, followed by decades of Soviet domination overcome in 1991.

TOP LEFT A rider passes a rainbow at Khui Doloon Khudag village on the eve of the Naadam festival. 10 July 2003. Claro Cortes IV

ABOVE LEFT Young Naadam wrestlers wait for their matches in Ulan Bator. 11 July 2003. Claro Cortes IV

TOP A wrestler trains for Naadam at a camp in the grasslands town of Suuj. 5 July 2006. Nir Elias

ABOVE Wrestlers take an outdoor shower at the end of a training session in Suuj. 5 July 2006. Nir Elias

## SUMO CEREMONY

ABOVE A sumo wrestler throws ceremonial salt before facing off in the first officially sanctioned Grand Sumo tournament in the United States in two decades. The giant wrestlers were treated like rock stars when Japan's ancient sport arrived at America's gambling and entertainment mecca of Las Vegas. 9 October 2005. Steve Marcus

RIGHT Japan's Kotomitsuki (top) heaves Tochinonada flat on to the sacred sumo ring at the New Year Grand Tournament in Tokyo. Historians say sumo began as entertainment for the gods, but there was nothing divine about a series of violent outbursts by some of the sport's heavyweights that tarnished its image in 2006. 17 January 2005. Toru Hanai

## OIL WRESTLING IN TURKEY

A young oil wrestler pins his rival to the grass as the referee signals for the end
of their match in the 645th annual oil wrestling tournament in Sarayici, western
Turkey. Wrestlers, clad in leather trousers and smeared with olive oil, grapple with
one another in a sport dating back to the middle ages. Putting a hand down the
opponent's trousers to get a better grip is a common tactic. 2 July 2006. Fatih Saribas

## ONE-LEGGED AFGHAN WRESTLING

BELOW  Afghan boys play Ghursay, a type of traditional Afghan wrestling, in Kabul. Players hold up one leg and attempt to push over their opponents while trying to reach a target on the ground. 17 February 2006. Ahmad Masood

## BOLIVIAN WOMEN TAKE TO THE RING

BOTTOM  Bolivian Aymara Indian female wrestlers are helped by experienced wrestler 'Mister Atlas' (left) to prepare for a bout in El Alto. To the horror of Bolivian machos, women have made a successful incursion into the professional wrestling ring. 19 December 2004. David Mercado

## INDIAN WRESTLER'S RESPITE

BELOW  A wrestler performs a headstand in a clay pit near the river Ganges in the eastern Indian city of Kolkata. 15 November 2006. Parth Sanyal

## BARE-KNUCKLE FIGHTING

BOTTOM  Fist-fighters slug it out in the annual Venda bare-knuckle tournament in Gaba village, Limpopo province, South Africa. Volunteers ranging from five-year-old boys to pensioners are randomly chosen to fight until one of them is knocked out or surrenders. 28 December 2006. Siphiwe Sibeko

## SCOTTISH HIGHLAND GAMES

Soldiers take part in the tug-of-war at the Braemar Highland Games in the
Grampian Highlands, the grand finale to the Games season. Athletes from
throughout Scotland gather on the first Saturday of September to compete in
traditional events such as caber-tossing, hammer throwing, highland dancing and
bagpipe playing, watched by Britain's royal family. 6 September 2003. Jeff J Mitchell

## INDIAN POLE EXERCISE

An Indian boy practises traditional pole mallakhamb at a training centre in Mumbai. The centuries-old sport involves performing exercises and poses on a wooden pole. Devotees say that it boosts all-round fitness, increases agility, builds muscle and improves mind and body coordination, and it has become a fashionable leisure pursuit in both Delhi and Mumbai. 26 September 2004. Arko Datta

LEFT An elderly Indian from Brazil's Surui nation looks through a traditional Cokar headdress, made with macaw feathers, during the sixth Indigenous Nations' Games in Palmas. 6 November 2003.

# INDIGENOUS SPORTS IN BRAZIL

From the Amazon rainforest, the open plains of the south and the coastal regions of the northeast, Brazil's diverse tribes congregate for the annual Indigenous Nations' Games to take part in unique events such as the 'toras' run, a relay race in which competitors shoulder a section of a tree trunk weighing up to 60 kg (130 lb). Singing, dancing and storytelling are part of the festival. The Indian population numbered an estimated six million when Portuguese explorers first landed in 1500 in what would become Brazil. Over the centuries, they have suffered enslavement, extermination campaigns, disease and neglect and by 2000 numbered about 734,000 in around 230 tribes, according to government figures.

All photos by Paulo Whitaker

BELOW LEFT Members of Brazil's Yawalapiti nation compete against another tribe in the tug-of-war at the sixth Games. 6 November 2003.

BOTTOM LEFT Members of Brazil's Matis nation, who live along the border with Peru, watch the Games in Palmas. 6 November 2003.

BELOW A child from the Kayapo tribe practises with a bow and arrow. 6 November 2003.

BOTTOM Xerente women train for the relay race carrying sections of tree trunks, called 'toras,' at the seventh Indigenous Nations' Games in Porto Seguro, Brazil. 24 November 2004.

## OPEN-AIR BILLIARDS IN TIBET

Ethnic Tibetans play billiards below a rain-threatening sky in Dangxiong County, Tibet. A battered billiard table is a common sight even in the smallest village in Tibet, where it is said one in six people play the game. The sport is popular across the region, and has been one of the disciplines in the Asian Games since 1998. 29 June 2006. Jason Lee

## THE GAY GAMES IN CHICAGO

Brought together under the slogan 'participation, inclusion and personal best', 12,000 athletes descended on Chicago in July 2006 for the seventh Gay Games, eight days of events mixing aerobics and same-sex ballroom dancing with traditional sports. Seventy nations were represented, including some where gay relationships are outlawed. The U.S. government eased immigration restrictions for non-citizens with HIV to attend. The event was one of two in North America due to a schism among organizers; Montreal hosted the first World Outgames with around 13,000 participants. The Gay Games movement was started in 1982 by Tom Waddell, a U.S. decathlete at the 1968 Mexico City Olympics. All photos by John Gress

TOP LEFT U.S. wrestlers Jake Whitehill (left) and Calvin Malone relax on the mat during a break. 17 July 2006.

ABOVE LEFT Janis Verrusa (right) of the U.S. laughs with compatriot Kathy Brennan before the Physique competition of the Games. 18 July 2006.

TOP RIGHT American Will Cater (left) and Arik Pou of the Philippines

embrace between wrestling bouts at the seventh Games. 17 July 2006.

ABOVE Frenchman Michel Jacq-Hergoualdh, 63, keeps an eye on the pre-judging for the Games' Master Physique event. 18 July 2006.

OPPOSITE Americans Jay Kobayashi (front) and Bradley Erickson perform a figure skating routine inspired by the film *Brokeback Mountain*. 19 July 2006.

## BUILDING THE BODY BEAUTIFUL

Bodybuilders believe their sport deserves a place at the Olympics but critics argue it is riddled with performance-enhancing drugs and is more akin to a beauty contest. Seven-times Mr Olympia Arnold Schwarzenegger, who went on to become the governor of California, has admitted using steroids during his bodybuilding career and said in 2007 he thought it likely that some contestants were still using banned drugs.

LEFT Male competitors wait backstage at the world fitness championships in the Greek town of Kavala. 5 November 2006. Grigoris Siamidis

BELOW LEFT In high heels and thongs, women compete at the world fitness championships in Kavala. 5 November 2006. Grigoris Siamidis

## MR AFGHANISTAN

Bodybuilders apply tanning lotion as they prepare to compete for the title of Mr Afghanistan in Kabul. Bodybuilding is the most popular sport in Afghanistan after soccer according to the sport's guardians, who organized the country's first Mr Afghanistan contest in 2005. Forty-eight bodybuilders flexed their muscles and showed off oiled torsos to compete for the title, which went to a 23-year-old businessman. Gyms have mushroomed since the days of Taliban rule. 18 September 2006. Ahmad Masood.

# A BREEDING GROUND FOR BOXING CHAMPIONS

For decades Mdantsane, a township of about half a million inhabitants just outside East London, regarded itself as South Africa's home of boxing and a breeding ground for champions. The township has produced more than 10 world champions since South Africa was readmitted into the international sporting fraternity. Trainer Mzi Mnguni converted his old hardware store into a gym and used his own cash to buy all the equipment, including punchbags, gloves and protective gear. Even so, the basic facilities contrast starkly with state-of-the-art studios in Johannesburg, which are luring away the best boxers.

OPPOSITE AND BELOW Boxers train at the Eyethu Boxing Club in Mdantsane township. 25 April 2006. All photos by Siphiwe Sibeko

## FINGER WRESTLING IN BAVARIA

In Bavarian beer cellars, men keep up the centuries-old tradition of finger wrestling. Using only their middle fingers for the tug-of-war they attempt to pull their opponent belly-first across the table. To strengthen their fighting fingers, some contestants train by hauling loaded carts up a hill or pulling a heavy lorry. The strain exerted in competition can induce nosebleeds.

ABOVE Two entrants in the Bavarian finger-wrestling championships wait for the referee to start their match in Mittenwald. 20 July 2003. Alexandra Beier

RIGHT A finger wrestler tries to drag his opponent over the table in the Bavarian village of Pflugdorf. 27 August 2006. Alexandra Beier

# AFGHANISTAN'S NATIONAL SPORT

There are few hard and fast rules in buzkashi, regarded by many as Afghanistan's national game, but the idea is simple. First the carcass of an animal, perhaps a calf, sheep or goat, is placed inside a chalk circle on the pitch. Two teams of horsemen throng round the dead animal, their horses nervously jostling each other, the riders hanging down from the saddles. When one rider gets a grip on the carcass he gallops away with it hanging at his side. His aim is to make it once around the stadium and deposit the animal back in the chalk circle to score, fighting off rival horsemen who try to seize the animal or block his route home.

OPPOSITE Afghan chapandaz, or horse rider, Sultan Mahmood practises his skills in Kabul. 27 February 2004. Ahmad Masood

RIGHT In Mongolia, where the game is also played, horsemen tussle over a goat skin at the Altai Eagle Festival in Sagsai. 1 October 2006. Zeev Rozen

RIGHT BELOW Afghan men compete in Kabul. Buzkashi was rarely seen in the capital under Taliban rule, partly because civil war closed routes to the north where the game is most popular. 3 November 2006. Ahmad Masood

## THE PALIO IN SIENA

To some it is just a trumped-up horse race, a multi-coloured tourist attraction. To the people of Siena, the Palio is the very essence of existence, the lifeblood of the Italian town. Each 2 July and 16 August, almost without fail since the mid-1600s, 10 riders have hurtled bareback around Siena's shell-shaped central square in a desperate bid to win the Palio, a silk banner depicting the Madonna and child. For the 75 or so seconds it takes horse and rider to lap three times around the sloping square's hard-packed earth, Siena is caught in the grip of a monstrous frenzy. The action is alarming, with jockeys, known locally as 'assassins' or 'mercenaries', free to ram and beat their rivals as they charge headlong around the course, inches from spectators and in constant danger of careering into the barriers that force them round the two absurdly tight right-angle turns.

TOP LEFT A priest blesses a horse and rider with the traditional exhortation 'Vai e torna vincitore' ('Go and return a winner'). 16 August 2006. Stefano Rellandini

ABOVE LEFT Selva parish jockey Alberto Ricceri embraces his horse after winning the 2006 Palio. 16 August 2006. Stefano Rellandini

TOP Jockey Alberto Ricceri of the Giraffa parish outruns Dino Pes of Bruco parish. Siena's 17 districts are awarded places in the Palio by lottery. 2 July 2004. Daniele La Monaca

ABOVE The flag of the Lupa parish is waved in front of Siena's Cathedral before the race. 2 July 2004. Daniele La Monaca

BELOW Siena's Piazza del Campo is packed with spectators on the last day of practice for the Palio. 15 August 2006. Stefano Rellandini

## ELEPHANT POLO

The Himalayan kingdom of Nepal is the venue for the annual World Elephant Polo Championship, an event dreamed up by two Britons over drinks while on holiday in St Moritz. Rules are the same as for horse polo, with a few important changes: elephants must not lie in the goalmouths, pick up the ball with their trunks or stand on it. Mahouts slap their legs on the elephants' sides to give directions and the players sit behind, wielding a stick at least two metres long. Men must control the stick with one hand but women can use both, a rule that threw referees at Thailand's King's Cup into confusion when the Screwless Tuskers team of Thai ladyboys arrived to play in the 2003 tournament. After some discussion, they were allowed to play as women but lost to Australia.

LEFT Elephants are prepared for the eight-team world polo competition in the Meghuli Forest in southern Nepal. 30 November 2006. Gopal Chitrakar

BELOW Scottish team Angus Estates (in blue and black) play National Park of Nepal in the 2006 final in Chitwan. The Scots won 8–6. 1 December 2006. Gopal Chitrakar

# EAGLE HUNTING IN KAZAKHSTAN

The people of eastern Kazakhstan have been hunting with golden eagles since the days of Genghis Khan. The tradition of a winter hunt is now preserved by a handful of families who have passed their skills from generation to generation. Clad in fur hats and embroidered tunics similar to those worn by their nomadic ancestors, the hunters, or berkutchi, take the eagles to the foothills of the Tien Shan mountains, where they hunt foxes. The eagles dive at speeds up to 300 kph (185 mph), using their razor-sharp talons to strike prey. People travel from all over the world to witness the majesty of the hunt. For visitors from central Asia, it is a rare chance to reconnect with their ancestors. All photos by Shamil Zhumatov

OPPOSITE ABOVE LEFT An eagle has its head covered by a leather cap before a hunt near the town of Taldykorgan, Kazakhstan. 23 January 2004.

OPPOSITE ABOVE RIGHT A Kazakh hunter rides with an eagle during a traditional two-day hunting competition near Taldykorgan. 24 January 2004.

OPPOSITE BELOW A golden eagle catches a fox during a hunting festival in Chengelsy Gorge, 150 km (93 miles) east of Almaty. 11 February 2006.

BELOW A Kazakh female hunter releases her eagle in Taldykorgan. The eagles have wingspans of up to two metres (6ft 6in). 23 January 2004.

## SPORTING NOVELTIES

ABOVE An orang-utan raises his arm after knocking out his fellow primate at a kickboxing match in Bangkok. Many of the apes in such events are imported illegally from the jungles of Malaysia and Indonesia, where fewer than 30,000 orang-utans are thought to remain. Environmentalists say that if the current rate of decline continues the species could become extinct in 20 years. 15 November 2003. Sukree Sukplang

OPPOSITE Kenyan jockeys race ostriches during the Jockey Club of Kenya's celebration of 100 years of thoroughbred horse racing at Ngong racecourse in Nairobi. The ostriches weigh between 180 and 200 kg (400–450 lb) and reach speeds of nearly 50 kph (30 mph). Other events at the Ngong celebrations included goat racing, helicopter rides and a fashion show. 31 October 2004. Radu Sigheti

## HORSE RACING ON ICE

BELOW  Skiers are towed by horses at speeds of up to 50 kph (30 mph) in the skikjöring event at the centenary White Turf meeting on a frozen lake at the glitzy Swiss ski resort of St Moritz. Over three consecutive Sundays, thousands of spectators sip champagne in lakeside marquees to watch the skikjöring, a 2.7-km (1.7-mile) race unique to the Engadine region of Switzerland, as well as other flat and trotting horse races. The skikjöring driver displaying the greatest courage, strength and stamina and gaining the most points over the three races is crowned King of the Engadine. 4 February 2007. Siggi Bucher

## MUD FLAT RACING

RIGHT  Jockeys race their horses through shallow water during the traditional horse-race meeting in Duhnen on the German North Sea coast near Cuxhaven. In 2006 some 30,000 spectators watched the annual event, held since 1902. The races begin when the ebbing tide exposes the mud flats. 6 August 2006. Christian Charisius

## EXTREME CYCLING IN MEXICO

A Mexican cyclist jumps with his mountain bike during the extreme cycling contest known as the Red Bull Down Taxco, in the city of that name, in the Mexican state of Guerrero. In 2005 dozens of daredevil competitors from all over the world took part in the competition, which saw riders racing downhill through the cobbled streets of Taxco, often flying high and sometimes diverting through the rooms and passages of houses on the route. Some cyclists found the downhill flight too much and were reduced to carrying their machines in front of large crowds who cheered Swiss mountain-biker René Wildhaber to victory. Such extreme events have gained great popularity among young people in many parts of the world, assisted by the patronage of the Red Bull drink brand. 20 August 2005. Luis Cortes

## WOMEN RACERS

LEFT Laleh Seddigh is reflected in a mirror of her racing car before the start of the Arjan rally outside Tehran. Seddigh was the first Iranian woman to compete against men in any sport since the Islamic revolution. Supported by her industrialist father, Seddigh fought against convention to become an elite performer in the male-dominated world of motorsport. Impressive in any context, her achievement is all the more remarkable in Iran, an Islamic theocracy where restrictions are imposed on women. 10 June 2005. Damir Sagolj

ABOVE Carla Barajas, 19, rides her motorcycle across the world's most famous high-speed salt flats at Bonneville in Utah at 250 kph (155 mph) during the annual World of Speed event. The event is the scene of many attempted land speed records in various different motorsport disciplines. Barajas, number 15069, clocked sufficiently fast times to claim membership of the elite 150 MPH Club at the event. 14 September 2006. Todd Korol

## SOLAR CAR RACING

ABOVE  For the North American Solar Challenge in 2005, 20 competing teams
from academic institutions all over North America took up the challenge to design,
build and then race their own vehicles. The event was the world's longest solar
car race and the first to go through both the United States and Canada, running
over 4,000 km (2,500 miles) from Austin, Texas, to Calgary, Alberta. Here,
Canadian Border Service Officer Lauren Lange clears driver Adam Vaccaro of the
Massachusetts Institute of Technology at the Emerson West Lynne Border Crossing
in Southern Manitoba, Canada. 21 July 2005. Stefano Paltera

## DIY FORMULA ONE

RIGHT  Zhao Xiuguo sits in his home-made model of a Formula One racing car
while his brother Zhao Xiushun looks on proudly outside their home in Tangshan,
Hebei Province, 180 km (112 miles) east of Beijing. The brothers, who worked
tirelessly on the project, constructed the full-size replica car from pieces of scrap
metal that they found. They said they were inspired to become the first Chinese
owners of a Formula One racing car. 21 July 2006. Claro Cortes IV

## THE WORLD OF SPEED

The World of Speed is an annual high-speed and endurance testing event held on Utah's sun-baked Bonneville Salt Flats, which have played host to land speed record attempts for decades. The Utah State Highway Department prepares and marks out a 16 km (ten-mile) stretch of straight land for speed trials and an oval track for distance races. The event features a broad selection of racing vehicles, many of them only seen at Bonneville. They include 'Lakesters', modified and street roadsters, vintage coupés, diesel trucks and hundreds of rare motorcycles. World of Speed has also featured a motorized skateboard. All photos by Todd Korol

LEFT Motorcycle racer Rod Henninger prepares to compete in the World of Speed event at the Bonneville Salt Flats, Utah. 14 September 2006.

LEFT BELOW Californians Keith Gaeth and Elaine Leach watch racers compete. 14 September 2006.

OPPOSITE ABOVE Randy Haubrich from New Hampshire takes loving care of his 1953 Studebaker. 14 September 2006.

OPPOSITE BELOW Roland Morrison races on a street luge board. 14 September 2006.

## POND HOCKEY IN THE UNITED STATES

LEFT Ice hockey players and fans attend the inaugural United States Pond Hockey Championships on Lake Calhoun in Minneapolis. The weekend event featured 116 teams on 25 rinks, making it the nation's largest outdoor ice hockey tournament. The success of the 2006 event caused it to be extended to three days the following year, although the 2007 Championships had to be moved from Lake Calhoun to Lake Nokomis because the original venue did not freeze over. 21 January 2006. Eric Miller

## BRITISH TOUGH GUYS

BELOW An athlete runs through flames as he competes in the Tough Guy Event in Preston, England, a biannual charity race designed to test physical and mental endurance on an obstacle course known as the Killing Fields. The course is a 12.9-km (eight-mile) combination of mud, brambles, ice cold water, underwater tunnels, smoke and climbing frames containing electric cables. Thousands of athletes strive to claim the coveted title of 'Toughest Guy in Britain.' 29 January 2006. Darren Staples

## POUNDING THROUGH WADI RUM

ABOVE Horse riders from the Middle East compete in the annual 120-km (75-mile) International Endurance Race in the spectacular desert of Wadi Rum in southern Jordan. Horses are stopped for rest and medical checks at regular intervals.
14 November 2006. Ali Jarekji

## GOLF IN THE NAMIBIAN DESERT

RIGHT Namibian Manfred Geinub plays a shot on a roadside desert golf track in Walvis Bay, Namibia. The nine-hole course dubbed the 'West Side Club' has no greens, tees, water or grass. Stinging sand and gusts of wind whistle through a lone row of palm trees on the edge of the forbidding Namib desert. Interest in golf is growing fast among the young people of the poor southern African nation.
16 May 2006. Howard Burditt

## AFGHAN GOLF OPEN

In 2004 Kabul Golf Club, a battlefield in the 1990s, hosted Afghanistan's first open golf tournament in more than 30 years. The first shot of the day went to the local militia commander, applauded by his men with shouldered Kalashnikovs. Organizers hoped their tournament, contested by 40 local caddies in a picturesque valley just outside the capital, would help usher in a new era in which the only risks were from golf balls, not bullets, flying down the fairways. The club describes itself as the best – and only – course in Afghanistan. The greens are brown, the club house is a bombed-out shell and hazards include the odd spent shell and scurrying lizard.

TOP LEFT A sign marks the entrance to Afghanistan's only golf course. 26 November 2004. Ahmad Masood

ABOVE LEFT Club professional Mohammad Afzal Abdul holds the Afghan Cup. 23 May 2004. Tim Wimborne

TOP A man stands in a doorway of the bombed-out club house at the Kabul course. 29 May 2004. Tim Wimborne

ABOVE Golfers line up before the start of the tournament. 26 November 2004. Ahmad Masood

BELOW A golfer plays at the Kabul club,
which promises 'golf with attitude'.
11 November 2005. Ahmad Masood

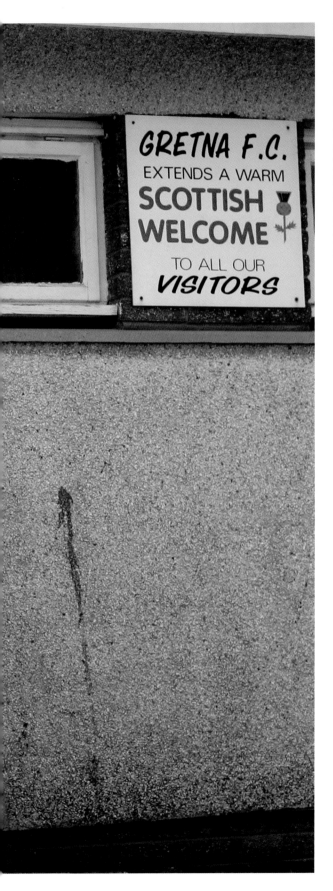

## GRETNA'S CUP RUN

Virtually the entire population of the tiny border town of Gretna headed to Hampden Park when their third-division club played in the Scottish FA Cup final in 2006. Four years earlier, Gretna had been playing before crowds of 60 in a minor English league. After gaining entry to the Scottish Football League they surged through the fourth and third divisions, then reached the cup final against Hearts. Millionaire owner Brooks Mileson, who also owns a private animal sanctuary, sold cup final tickets from a cabin in the club car park and gave away hundreds to local children. Though Hearts won on penalties, there was still a happy ending for Gretna, who qualified for the UEFA Cup as Hearts had secured a Champions League spot by finishing second in the Scottish Premier League.

LEFT Gretna player John O'Neil carries away the Scottish Cup after posing for photographers at the club's Raydale Park four days before the final. 9 May 2006.
David Moir

## BOSNIA UNITED

No other team in Bosnia depends more on unity than FC Guber Srebrenica. The mixed line-up of Muslims, Serbs and one Croat are still viewed with suspicion by some in the town, which had a Muslim majority before the 1992–95 war but was included in the Serb half of Bosnia in the peace accord that ended it. The amateur players are usually greeted with a torrent of nationalistic abuse when they play all-Serb teams in the country's basement league. Their biggest problem, though, says left-back Emir Jasarevic, is the referees. 'They're always against us regardless of where we play. This team is different and they can't stand it.'

All photos by Damir Sagolj

TOP LEFT Muslim and Serb players of FC Guber warm up together before a match in Srebrenica. 17 September 2006.

ABOVE LEFT The players greet a turnout of 20 supporters as they take to the pitch. 17 September 2006.

TOP Players of FC Guber (right) and FC Buducnost Pilicea wait to start their match in Bosnia's bottom league. 17 September 2006.

ABOVE Guber supporters sit on the grass to watch their team's game. 17 September 2006.

BELOW Coach Jusuf Malagic, the club's goalkeeper before the war and the man who revived the team, instructs his players. 17 September 2006.

BOTTOM Players listen to the team talk at half-time. 17 September 2006.

BELOW Stojan Milinkovic, Guber's 39-year-old Serb goalkeeper and one of five members of an extended family in the squad, saves a shot. 17 September 2006.

BOTTOM A Guber player looks from a window of the team bus after a derby match in Tabanci. 10 November 2006.

## THE MUD OLYMPICS

Enthusiastic participants battle for the ball during the Mud-Soccer World
Championships on the mudflats of the river Elbe in Brunsbüttel near Hamburg.
Approximately 300 athletes take part in the so-called 'Wattolümpiade' or Mud
Olympics. Other events include volleyball, cycle racing and Nordic mud-walking.
4 June 2006. Christian Charisius

## CHASING THE CHEESE

Blair Matheson wins the cheese during the Whitestone Cheese Rolling New Zealand championships at Waikaka, near Invercargill. Cheese rolling originated as a festive tradition in England. Competitors chase large cheese wheels that are rolled down a hill, and the person who reaches the cheese first gets to keep it. 6 February 2007. Simon Baker

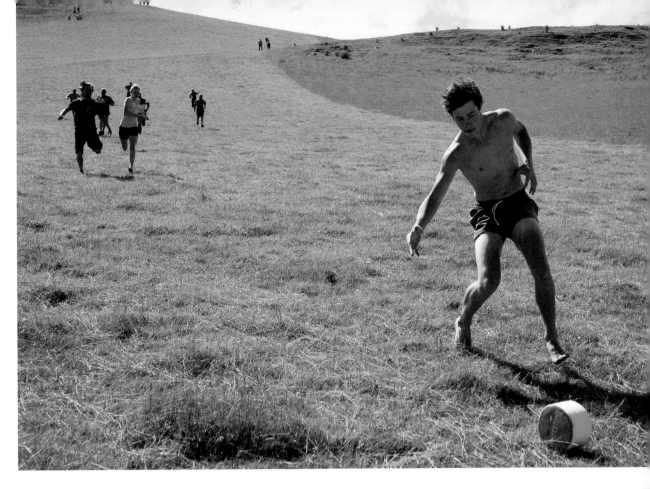

## BOG SNORKELLING

A competitor takes part in the 2006 World Bog Snorkelling Championship at Llanwrtyd Wells in Powys, mid Wales. One hundred entrants from around the world participated in the event, wearing snorkels and flippers to complete a course in a muddy trench 1.2 metres (four feet) deep. To make matters worse, conventional swimming strokes are banned. 28 August 2006. Phil Noble

## HUGE SURF IN SYDNEY

Unusually large swells, not seen in the district for many months, hit Sydney's beaches in late February 2004. They were caused by strong winds combining with a low-pressure cell off the east coast of Australia.

LEFT A group of young boys crouch behind a sea-pool wall as they play in massive surf at Sydney's Narrabeen Beach. 26 February 2004. David Gray

LEFT BELOW A man prepares to brave the massive surf at Sydney's Narrabeen Beach. 26 February 2004. David Gray

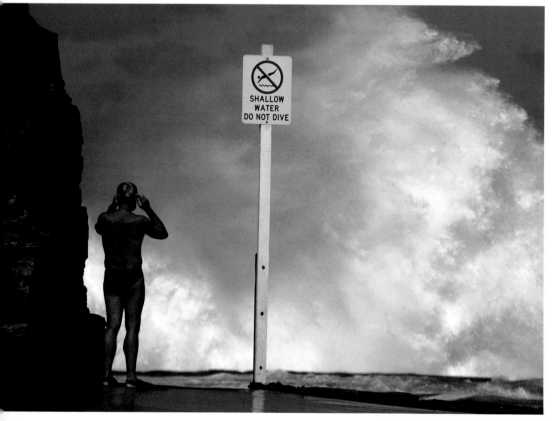

## MUD RACERS IN THE NETHERLANDS

OPPOSITE An exhausted participant climbs out of one of 22 energy-sapping ditches along the testing 3-km (1.8-mile) course by the meadow lands near Monnickendam in the Netherlands. In 2005 more than 200 runners took part in this traditional Dutch mud race that takes place annually at the start of the summer. 26 June 2005. Koen van Weel

## WINDSURFING IN THE CANARY ISLANDS

OPPOSITE Douglas Diaz from Venezuela (left) and Tonky Frans from Bonaire Island narrowly avoid a potentially catastrophic collision during a freestyle training session at the Fuerteventura Windsurfing and Kiteboarding World Cup. This annual event, which is open to amateurs as well as professionals, plays host to a number of world championship contests. Judges rate the competitors on their adventurous jumps and daredevil moves to decide who will be the World Cup winner. 22 July 2006.

Juan Medina

## EXTREME SPORTS IN LOS ANGELES

ABOVE Seventeen-year-old Rob Lorifice is separated from his skateboard as he competes at the 11th annual X Games in downtown Los Angeles. This incident happened when the rookie flew out of the quarter-pipe at the end of a Big Air ramp. More than 150 athletes compete in extreme action sports including surfing, BMX racing and rally car racing at the weekend-long annual event. 4 August 2005.

Lucy Nicholson

## SURFING ACROSS CONTINENTS

LEFT Hundreds of surfers take to the water in preparation for a Guinness World Record attempt for the most surfers to ride on one wave. The organizers in Muizenberg, Cape Town, claimed a record after 73 surfers, from an original 300 entries, caught and rode a wave for at least five seconds. This beat the previous record total of 53 surfers. 17 September 2006. Mike Hutchings

ABOVE Pancho Sullivan of the United States is just visible, a picture of concentration, as he surfs through a huge wave during the Quiksilver Pro France tournament at Hossegor in southwest France. The autumn event, which forms one leg of the ASP Men's World Champion Tour of Surfing, brings together a wealth of surfing talent from across the world. 28 September 2006. Victor Fraile

## DRAGON BOAT RACING

Widely popular throughout Asia, dragon boat racing originated in China where, according to tradition, races are held to commemorate the death of Qu Yuan (also known as Ch'u Yuen), a famous patriotic poet closely associated with the classical age and the creation of China itself. In the year 278 BC, according to legend, Qu Yuan carried a great rock into the river Miluo and took his own life in an act of ritual suicide. Learning of this, many ordinary people in fishing boats rushed to the middle of the river first to try to save him, and then to protect his body from fish and evil spirits by splashing the water with their paddles. The modern sport inspired by that moment involves long, narrow, human-powered boats in paddling contests for which the boats are always rigged with decorative Chinese dragon heads and tails. Each boat carries a drummer, a steering helmsman and 18 or 20 paddlers.

LEFT ABOVE Competitors participate in a dragon boat race at Hong Kong's Tolo Harbour. 18 June 2005. Bobby Yip

LEFT BELOW A dragon boat race at Hong Kong's Aberdeen fishing port. 11 June 2005. Kin Cheung

OPPOSITE ABOVE Dragon boat crews paddle in a race in Sydney Harbour during Chinese New Year celebrations. 20 February 2005. David Gray

OPPOSITE BELOW A Taiwanese dragon boat leader reaches out to take the victory flag during a boat race in Taipei. 26 May 2006. Richard Chung

# MARATHON RUNNING ACROSS THE WORLD

From elite athletes to charity fundraisers to club runners, people of all ages and all walks of life, all over the world, have given enormous support to public marathons and fun runs. Tens of thousands take part in the annual big-city public marathons in London, New York, Paris, Sydney, Berlin, Tokyo and Singapore, to mention but a few. For some runners, the necessary training period provides a motivation to get fit. For others, each event is a part of a carefully scheduled long-distance racing calendar. Huge crowds of spectators turn out and create a carnival atmosphere in the host city for a day. Marathon running originated in Greece, but the 42.2-km (26.2-mile) test of fitness, speed and endurance now belongs to millions of runners worldwide.

BELOW A photographer holds on to a traffic light pole at the start of the annual City to Surf fun run in Sydney. 14 August 2005. David Gray

OPPOSITE, CLOCKWISE FROM TOP LEFT The 2006 Beijing International Marathon. 15 October 2006. Grace Liang. The 2005 New York City Marathon. 6 November 2005. Seth Wenig. The 30th Paris Marathon. 9 April 2006. Victor Tonelli. The 2006 Barcelona Marathon. 26 March 2006. Albert Gea

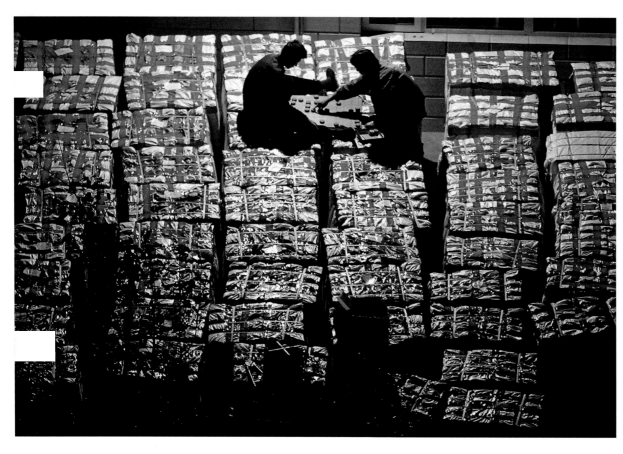

## CHINESE CHESS BREAK

ABOVE Beijing workers relax by playing Chinese chess while sitting on packages of garments awaiting shipment to Russia during the early hours of the morning. 5 May 2002. Andrew Wong

## SETTING A NEW CHESS RECORD IN MEXICO

RIGHT Fourteen thousand chess enthusiasts gather to enjoy playing one of the world's most popular games and in doing so earn a place in the *Guinness Book of World Records*. The successful attempt for the most simultaneous games of chess took place in Mexico City's Zocalo plaza. 22 October 2006. Tomas Bravo

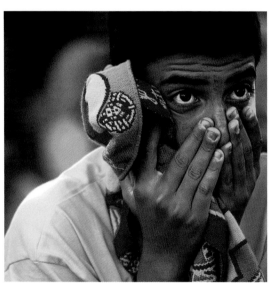

## WORLD CUP FEVER

No major sports tournament stirs the passions like the month-long finals of soccer's World Cup. Held every four years on a different continent, the World Cup inspires national fervour, manifested by fans in their national colours, songs, music, poetry and loud massed support inside and outside the stadiums when games are played. The finals create a fiesta atmosphere and fans party together as if the World Cup has taken over their lives. The excitement can lead to intoxication, extreme behaviour and even tragedy. Joy and despair are shared across nationalities and colours swirl in a rare sporting cocktail.

TOP LEFT An Italian soccer fan in Milan celebrates after Italy score during their World Cup Group E match against the Czech Republic in Hamburg, Germany. 22 June 2006. Stefano Rellandini

TOP CENTRE Daniel Dressel poses with his new special German soccer hairstyle in Munich. 14 June 2006. Michaela Rehle

TOP RIGHT A fan awaits the start of the second round World Cup 2006 soccer match between Spain and France in Hanover. 27 June 2006. Alessandro Bianchi

ABOVE LEFT A journalist wears a yarmulka with the pattern of a soccer ball during a news conference in Berlin. 20 June 2006. Alexandra Beckstein

ABOVE CENTRE A Czech Republic fan waits before his country's Group E World Cup match against the U.S. 12 June 2006. Carlos Barria

ABOVE RIGHT A Portugal fan watches the World Cup 2006 semi-final between Portugal and France in Lisbon. 5 July 2006. Nacho Doce

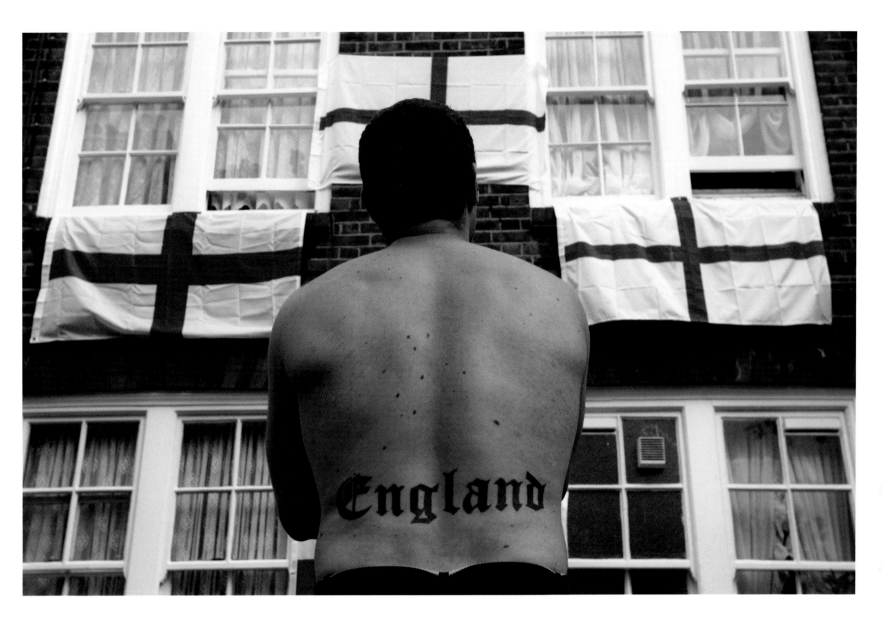

ABOVE A soccer fan looks at a building covered with England flags during the World Cup. 8 June 2006. Luke MacGregor

## WOMEN'S SOCCER IN THAILAND

Female Thai soccer fans gather at the Rajamangala National Stadium in Bangkok to support FIFA's U-19 Women's World Championship. Soccer has grown rapidly in popularity in Thailand, where many fans, both male and female, follow the fortunes of European clubs and watch televised games beamed to them from Britain and other countries. 10 November 2004. Lee Mills

## DISTRACTING THE OPPOSITION

German basketball player Dirk Nowitzki shoots a free throw for the Dallas Mavericks during their NBA Finals tie against the Miami Heat. In the background, Miami Heat fans try to distract him by holding up photographs of actor and singer David Hasselhoff after Nowitzki admitted he likes to hum Hasselhoff's song 'Looking for Freedom' during visits to the free throw line. Hasselhoff returned the compliment to Nowitzki by offering his support for the German's bid to claim the Most Valuable Player of the season award. 15 June 2006. Marc Serota

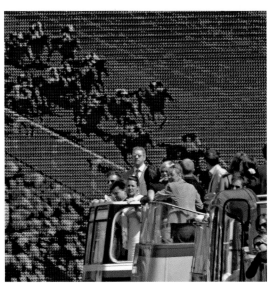

# BIG-SCREEN VIEWING

For sports-lovers who cannot attend a major event because it is sold-out, there is an increasingly popular alternative: join other fans in front of a big-screen showing. The phenomenon of big-screen viewing has grown rapidly and been adopted by many international sports organizing bodies. Fan parks, set up in town squares, fields and other big open spaces, can often generate as much atmosphere as inside a stadium. At the 2006 FIFA World Cup soccer finals in Germany, up to half a million ticketless fans congregated in Berlin to share in the big-screen experience set up for them. Many soccer clubs also beam back action from their away games to their home stadium to give fans a chance to follow them when they cannot buy tickets or travel. This new habit of sports-watching has been adopted across several sports including soccer, cricket, cycling and rugby union.

OPPOSITE TOP, LEFT TO RIGHT
Paris, 22 June 2002. Charles Platiau
Austin, Texas, 24 July 2005. Jeff Mitchell
Kabul, 22 June 2002. Beawiharta

OPPOSITE CENTRE, LEFT TO RIGHT
Munich, 30 June 2006. Alexandra Beier
Turin, 28 May 2003. Claudio Papi
Saitama, Tokyo, 12 June 2006.
Toru Hanai

OPPOSITE BELOW, LEFT TO RIGHT
Accra, 22 June 2006. Yaw Bibini
Berlin, 9 July 2006. Christian Charisius
Nice, 23 June 2006. Eric Gaillard

THIS PAGE TOP, LEFT TO RIGHT
Havana, 21 March 2006. Claudia Daut
Tokyo, 13 June 2006. Yuriko Nakao
The separation wall at the West Bank village of Abu Dis, 8 June 2006.
Ronen Zvulun

THIS PAGE ABOVE, LEFT TO RIGHT
Frankfurt, 21 June 2006. Toby Melville
Hong Kong, 14 June 2006. Bobby Yip
Epsom Downs, England, 4 June 2005.
Toby Melville

## STREAKER STEALS THE LIMELIGHT

New Zealand policemen struggle to get to grips with a streaker during a rugby match on a British and Irish Lions tour. The interruption did not disrupt the rhythm of the touring side who ran out 109–6 winners against the amateurs of Manawatu, winger Shane Williams scoring five tries. The match, in Palmerston North, provided one of the highlights of a miserable tour on which the Lions lost the test series 3–0 to the New Zealand All Blacks. In recent years streakers have disrupted play on Wimbledon's Centre Court, at the Turin Winter Olympic curling competition, NHL games and the French Open men's tennis final, and an online casino has used streakers as 'human billboards' at the U.S. Open golf and the 2004 Super Bowl. 28 June 2005. David Gray

## EXUBERANCE SPILLS OVER IN TURIN

Supporters of Italian soccer team Juventus invade the pitch, snatching the shorts and shirt of striker Filippo Inzaghi during a match against Atalanta at Delle Alpi stadium in Turin. The match was the final league fixture of the season. Despite defeating Atalanta 2–1, Juventus could only claim second place. The championship went to AS Roma who beat Parma 3–1 earlier in the day. The Rome club's first 'Scudetto' title in 18 years sparked a similar pitch invasion in Rome's Olympic Stadium. 17 June 2001. Stefano Rellandini

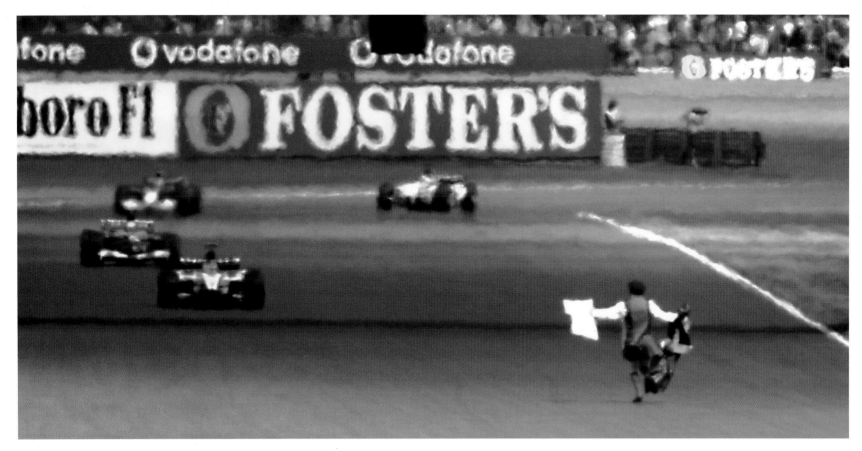

## MAVERICK RUNS AMOK

ABOVE Defrocked Irish priest Cornelius Horan is infamous for disrupting sporting events. He ran on to the track at Silverstone during the British Grand Prix carrying a sign that read 'Read the Bible. The Bible is always right.' Cars travelling at speeds of up to 320 kph (200 mph) were forced to swerve to avoid him. 20 July 2003. Jim Tanner

RIGHT Horan grabs leader Vanderlei de Lima during the men's marathon at the Athens Olympics. The Brazilian was leading by about 45 seconds but after being held up by Horan, was only able to claim the bronze medal. De Lima later unsuccessfully appealed to the Court of Arbitration for Sport to be awarded the gold medal won by Italy's Stefano Baldini. 29 August 2004. Ruben Sprich

## THE BRITISH SUMMER SOCIAL SEASON

Traditional sporting events provide some of the highlights of the British summer social calendar. The five-day Royal Ascot horse race meeting, the Henley Regatta and Wimbledon's tennis championships are all part of a tradition enjoyed by the social elite. These cherished occasions are as famous for their costumes, food and drink as the sport. Luminaries travel from all over the world to be involved, with Queen Elizabeth and Prince Phillip among the regular attendees on most days at Royal Ascot.

LEFT  Race-goers await the start of the first race at the Royal Ascot race meeting in Berkshire, England. 15 June 2004. Peter Macdiarmid

TOP  Race-goers, sporting classic and eye-catching hats, arrive for the second day at Royal Ascot. 21 June 2006. Alessia Pierdomenico

ABOVE  Spectators watch proceedings at the Henley Regatta, Henley-on-Thames, Oxfordshire. 30 June 2004. Toby Melville

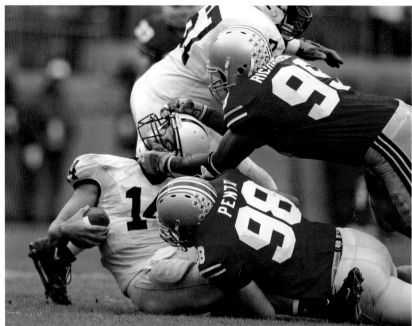

## OUCH!

Whether it involves taking a hockey stick in the face, being set upon by a gang of aggressive defenders or crashing your motorbike at high-speed, there is no doubt that the world of competitive sport can be a painful and even dangerous place. However, such risks and sacrifices are what make sporting achievements all the more satisfying.

Bayern Munich's Mark van Bommel (right) tussles with Inter Milan's Fabio Grosso during a soccer match in Milan. 27 September 2006. Alessandro Garofalo

Penn State quarterback Anthony Morelli is set upon by Ohio State defenders during a football game in Columbus, Ohio. 23 September 2006. Matt Sullivan

Germany's Timo Wess is challenged by India's Tushar Khandker during their Field Hockey World Cup match in Mönchengladbach. 6 September 2006. Pascal Lauener

Racing Lens' forward Eric Carrière takes it on the nose during a UEFA Cup soccer match against Groclin Grodzisk in Lens. 15 September 2005. Pascal Rossignol

Sevilla goalkeeper Andres Palop shields himself as fans throw objects at Atlético Madrid's Vicente Calderón soccer stadium. 23 March 2006. Alejandro Ruesga

MotoGP rider Alex Barros of Brazil crashes his Yamaha during the Australian Grand Prix at Phillip Island circuit near Melbourne. 16 October 2005. Mark Horsburgh

Brazilian official Lia Mara Lourenco is treated after being pierced by a javelin during warm-ups in a São Paulo competition. 24 September 2006. Jonne Roriz-Agencia Estado

Australia's Shane Rose, riding All Luck, crashes into a jump at the World Equestrian Games in Aachen. 26 August 2006. Caren Firouz

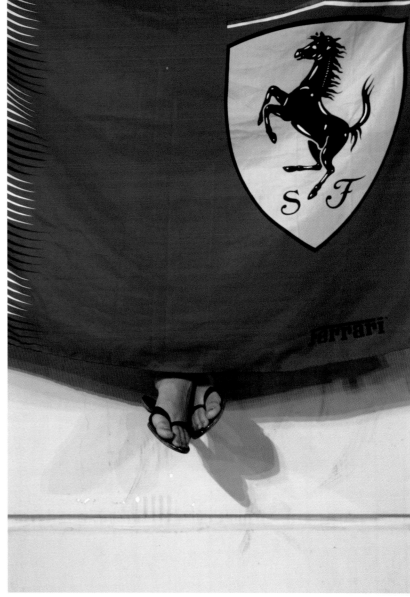

## FLYING THE FLAG

TOP A Benfica fan proudly waves his club's flag before the Portuguese Premier League soccer match against Belenenses at the Estádio da Luz in Lisbon. The match ended 0–0. 27 November 2005. Nacho Doce

ABOVE A Trabzonspor fan waves his team's colours standing in front of a Turkish flag before Trabzonspor's UEFA Cup second qualifying round soccer match against APOEL Nicosia of Cyprus. The match took place in the Turkish Black Sea city of Trabzon. 24 August 2006. Umit Bektas

ABOVE A fan sits behind a Ferrari flag at a charity soccer match between the Nazionale Piloti, including Ferrari driver Michael Schumacher, and a Greek All-Star team in Athens. 23 August 2006. Yiorgos Karahalis

TOP A mass gathering of South Korean soccer supporters watch their team's World Cup match against Portugal on a large screen in central Seoul. South Korea were joint hosts of the tournament with neighbours Japan. 14 June 2002. Noh Soon-taek

ABOVE Japanese supporters shelter from the rain under a giant sheet as they wait for the start of the World Cup Finals game between Japan and Turkey in Sendai. Turkey won the second-round match 1–0. 18 June 2002. Ian Waldie

TOP A Berlin apartment block is adorned with the flags of some of the nations competing at the 2006 FIFA World Cup in Germany. Italy went on to win the world's most important soccer competition. 12 June 2006. Pawel Kopczynski

ABOVE Portuguese and Angolan fans wait in the stands before their countries' World Cup Finals encounter in Cologne. Pedro Pauleta's fifth-minute goal proved enough for Portugal to overcome their African opponents 1–0. 11 June 2006. Albert Gea

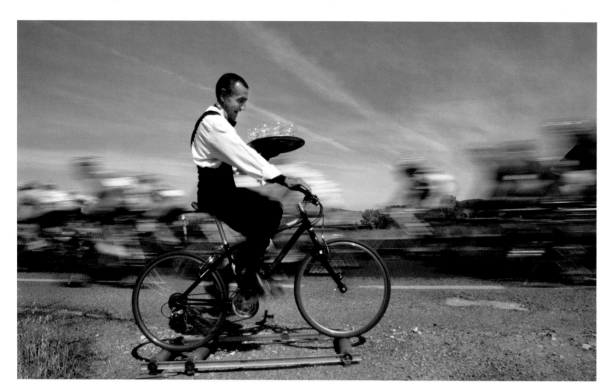

## TURNING OUT IN SUPPORT

LEFT Waiter Saturnino Gonzalez cycles on the spot holding a tray loaded with glasses to galvanize the competitors during stage eight of the Tour of Spain cycling race between Ponferrada and Lugo. 2 September 2006.
Dani Cardona

BELOW An Italy fan celebrates in the streets of downtown Frankfurt after the World Cup soccer match between Italy and Australia. A last-minute penalty from Francesco Totti helped the Italians claim a 1–0 victory in the second round en route to winning the cup. 26 June 2006.
Miro Kuzmanovic

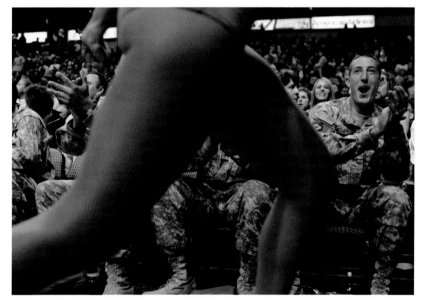

TOP Rugby fans dressed as nuns and bishops sing and dance on the second day of the Hong Kong Sevens tournament. This annual three-day international sporting event is popular with supporters from around the world who congregate in celebration of a feast of rugby. 27 March 2004. Bobby Yip

ABOVE A supporter leans through the net to celebrate with Sevilla's Frédéric Kanouté after the Malian scored a goal against Deportivo la Coruña in a Spanish Primera Liga soccer match at Ramón Sánchez Pizjuán stadium in Seville. 20 December 2006. Alejandro Ruesga

TOP German Didi Senft, 'the Devil', is a Tour de France supporter who has followed the cycling race for years. Here he supports riders on the Tourmalet pass during the 15th stage of the Tour between Bagnères-de-Bigorre and Luz-Ardiden. 21 July 2003. Jacky Naegelen

ABOVE Specialist Larry McFarland (far right) cheers as a Dallas Mavericks dancer leaves the court during NBA action between the Dallas Mavericks and Detroit Pistons in Dallas, Texas. The Pistons won the fixture 92–82. 7 December 2006. Jessica Rinaldi

# Off the Field
## Media / Marketing / Behind the Scenes

A soccer player's silhouette is projected on to the floor at the exhibition 'Pelestation – The Legend in Action', opened by the Brazilian great himself in Berlin. 7 June 2006. Michaela Rehle

## PAGEANTRY AND POP STARS

Showbusiness meets sport in opening ceremonies which have become ever more spectacular and expensive. At every Olympic Games national pride is at stake. With billions of people watching as the curtain rises on its Games, each host city wants to put on the biggest show on earth. Pageantry and pop stars are the order of the day, as well as seemingly endless parades of athletes, massed ranks of costumed dancers and fireworks that last well into the night. Only then do the ceremonies come to the business of the swearing of the Olympic oath and lighting of the Olympic flame by a personality whose identity has been a carefully guarded secret until the last moment. Sydney organizers chose Aboriginal runner Cathy Freeman in 2000, in a moving gesture of national reconciliation. The city's opening ceremony, which featured a band of 2,000 musicians, fire eaters and a cavalry charge by 120 stockmen, was the most watched television programme in Australian history. The 2004 Athens opener, a three-hour pageant reviewing Greek civilization, attracted four billion viewers across the world, though a handful in the United States lodged complaints about actors portraying nude statues. Other sports events have copied the Olympics, spending months and vast sums developing elaborate opening events with acrobats, dancers, opera singers and more fireworks. All the extravagance prompted former Olympic chief Juan Antonio Samaranch to suggest to Beijing organizers that they show a bit more restraint and try to keep their 2008 opening ceremony down to under two-and-a-half hours.

LEFT Fireworks explode over the Olympic stadium during the opening ceremony of the Athens 2004 Olympic Games. 13 August 2004. Yannis Behrakis

Israeli athletes participate in the opening of the Maccabiah games, dubbed the 'Jewish Olympics', in Tel Aviv. 11 July 2005. Oleg Popov

Colombian dancers entertain spectators at the opening of the Central American and Caribbean Games in Cartagena, Colombia. 15 July 2006. Jose Miguel Gomez

Artists perform during the opening ceremony of the Turin Winter Olympics in Italy. 10 February 2006. Petr Josek

Performers light up the arena with giant torches at the Asian Games in Pusan, South Korea. 29 September 2002. Bobby Yip

Theatrical group La Fura del Baus, dressed as pawns, perform at the opening of the 36th Chess Olympiad on the Spanish island of Mallorca. 14 October 2004. Dani Cardona

Chinese dancers create a field of green during the opening ceremony of the 21st University Games in Beijing. 22 August 2001. Claro Cortes IV

South Korean performers run with flags in the opening ceremony of the 8th Far East and South Pacific Games for the disabled in Pusan. 26 October 2002. Busan Ilbo

Dancers take part in the closing ceremony at the 18th Commonwealth Games in Melbourne. 26 March 2006. Anthony Phelps

Australian Aboriginal dancers join in the opening celebrations at the Sydney Olympics. 15 September 2000. Sergio Perez

BELOW Greek dancers, acting the part of priestesses, hold olive branches as they rehearse for the ceremony in Ancient Olympia to light the torch for the Turin Winter Olympics. 26 November 2005. Yannis Behrakis

Russian tennis player Maria Sharapova looks at two of the male models chosen to act as ballboys at the WTA championships in Madrid. 11 May 2006. Andrea Comas

At the Indianapolis Motor Speedway, Americans Elizabeth Cannon and Ashley Haub wear matching stars and stripes outfits in front of a replica of a Ferrari Formula One car. 16 June 2005. Jason Reed

## WORKING TO MAKE IT ALL HAPPEN

Away from the spotlight at every sporting event, an army is at work preparing courts, pitches and tracks, keeping players fed and happy and acting as ushers, interpreters, chauffeurs, score-keepers and water-carriers. Some, like the team who tend Wimbledon's manicured lawns, are paid. Others, like the tens of thousands of volunteers mobilized by every Olympic host city, work for nothing.

BELOW Workers dry the court in Arthur Ashe Stadium at the 2003 U.S. Open in Flushing Meadow, New York, after three days of delays due to rain. 3 September 2003. Shaun Best

OPPOSITE, CLOCKWISE FROM TOP LEFT A groundsman makes preparations for the Commonwealth Games athletics events at the Melbourne Cricket Ground. 18 March 2006. Russell Boyce.

Workers spray the clay court during a break in a Davis Cup match in Costa do Sauípe. 9 April 2004. Paulo Whitaker

A ball boy retrieves the ball during the WTA tennis championships in Madrid. 7 November 2006. Susana Vera

Installing fencing to separate fans at Sarajevo's Kosevo Olympic Stadium before a World Cup qualifier between Bosnia and Serbia & Montenegro. 8 October 2004. Danilo Krstanovic

Performers line up before a match during the soccer World Cup in Berlin. 20 June 2006. Damir Sagolj

A security guard stands next to the World Cup during the 2006 final in Berlin. 9 July 2006. Alessandro Bianchi

ABOVE San Diego's chicken mascot is carried off after
pretending to be hurt in an attack by the Cincinnati
Reds bullpen during a Major League Baseball game
in San Diego. 2 September 2006. Mike Blake

RIGHT A junior cheerleader cries during the
introductions to the NFL game between the Green
Bay Packers and the Miami Dolphins in Miami.
22 October 2006. Marc Serota

## THE VALUE OF SPORTING SUCCESS

Soccer stars, golfers and tennis champions of the 21st century have become gods in the global religion of consumerism. Instantly recognizable across the world, their images appear everywhere. David Beckham's personal brand, buoyed up by his celebrity lifestyle with ex-Spice Girl wife Victoria, helped Real Madrid to move into the lucrative Asian market, where his popularity transcends his soccer skills. Part of his appeal to the Los Angeles Galaxy, the Major League Soccer club with which the Englishman signed a $250-million deal in 2007, was his potential to transform them into a global brand.

In the soccer league of superstar value, however, even Beckham has been outshone by Brazil and Barcelona forward Ronaldinho, who was declared the most commercially valuable soccer player in the world by a study in 2006. It put Ronaldinho's brand value at 47 million euros ($56.4 million) followed by Beckham at 44.9 million euros ($53.88 million). The early years of the 21st century have seen a scramble for the hearts and wallets of Asian sports fans as markets in China and elsewhere open up. The New York Yankees baseball team sent coaches, scouts and marketing personnel to China, Brazil's leading soccer clubs signed an accord to help sport in Singapore, Japanese pitcher Daisuke Matsuzaka went to the Boston Red Sox in a record-breaking $103.1-million deal and the NBA cultivated a Chinese fan base with Yao Ming at the Houston Rockets.

No one personifies the global brand better than Tiger Woods, the multi-major golf champion whose African-American and Thai heritage, good looks and charm – combined with extraordinary sporting ability – have made him one of the most marketable icons in sport.

OPPOSITE LEFT A security officer sits in front of a billboard showing Brazil soccer player Ronaldinho in Shanghai. 8 June 2006. Aly Song

OPPOSITE RIGHT ABOVE A poster of Argentina's Lionel Messi hangs on the side of a building in Hamburg, one of the 2006 World Cup venues. 9 June 2006. Carlos Barria

OPPOSITE RIGHT BELOW An Indian couple celebrate Valentine's Day in front of a poster of Indian cricket captain Saurav Ganguly at a food pavilion in Kolkata. 14 February 2005. Jayanta Shaw

BELOW LEFT The face of France and Arsenal striker Thierry Henry looms over visitors to the China Soccer Expo in Beijing. 15 July 2004. Andrew Wong

BELOW A 65-metre (213-foot) wide poster of German goalkeeper Oliver Kahn greets travellers at Munich's airport ahead of the 2006 soccer World Cup. 29 May 2006. Michaela Rehle

BOTTOM Pedestrians in Paris walk past an advertisement featuring French Open tennis defending champion Justine Henin of Belgium. 22 May 2004. Charles Platiau

## BRING ON THE MONEY

'Bring on the money,' said Maria Sharapova in 2006 when asked about her endorsement earnings. 'It is never enough. I always look for more.' Reportedly the world's highest-paid female athlete at the age of 19, the Russian 2004 Wimbledon champion has traded on her tennis talent and good looks to earn an estimated $25.4 million a year thanks to contracts to promote the goods of a string of multinational companies.

Sponsors from airlines to mobile phone companies queue up to buy association with the latest sporting phenomena. American golf prodigy Michelle Wie was earning $20 million from endorsements while still at school. However, sponsors and their cheque books can disappear just as quickly at the whiff of scandal. In

cycling, 2006 Tour de France winner Floyd Landis's Phonak team were disbanded when the Swiss hearing aid company pulled out after the American failed a dope test. NBA guard Kobe Bryant lost millions of dollars in endorsements after he was charged with sexual assault in 2003, though the charges were later dropped and his star rose again.

The money-making route is not open to everyone, however. China banned its athletes preparing for the 2008 Olympics from taking on commercial endorsements, saying they were a distraction.

OPPOSITE LEFT Images of Chinese basketball players Mengke Bateer, Yao Ming and Guo Shiqiang adorn bottles of cola in a Shanghai supermarket. 27 May 2003. Claro Cortes IV

OPPOSITE BELOW LEFT Los Angeles Lakers guard Kobe Bryant appeared on jars of hazelnut spread before the manufacturers dropped the promotion when he was charged with sexual assault. 5 August 2003. Tim Shaffer

OPPOSITE RIGHT Phoenix Suns guard Steve Nash became only the third Canadian to adorn Wheaties cereal boxes. 17 April 2006. Jeff Topping

OPPOSITE BELOW RIGHT Two Chinese men pass a huge billboard of soccer player David Beckham promoting a U.S. soft drink in Shanghai. 15 March 2002. Claro Cortes IV

BELOW Russia's 2004 Wimbledon tennis champion Maria Sharapova promotes a car at a pre-Wimbledon party in London. 22 June 2006. Leon Neil

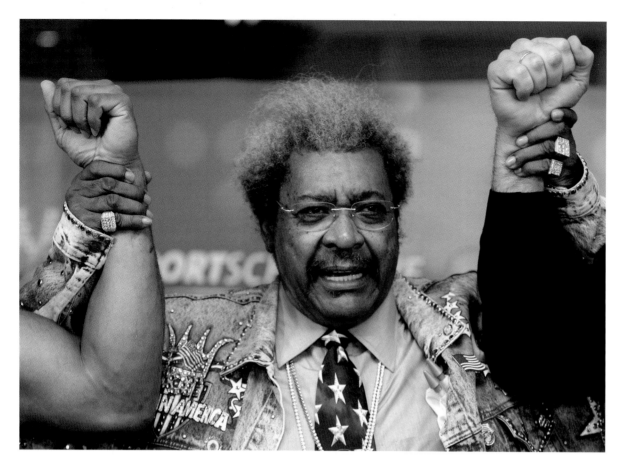

## DON KING

American boxing promoter Don King, who blends ruthless business acumen with a captivating eccentricity, claims to have promoted more than 500 world championship bouts. King had his break as a promoter in 1972 when he persuaded Muhammad Ali to take part in a charity exhibition match for Forest City Hospital, Cleveland. He went on to arrange the classic 1974 'Rumble in the Jungle' between Ali and George Foreman in Zaire. The fight was the first to attract a worldwide television audience of one billion people and the first with a guaranteed purse of $10 million to be split between the boxers. King has promoted most of the world's greatest boxers including Ali, Foreman, Roberto Duran, 'Sugar' Ray Leonard, Joe Frazier and Mike Tyson. In 1994 *Sports Illustrated* magazine named him one of the 40 most influential figures in sport in the previous 40 years.

LEFT  King raises the arms of Russian champion Nikolai Valuev and Jameel McCline of the U.S. before their fight in Basel, Switzerland. 19 January 2007. Vincent Kessler

## MALCOLM GLAZER

American tycoon Malcolm Glazer rocked the soccer world when in May 2005 he completed his long battle to gain a controlling stake in England's biggest club, Manchester United. Valuing the club at £800 million Glazer managed to acquire the 75 percent of shares necessary to de-list from the stock market. The Glazer takeover was bitterly contested by many fans due to concerns over the level of debt he would create. Glazer and his sons, who were appointed board directors, kept a low profile after the purchase and helped to fund new signings to generate new success for the team. This went some way to quelling the unrest. Since 1995, Glazer has also had a controlling stake in the NFL team the Tampa Bay Buccaneers. The Florida franchise had been perennial losers, but under Glazer they achieved their first Super Bowl championship in 2002.

LEFT  Arsenal fans, wearing Malcolm Glazer masks, mock his takeover of Manchester United. 21 May 2005. John Sibley

## ROMAN ABRAMOVICH

Russian billionaire Roman Abramovich bought English soccer club Chelsea in 2003 and immediately embarked on a spending spree unprecedented in English soccer to establish Chelsea as the top club in England and a major power in Europe. His extravagant investment in players combined with the astute tactics of Portuguese manager José Mourinho saw the club dubbed 'Chelski' by the English tabloids win Premier League titles in 2005 and 2006. Reported to be the richest man in Russia, Abramovich built up his estimated $18.5-billion fortune mostly from oil and aluminium businesses. By 2007, he had invested more than $1 billion in Chelsea, including $60 million on Ukrainian Andriy Shevchenko. Abramovich is notoriously shy of the media, but has been a regular spectator at Chelsea matches. He often visits the team dressing rooms, and has rewarded key players by allowing them the use of his luxury yacht.

RIGHT Abramovich celebrates winning the FA Barclays Premiership with John Terry, Frank Lampard and Eidur Gudjohnsen. 30 April 2005. Darren Walsh

## GEORGE STEINBRENNER

New York Yankees owner George Steinbrenner is one of the most controversial figures in American sport. Steinbrenner's involvement with the Yankees began in 1973 when he headed a group of investors who bought the baseball club. Since then, success and controversy have gone hand in hand for Steinbrenner. Known for his willingness to spend huge sums on bringing the best players to his club, the man often called 'The Boss' has never been shy of making a tough decision. During his first 23 seasons in charge, he changed the Yankees' manager 20 times. While he has ruffled more than a few feathers, Steinbrenner's actions are clearly aimed at what he thinks is best for the Yankees, who won six world titles between 1973 and 2000.

RIGHT Steinbrenner responds to reporters at the Yankees minor league complex in Tampa, Florida. 17 February 2004. Peter Muhly

## SEPP BLATTER

Joseph 'Sepp' Blatter is the authoritative and often-controversial president of world football's governing body, FIFA. The Swiss was elected to the role in June 1998, and survived allegations of corruption surrounding his election victories in both 1998 and 2002. He also faced criticism when he suggested women soccer players should wear tighter shorts and skimpier clothes to boost their game's popularity. But he has championed soccer in all regions of the world and worked hard on developing the game in poor countries. He has also fought to preserve the importance of international soccer in an era when the club game, buoyed up by enormous television revenues, has grown in power. He has been responsible for a number of new initiatives in world soccer including awarding a yellow card to players who perform over-zealous goal celebrations and scrapping automatic qualification to the World Cup finals for the previous winners.

LEFT Blatter attends a news conference at FIFA's headquarters in Zurich, Switzerland. 11 April 2006. Siggi Bucher

## BERNIE ECCLESTONE

Englishman Bernard Charles Ecclestone rose from humble origins to become the very rich head of the multi-billion dollar Formula One racing empire. He developed F1 from a fun sport for rich playboys into a global sports business circus with high television audiences. His personal fortune is reported to be more than $4 billion. As the president and CEO of F1 Management Ecclestone has almost total control over the sport. He has promoted F1 all over the world, most recently introducing Grands Prix in China, Bahrain and Abu Dhabi. Despite selling off his 25 percent stake of the F1 business for £1 billion, Ecclestone strengthened his position in the sport by investing in the company that owns the commercial rights of F1. His famous determination has helped him overcome obstacles including a triple coronary bypass in 1999 and, more recently, a bid to oust him by three banks that own a 75 percent share in F1.

LEFT Ecclestone attends the U.S. Grand Prix in Indianapolis. 19 June 2005. Crispin Thruston

## JACQUES ROGGE

President of the International Olympic Committee Jacques Rogge is a former sportsman who competed for Belgium in sailing competitions at the 1968, 1972 and 1976 Olympics and also represented his country at rugby. Between 1989 and 1992 he served as president of the Belgian Olympic Committee and was president of the European Olympic Committee from 1989 to 2001. He became an International Olympic Committee (IOC) member in 1991 and was elected to his current position in 2001, becoming the eighth IOC president. An orthopedic surgeon by profession, Rogge was knighted and given the title of Count by King Albert II of Belgium in recognition of his contribution to sport. His presidency has been characterized by a strong stance against performance-enhancing drugs and a commitment to making it easier for developing nations to bid for and host the Olympic games. He has also proposed a Youth Olympic Games for athletes aged 14 to 18.

RIGHT Rogge at the re-opening of Sarajevo's Olympic museum. 9 February 2004.
Damir Sagolj

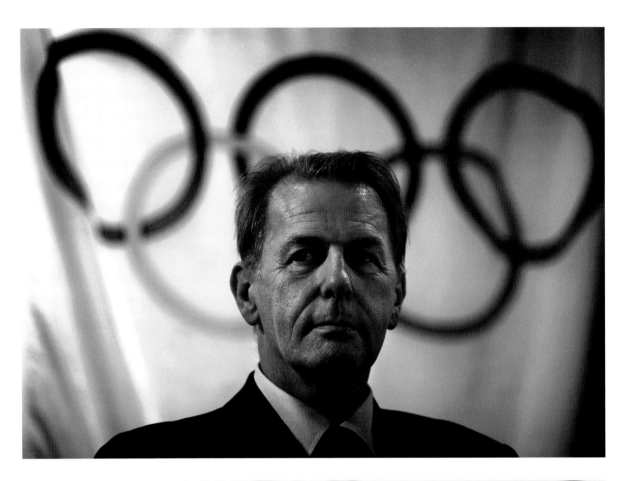

## DICK POUND

Dick Pound has been Chairman of the World Anti-Doping Agency (WADA) since it was established by the IOC in 1999. Pound runs WADA from Montreal, where he juggles his time to be a partner at a top law firm and chancellor of McGill University as well as a member of the IOC. WADA is responsible for overseeing the drugs testing undertaken by the world's sports federations. As chairman Pound has confronted some of the biggest institutions in world sport in his fight against performance-enhancing drugs. WADA has an annual budget of more than $20 million, but the performance-enhancing drugs industry wields far greater resources, meaning Pound faces an uphill struggle. However, 191 nations have so far been persuaded to commit to WADA's Anti-Doping Code. This prohibits most of the world's athletes from taking substances banned by WADA.

RIGHT Pound speaks at a WADA symposium at the Olympic Museum in Lausanne. 29 January 2004. Dominic Favre-Arc

## POLITICAL POINT SCORING

Cynics may say politicians show an interest in sport only when they think they can squeeze political mileage out of it. British Prime Minister Tony Blair was accused of opportunism when he invited England's cricket team to 10 Downing Street after they beat Australia in the 2005 Ashes series. There were also some raised eyebrows when he announced his allegiance to soccer team Newcastle United. American president George W. Bush seems to have a slightly more authentic interest in sport. A keen runner, Bush completed the 1993 Houston marathon. He also previously owned a share in baseball team the Texas Rangers.

ABOVE Britain's Prime Minister Tony Blair plays cricket with children at 10 Downing Street in London. 22 November 2006. Alessia Pierdomenico

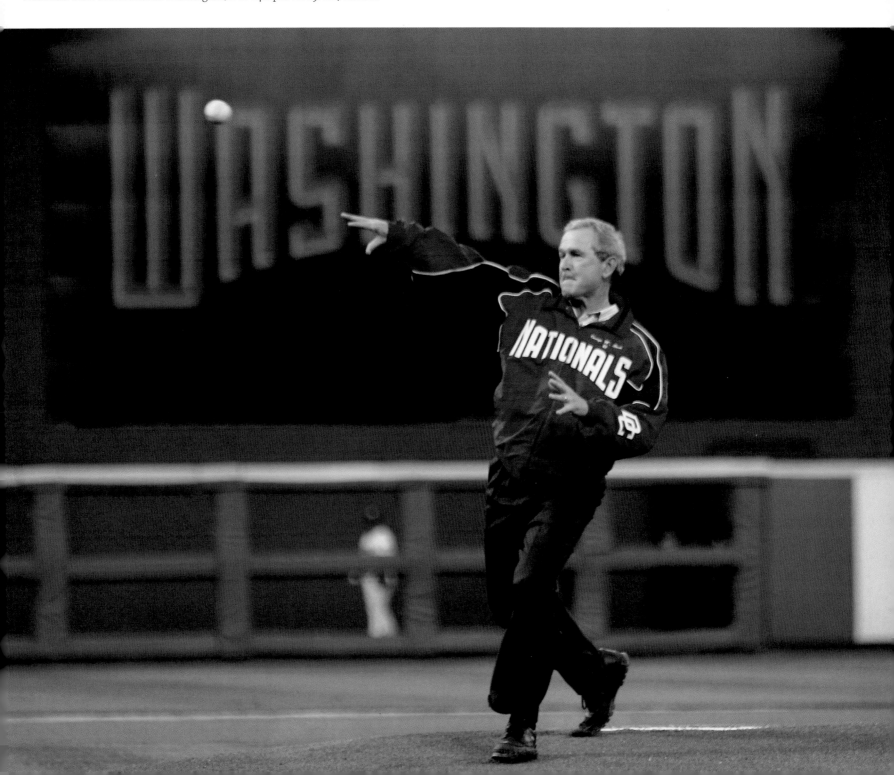

BELOW U.S. President George W. Bush throws out the first pitch for the Washington Nationals at RFK Stadium in Washington, DC. 14 April 2005. Gary Cameron

# HOOLIGANISM

Hooliganism is an unfortunate blight on many sports, especially soccer. It erupts, often unexpectedly, at events all over the world. In soccer, hooliganism developed into a serious problem in the 1980s. It usually features destructive, violent and criminal behaviour by supporters, often fuelled by alcohol. Rivals gangs meet to fight and cause trouble through vandalism and wild behaviour, before, during and after matches. This behaviour has repeatedly resulted in serious injuries and death. Soccer's international ruling bodies have waged their own war on hooliganism with assistance from expert police forces, but have yet to eradicate its menace. One of the most harrowing examples occurred at the 1985 European Cup final between English champions Liverpool and Italian champions Juventus. Thirty-nine mainly Italian supporters died when a dilapidated wall collapsed after English fans broke a fence and charged at the Italians, forcing them to retreat. The incident sparked widespread fury and resulted in English teams being banned from European competition for five years, with Liverpool expelled for six. Since then, hooliganism has marred many other major soccer occasions and championships.

Aggressive behaviour is not restricted to soccer. Other sports including tennis and basketball have witnessed ugly scenes. In 2000, Los Angeles Lakers basketball fans went on a rampage through the city's streets following their team's first NBA championship title in 12 years. In 2007, the Australian Open tennis tournament was marred when fighting broke out between Croatian and Serbian supporters. Hopes that the 21st century would see an end to such violent outbursts have not been realized. In Italy in 2007, Italian soccer fans were banned from attending top matches after a policeman was killed during fighting between fans of rival Sicilian clubs. Much blame for modern hooliganism has been heaped on books and films such as The Football Factory and Green Street, which appeared to glorify thuggish behaviour, although this has been denied by the films' directors.

OPPOSITE LEFT Supporters gesture angrily at a Cardiff City v. Leeds United soccer match in Wales. 6 January 2002. Alex Morton

OPPOSITE BELOW LEFT An England soccer fan and a German riot policeman stare at each other in Stuttgart during the 2006 World Cup. 24 June 2006. Toby Melville

OPPOSITE RIGHT A CSKA Sofia soccer fan throws a seat following a 2–0 defeat by rivals Levski Sofia in Sofia. 30 September 2001. Dimitar Dilkoff

OPPOSITE BELOW RIGHT Supporters of CSKA Moskva and Vardar fight at the Skopje City stadium, Macedonia. 6 August 2003. Ognen Teofilovski

BELOW Members of the Serbian police clash with Red Star fans during a basketball game against Partizan in Belgrade. 15 June 2006. Milan Rasic

## COMPUTER GAMING

Computer game manufacturers provide large revenue streams to sporting organizations in return for using the names and logos of players and teams. High-profile players including soccer star Ronaldinho are involved in games such as FIFA Street, which used the Brazilian's movements in its production. Golfing superstar Tiger Woods is another figure heavily involved in the computer game industry, putting his name to a golf game. American football coach and commentator John Madden lent his name to the most financially profitable sporting game series, which from its conception in 1990 to 2007 sold 51 million copies worldwide, more than any other sports game in history.

The $7-billion U.S. video game market has often been criticized for failing to promote physical activity in young people. It is said to be partly responsible for ever-increasing levels of childhood obesity across the world.

ABOVE Satoru Iwata, president of Nintendo (left), and Shigeru Miyamoto, senior managing director and general manager of the entertainment analysis and development division, play a game of tennis on a video screen with the new 'Wii' remote control in Hollywood, California. 9 May 2006. Robert Galbraith

OPPOSITE Two gamers play on a Sony Playstation 3 in Beverly Hills. 8 November 2006. Fred Prouser

# SPORT AND THE MEDIA

The huge growth and variety of the modern media, and the high stakes involved in top sport, have turned the relationship between the two into a professional and often commercial arrangement. Television, radio, the Internet and print media now deliver non-stop news on world sport all over the globe. In turn, sport has exploited this interest by introducing high levels of advertising and by charging the media for their coverage. Huge modern media companies such as Sky and Fox have invested heavily in technology and altered radically the way in which sport is televised – and the international viewer's expectations. Fans in Thailand, Malaysia and Indonesia enjoy live coverage of European soccer, with kick-offs timed to suit their lifestyles. The Australian Open tennis men's final is played in the evening to meet the demands of the European television market. The English Premier League has become the world's most lucrative soccer league with television rights sold for more than $4 billion. The money has funded the construction of modern stadiums and the recruitment of big-name international players. The media expects almost intimate access in return. Thanks to the huge modern media, sport has become a very big business.

OPPOSITE CLOCKWISE FROM TOP LEFT Fans and a television cameraman watch the British Grand Prix at Silverstone circuit in Northamptonshire, England. 10 June 2006. David Moir

A camera operator films Kenyan Rita Jeptoo as she leads the 110th Boston Marathon. 17 April 2006. Mike Segar

American Lindsey Kildow is caught in the glare of a camera light after finishing second in a super-G Alpine ski race in St Moritz. 21 December 2004. Andreas Meier

Photographers squeeze to capture Australian golfer Nicholas Flanagan competing in the British Open at St Andrews. 13 July 2005. Eddie Keogh

Formula One world champion Michael Schumacher appears on television screens during a news conference in Spielberg, Austria. 15 May 2003. Leonhard Foeger

BELOW Journalists surround Oscar Pereiro of Spain as he awaits the start of the 17th stage of the Tour de France. 20 July 2006. Stefano Rellandini

## OLYMPIC PREPARATIONS IN BEIJING

Beijing's preparations for the 2008 Olympic Games have included building 31 different venues, among them the iconic $400-million 'Bird's Nest' main stadium and the $155-million 'Water Cube' Aquatic Centre. The city has invested an estimated $40 billion in upgrading its creaking infrastructure in time to welcome the world for the sporting extravaganza. Nine new lines have been added to the city's archaic subway system and a host of roads constructed, as well as a new airport terminal designed by Norman Foster. Games preparations have helped to fuel an economic boom that pushed Beijing's output per head above the $6,000 mark in 2006, double the level in 2001 and more than three times the national average, city officials said.

Beyond the construction sites, Beijing has designated the 11th day of every month as 'voluntarily wait in line' day in an attempt to eradicate the habit of queue-jumping, and has run campaigns to persuade its citizens not to dump litter or spit in the streets. More than 5,580 public toilets in Beijing have been spruced up, unsanitary restaurants closed and the exterior of 20,000 buildings earmarked for cleaning. Officials spent $2.5 billion fighting pollution in 2006, taking 15,000 old taxis and 3,000 old buses off the road, closing down a large chemical factory and upgrading 15,000 industrial boilers.

Beijing organizers have set new standards in Olympic preparations, the International Olympic Committee's chief inspector Hein Verbruggen said in the run-up to the 2008 Games. The IOC, which was increasingly exasperated by construction delays and last-minute scrambles ahead of the 2004 Athens Games, was happy to give China a glowing report.

OPPOSITE LEFT  Behind the Olympic rings, work continues on the 91,000-seat National Olympic Stadium in Beijing. 26 September 2006. Russell Boyce

OPPOSITE BELOW LEFT  Construction workers, clad in plastic raincoats, attend the ground-breaking ceremony at the site of the Beijing Olympic athletes' village. 26 June 2005. Alfred Cheng Jin

OPPOSITE RIGHT  A man works on construction of the National Olympic Stadium, nicknamed the 'Bird's Nest' for its criss-crossing bands of steel, which cost Beijing $400 million. 4 September 2006. Jason Lee

OPPOSITE BELOW RIGHT  Workers install the final piece of plastic film on the outside of Beijing's National Aquatics Centre, venue for swimming, diving, synchronized swimming and water polo events. 26 December 2006. Paul Zhang

BELOW  A security guard watches over the construction site of the National Olympic Stadium. 28 March 2006. Reinhard Krause

# World Timeline of Sport

# WORLD TIMELINE OF SPORT 2000

## January

**30 January UNITED STATES**
Quarterback Kurt Warner guides the St Louis Rams, 200–1 long shots at the start of the season, to a 23–16 Super Bowl win over the Tennessee Titans.

## March

**27 March JAMAICA**
West Indies cricket fast bowler Courtney Walsh dismisses Zimbabwe's Henry Olonga to become the world's leading wicket taker with 435 victims at his home ground of Sabina Park, prompting a joyous reggae party which lasts deep into the night.

## June

**18 June UNITED STATES**
American Tiger Woods wins the U.S. Open by 15 strokes, beating the previous record at any major golf championship set by Tom Morris at the British Open in 1862.

## July

**9 July UNITED KINGDOM**
In a rain-delayed Wimbledon final, playing in constant pain after a foot injury, American Pete Sampras recovers from dropping the first set to win a record 13th grand slam title, defeating Australia's Patrick Rafter.

**23 July FRANCE**
Texan Lance Armstrong becomes the first cyclist since Spaniard Miguel Indurain five years earlier to win consecutive Tours de France.

**23 July UNITED KINGDOM**
Tiger Woods becomes only the fifth player in history to win all four golf majors with an eight-stroke victory in the British Open at St Andrews. The American's 19-under total is the lowest score in relation to par in a major championship.

**15 September–1 October AUSTRALIA**
Australian Ian Thorpe wins three Olympic golds and two silvers in the pool, breaking three world records. Celebrations are muted, however, by his loss to Dutchman Pieter van den Hoogenband in the 200 metres freestyle.

**15 September–1 October AUSTRALIA**
American Marion Jones wins three Olympic golds and two bronzes in track and field events, but also has to endure a fraught news conference after a revelation that her shot putter husband C.J. Hunter had tested positive four times for a steroid in the previous year.

## October

**8 October JAPAN**
German Michael Schumacher wins his third Formula One title while handing the famous Italian team Ferrari their first title for 21 years. He goes on to equal the record of nine wins in a season held by himself and Briton Nigel Mansell.

**26 October UNITED STATES**
The New York Yankees beat the New York Mets 4–2 in game five of the Subway Series to win their third straight Major League Baseball (MLB) World Series and their fourth in five years.

## April

**7 April INDIA**
South Africa cricket captain Hansie Cronje and three team mates are charged with involvement in match-fixing by Delhi's joint commissioner of police after a one-day series in India the previous month. The four deny the charge.

## May

**24 May ISLAMABAD**
Former Pakistan cricket captain Salim Malik is banned for life for match-fixing. Several team mates, including the 1999 World Cup captain Wasim Akram, are censured and fined. Hansie Cronje and former India captain Mohammad Azharuddin are also banned for life later in the year.

**2 July NETHERLANDS**
France win the European soccer championship to add to their World Cup, beating Italy 2–1 on a golden goal by David Trézéguet. Midfielder Zinedine Zidane, later named the World Player of the Year, is the player of the tournament.

**6 July ZURICH**
South Africa fails in its bid to host the 2006 soccer World Cup, losing by one vote to Germany after Oceania Football Confederation president Charlie Dempsey of New Zealand, who had been instructed to vote for South Africa, abstains.

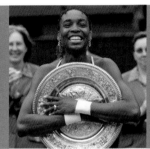

**8 July UNITED KINGDOM**
Venus Williams defeats fellow American Lindsay Davenport at the Wimbledon tennis championships to win her first major. She goes on to win the Olympic gold in both singles and doubles and becomes only the seventh player to win the Wimbledon and U.S. titles in the same year.

## August

**20 August UNITED STATES**
Tiger Woods clinches his third major of the year by winning the U.S. PGA in a three-hole playoff of escalating tension against fellow American Bob May.

## September–October

**15 September AUSTRALIA**
Cathy Freeman lights the Sydney Olympic flame in a symbol of reconciliation between Aboriginal Australians and European settlers. She goes on to win Australia's only track gold in the women's 400 metres.

**23 September AUSTRALIA**
At the age of 38, British rower Steve Redgrave helps the men's coxless fours to an emotional victory and his fifth consecutive Olympic gold in as many Games.

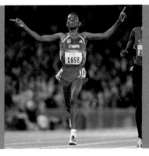

**25 September AUSTRALIA**
Haile Gebrselassie of Ethiopia just holds off his great Kenyan rival Paul Tergat in the 10,000 metres after an agonizing sprint finish in the best race of the Sydney Olympic Games.

## December

**10 December SPAIN**
Spain's tennis players land their first Davis Cup with Juan Carlos Ferrero defeating world number seven Lleyton Hewitt of Australia before King Juan Carlos and Queen Sofia in Barcelona.

## January

**27 January AUSTRALIA**
American Jennifer Capriati, who dropped from view during her troubled teenage years, completes a remarkable comeback by beating Swiss Martina Hingis 6–4 6–3 in the final of the Australian Open tennis tournament. It is her first grand slam title.

## February

**18 February UNITED STATES**
Dale Earnhardt dies of head injuries in a last-lap crash during the Daytona 500. He is the fourth NASCAR driver to die within a year.

## April

**8 April UNITED STATES**
American Tiger Woods becomes the first man to hold all four golf major titles at the same time, sealing a two-stroke win in the Masters at Augusta with a birdie.

## July

**9 July UNITED KINGDOM**
Goran Ivanišević of Croatia, three times a losing finalist, becomes the first wildcard entrant to win the Wimbledon tennis men's singles title with an emotional five-set win over Australian Patrick Rafter.

**14 July AUSTRALIA**
World rugby union champions Australia recover from losing the first of a three-test series to defeat the British Lions for the first time in a series.

## September

**9 September UNITED STATES**
Twenty-year-old Australian Lleyton Hewitt wins the U.S. Open with a straight-sets win over four-times champion Pete Sampras of the United States. Hewitt finishes the year as the youngest tennis number one ever.

**16 September UNITED KINGDOM**
The biennial Ryder Cup team golf match between the United States and Europe scheduled to take place at The Belfry is postponed for 12 months following the September 11 attacks on the United States.

**14 October JAPAN**
German Michael Schumacher completes a second Formula One championship for Ferrari and a fourth overall. At the end of the 17-race series he has amassed 53 Grand Prix career victories, two ahead of former leader Alain Prost of France.

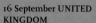

**30 October UNITED STATES**
Michael Jordan comes out of retirement at the age of 38 to play for the Washington Wizards in the National Basketball Association (NBA), scoring 19 points against the New York Knicks at Madison Square Garden. He finishes the season on the injured list.

**25 February AUSTRALIA**
Australian Don Bradman, the greatest batsman in the history of cricket, dies in Adelaide at the age of 92. Although he was dismissed without scoring in his final test innings, Bradman's average of 99.94 is still nearly 40 runs higher than his nearest rivals.

**March**

**15 March INDIA**
India end Australia's record streak of 16 consecutive cricket test victories in the second test in Calcutta despite being asked to follow on.

**22 April SOUTH AFRICA**
Boxer Lennox Lewis loses three of his four heavyweight title belts when he is knocked out by American Hasim Rahman in the fifth round. The Briton takes his revenge with a fourth-round knockout in the return bout in Las Vegas seven months later.

**May**

**21 May SWITZERLAND**
ISMM-ISL, the company that marketed soccer worldwide, collapses with debts of more than $430 million.

**June**

**6 June ITALY**
Two hundred police officers raid the hotel rooms of all 20 cycling teams after the 17th stage of the Giro d'Italia and confiscate a variety of illegal drugs. The riders retaliate by refusing to start the next stage.

**29 July JAPAN**
Australian Ian Thorpe finishes the world swimming championships in Fukuoka with a record six gold medals. He breaks his own world records in the 200, 400 and 800 metres freestyle and shares another world record in the 4x200 metres freestyle relay.

**August**

**6 August CANADA**
Edmonton stages the first North American world athletics championships. American Stacy Dragila, who sets seven world women's pole vault records during this year, wins the world title after a four-hour duel with Russian Svetlana Feofanova.

**October**

**5 October UNITED STATES**
Barry Bonds of the San Francisco Giants hits two homers against the Houston Astros to break Mark McGwire's 1998 Major League Baseball (MLB) single-season home-run record of 70. He finishes the year with 73.

**6 October UNITED STATES**
Cal Ripken, who broke Lou Gehrig's 56-year-old mark of 2,130 consecutive baseball games in 1995, closes his career at the age of 41 before former President Bill Clinton, Baseball Commissioner Bud Selig and a host of Baltimore Orioles fans.

**November**

**4 November UNITED STATES**
The Arizona Diamondbacks beat the New York Yankees 4–3 in their first baseball world series and the first to stretch into November.

**27 November JAPAN**
Bayern Munich, winners of the soccer Bundesliga and the European Champions League, add the World Club Cup to their trophy cabinet with an extra-time win over Argentina's Boca Juniors.

## January

**26 January AUSTRALIA**
American Jennifer Capriati saves four championship points against Martina Hingis of Switzerland to retain the Australian Open tennis title.

## February

**3 February UNITED STATES**
The New England Patriots win Super Bowl XXXVI, the first major sporting event staged in the United States since the September 11 attacks of the previous year, with an upset 20–17 win over the St Louis Rams.

**24 February UNITED STATES**
Canada beat the United States 5–2 in the ice hockey Olympic final to end a 50-year gold medal drought.

**24 February UNITED STATES**
Three cross-country skiers, including Spanish triple gold medallist Johan Mühlegg, are thrown out of the Games after positive tests for a new blood-boosting drug.

## April

## June

**1 June SOUTH AFRICA**
Former South Africa cricket captain Hansie Cronje dies in a plane crash, two years after he was banned from professional cricket for his part in a match-fixing scandal.

**8 June UNITED STATES**
Briton Lennox Lewis systematically destroys American Mike Tyson in eight rounds to retain two versions of the world heavyweight title and confirm beyond doubt he is the best fighter of his era.

## July–August

**21 July FRANCE**
German Michael Schumacher equals Argentine Juan Manuel Fangio's record with his fifth Formula One drivers' title. His victory in the French Grand Prix at Magny-Cours gives him the championship at an earlier stage than any of his predecessors.

**25 July–4 August UNITED KINGDOM**
Ian Thorpe picks up six gold medals and a silver as Australia dominate the Commonwealth Games in Manchester, comfortably topping the medals table ahead of England and India.

**14 September FRANCE**
American Tim Montgomery, the new partner of triple Olympic champion Marion Jones, sets a world 100 metres record of 9.78 seconds at the grand prix athletics final in Paris. Jones completes her first unbeaten season.

**29 September UNITED KINGDOM**
Irishman Paul McGinley sinks a nine-foot birdie putt on the 18th to secure the Ryder Cup for Europe at The Belfry in the biennial team match against the United States.

**8 February UNITED STATES**
U.S. President George Bush opens the Salt Lake City winter Olympics amid unprecedented security.

**8–24 February UNITED STATES**
Croatian Alpine skier Janica Kostelić wins three gold medals and one silver, a record for her sport, while Norway's Ole Einar Bjørndalen also sets a record with golds in all four biathlon events.

**17 February UNITED STATES**
Duplicate gold medals are awarded to Canadian skaters Jamie Sale and David Pelletier after a French judge admits she had been pressured by her federation to vote for the original winners, Russians Yelena Berezhnaya and Anton Sikharulidze.

**14 April UNITED KINGDOM**
Moroccan-born American Khalid Khannouchi breaks his own world record in the London marathon. Briton Paula Radcliffe clocks the second fastest women's time ever on her marathon debut.

**May**

**31 May SOUTH KOREA**
Senegal provide a sensational start to the first World Cup to be staged in Asia by beating their old colonial masters and defending champions France 1–0 in the opening match.

**29 June SOUTH KOREA**
Turkey's Hakan Sukur scores the fastest goal in World Cup history just 11 seconds into the game against South Korea in the third-place playoff. Turkey win 3–2.

**30 June JAPAN**
Ronaldo, battling against injury for the past 2½ years, scores the two goals which give Brazil victory over Germany in the final for an unprecedented fifth World Cup. His eighth goal of the tournament means he equals compatriot Pelé's World Cup tally of 12.

**28 July FRANCE**
Lance Armstrong wins a fourth successive Tour de France title, breaking the U.S. record of Greg LeMond who won three.

**September**

**7 September UNITED STATES**
American Serena Williams, forced to miss the Australian Open with an ankle injury, completes a sweep of the other three tennis grand slam titles by beating sister Venus for a third consecutive time to win the U.S. Open.

**October**

**13 October UNITED STATES**
Britain's Paula Radcliffe shatters the world women's marathon record by 89 seconds in Chicago, reducing the mark to two hours 17 minutes 18 seconds.

# WORLD TIMELINE OF SPORT 2003

## January

**25 January AUSTRALIA**
American Serena Williams beats sister Venus to win the Australian Open tennis tournament and become the fifth woman to hold all four grand slam singles titles simultaneously.

## March

**2 March NEW ZEALAND**
Renegade New Zealander Russell Coutts skippers Swiss yacht Alinghi to a 5–0 victory over Team New Zealand to bring the America's Cup to a landlocked European nation.

## May

**22 May UNITED STATES**
Swede Annika Sörenstam becomes the first woman for 58 years to compete in a PGA Tour event when she takes part in the Colonial tournament in Fort Worth, Texas. She misses the cut by four shots.

## June

**13–27 July SPAIN**
American Michael Phelps sets an unprecedented five individual world swimming records at the world championships in Barcelona, surpassing compatriot Mark Spitz who broke four, as well as contributing to three relay team world records, en route to winning seven golds at the 1972 Munich Olympics.

**20 July UNITED KINGDOM**
A kilted protester waving placards is dragged from the track at the British Grand Prix at Silverstone, overshadowing Brazilian Rubens Barrichello's first win of the season for Ferrari.

## August

**23–31 August FRANCE**
American Kelli White wins the 100–200 double at the world athletics championships in Paris but then tests positive for a stimulant used to treat narcolepsy, or sleeping sickness.

**24 August FRANCE**
Double world cross-country champion Kenenisa Bekele of Ethiopia outsprints his mentor Haile Gebrselassie to win the 10,000 metres gold medal at the Paris world athletics championships.

**28 September GERMANY**
Five-times world cross-country champion Paul Tergat of Kenya sets a world men's marathon record of two hours four minutes 55 seconds in Berlin.

## October

**10 October AUSTRALIA**
Australia's opening batsman Matthew Hayden strikes a world test record 380 against Zimbabwe in Perth. The powerful Queensland left-hander strikes 11 sixes, one short of the world record.

**23 March SOUTH AFRICA**
Australia cruise to a 125-run victory over India in the cricket World Cup final in Johannesburg after an unbeaten campaign, despite losing leg-spinner Shane Warne before the start of the tournament following a failed drugs test.

April

**13 April UNITED KINGDOM**
Briton Paula Radcliffe shatters her own world record in the London marathon, reducing her mark by one minute 53 seconds to two hours 15 minutes 25 seconds.

**26 June FRANCE**
Cameroon soccer international Marc-Vivien Foe collapses and dies on the pitch during a Confederations Cup semi-final against Colombia in Lyon.

July

**2 July UNITED KINGDOM**
Russian billionaire Roman Abramovich buys English Premier League soccer club Chelsea, in a deal worth 140 million pounds ($233 million).

**24 July SPAIN**
Russian swimmer Alexander Popov, 31, wins the 100 metres freestyle for a record third time at the world championships in Barcelona.

**27 July FRANCE**
American Lance Armstrong joins France's Jacques Anquetil and Bernard Hinault, Belgian Eddy Merckx and Spaniard Miguel Indurain as the only riders to win the Tour de France five times.

**25 August UNITED STATES**
American Pete Sampras retires at the age of 32 after winning a record 14 grand slam tennis titles. His perennial rival Andre Agassi won the Australian Open back in January and the best of the new American generation Andy Roddick was to take the U.S. Open title two weeks later.

September

**3 September UNITED STATES**
Federal agents raid the BALCO laboratory in California after scientists in Los Angeles discover a new designer steroid, THG. World 100 metres record holder Tim Montgomery, his partner Marion Jones, sprinter Kelli White and baseball slugger Barry Bonds are listed as clients.

**14 September UNITED STATES**
Yetunde Price, the eldest sister of tennis champions Venus and Serena Williams, is shot dead in the crime-ridden suburb of Los Angeles where the family grew up. She was 31.

**12 October JAPAN**
German Michael Schumacher takes the point he needs at the Japanese Grand Prix at Suzuka to break Juan Manuel Fangio's record with his sixth Formula One drivers' title.

November

**22 November AUSTRALIA**
England flyhalf Jonny Wilkinson drop-kicks the winning goal with his weaker right foot during the final minutes of extra time in the rugby World Cup final against Australia in Sydney.

# WORLD TIMELINE OF SPORT 2004

## January

**6 January AUSTRALIA**
Steve Waugh retires after leading the Australia cricket team to 41 victories in 57 tests, making him the most successful captain in history.

## April

**24 April UNITED STATES**
Ukrainian Vitali Klitschko avenges his brother Vladimir's upset loss to Corrie Sanders the previous year by stopping the South African in the eighth round in Los Angeles to win the World Boxing Council heavyweight title.

**25 April UNITED KINGDOM**
Arsenal clinch the English Premier League title with a 2–2 draw to north London rivals Tottenham. They go on to finish the 38-game season unbeaten, the first team to do so since Preston North End in the 1888–89 season.

## June

**15 June UNITED STATES**
Detroit Pistons upset the favoured Los Angeles Lakers with a 4–1 victory in the NBA best-of-seven finals. Defeat means the end of an era for the Lakers with coach Phil Jackson and leading player Shaquille O'Neal departing.

## July

## August

**13–29 August GREECE**
Briton Kelly Holmes, dogged by injury throughout her career, completes the 800–1,500 metres Olympic gold double in Athens.

**13–29 August GREECE**
American swimmer Michael Phelps wins six of the U.S. team's 35 gold medals plus two Olympic bronzes.

## September

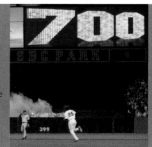

**12 September UNITED STATES**
Swiss Roger Federer completes his best year on the tennis circuit by winning the U.S. Open to give him victory in three of the four grand slam tournaments. He is the first man to complete the treble since Swede Mats Wilander in 1988.

**17 September UNITED STATES**
Barry Bonds hits his 700th career home run. Only Babe Ruth (714) and Hank Aaron (755) have ever scored more.

**11 April UNITED STATES**
Phil Mickelson finally fulfils his talents with victory in the U.S. Masters golf. Less happily, he teams up with Tiger Woods later in the year in an unsuccessful pairing as the United States lose 18½ to 9½ in the Ryder Cup.

**12 April ANTIGUA**
West Indies' cricket captain Brian Lara reclaims the world test individual batting record with an unbeaten 400 against England in the fourth test.

## May

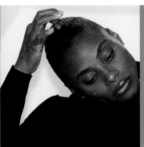

**19 May UNITED STATES**
American double world sprint champion Kelli White is banned after admitting taking the designer steroid THG and a variety of other prohibited drugs.

**26 May GERMANY**
Porto complete a golden season with a 3–0 victory over Monaco in the European Champions League soccer final in Gelsenkirchen after winning Portugal's league and Cup double.

**3 July UNITED KINGDOM**
Maria Sharapova wins the Wimbledon women's singles title at the age of 17 in only her second year on the tennis circuit. Russians take three of the year's four grand slam titles.

**4 July PORTUGAL**
Greece, who had not previously won a single game at a major soccer tournament, beat hosts Portugal 1–0 through a 57th-minute header from Angelos Haristeas to win the European championship.

**25 July FRANCE**
American Lance Armstrong succeeds where his distinguished predecessors Jacques Anquetil, Bernard Hinault, Miguel Indurain and Eddy Merckx failed by winning a sixth Tour de France.

**13–29 August GREECE**
Moroccan Hicham El Guerrouj wins the 1,500 metres Olympic gold medal at his third attempt and goes on to complete the first 1,500–5,000 double for 80 years.

**18 August GREECE**
Leading Greek medals hopes Costas Kenteris, the defending 200 metres champion, and Katerina Thanou withdraw from the Athens Olympics after missing a drugs test on the eve of the Games.

**29 August BELGIUM**
German Michael Schumacher wins his seventh Formula One world championship, finishing second at Spa-Francorchamps in Ferrari's 700th race.

## October

**27 October UNITED STATES**
The Boston Red Sox beat the St Louis Cardinals 4–0 to win the city's first baseball World Series since Babe Ruth was sold to the hated New York Yankees in 1920.

**31 October UNITED STATES**
Fijian Vijay Singh becomes the first man to win $10 million on the U.S. golf tour. He joins Byron Nelson, Ben Hogan, Sam Snead and Tiger Woods as the only players to record nine victories in a year.

# WORLD TIMELINE OF SPORT 2005

## January

Melbourne

**30 January AUSTRALIA**
Russian Marat Safin keeps his volatile temper under control long enough to end Swiss Roger Federer's grand slam dream before it has properly begun. Safin knocks out Federer in the Australian Open tennis semi-finals then defeats hometown favourite Lleyton Hewitt 1–6 6–3 6–4 6–4 in the final.

## February

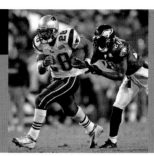

**6 February UNITED STATES**
The New England Patriots win their third Super Bowl in four years with a 24–12 win over the Philadelphia Eagles, a ninth consecutive post-season victory to equal the record of Vince Lombardi's Green Bay Packers.

## May

**25 May TURKEY**
Captain Steve Gerrard sparks an extraordinary comeback by Liverpool at the soccer European Cup final in Istanbul after AC Milan have strolled to a 3–0 lead at halftime. Liverpool fight back to level the score, then win the penalty shootout to claim the trophy for the fifth time.

## June

**14 July BRAZIL**
São Paulo destroy fellow Brazilians Atlético Paranaense 4–0 in the second leg to win the Libertadores Cup and become South American soccer club champions for the third time.

**22 July UNITED KINGDOM**
Russian Yelena Isinbayeva, the former gymnast who has redefined the women's pole vault record, breaks the five metres barrier at London's Crystal Palace.

**24 July FRANCE**
U.S. cyclist Lance Armstrong narrowly avoids a crash just before entering the Champs Élysées in Paris to win his seventh successive Tour de France in his final race before retiring at the age of 33.

**21 September MEXICO**
Argentine-born Rubén Omar Romano, the coach of one of Mexico's richest soccer clubs, Cruz Azul, is freed after a 65-day kidnap ordeal. Less than three months later he is fired.

**25 September BRAZIL**
Fernando Alonso takes over from Michael Schumacher as the world Formula One champion, winning the title in São Paulo after the longest season in history, comprising 19 races. He celebrates again in Shanghai by giving Renault their first constructors' title.

## November

**17 November GERMANY**
Soccer referee Robert Hoyzer is sentenced to two years and five months in jail for his part in Germany's biggest match-fixing scandal.

**25 November UNITED KINGDOM**
Northern Irishman George Best, possibly the most gifted soccer player the British Isles ever produced, and certainly the most glamorous, dies in a London hospital at the age of 59 after years of alcohol abuse.

## March

**19–20 March FRANCE**
Ethiopian Kenenisa Bekele, still devastated by the death of his 18-year-old fiancée during a training run at the start of the year, completes a fourth successive long and short-distance cross-country double near Saint-Étienne in central France. No other man has won both races since the short race was introduced in 1998.

## April

**10 April UNITED STATES**
Tiger Woods, who has remoulded his swing in the relentless quest for perfection, holes a 15-foot birdie putt to beat Chris DiMarco on the first playoff hole to win the U.S. Masters.

**14 June GREECE**
Jamaican Asafa Powell, a soft-spoken son of a preacher man, reduces the world 100 metres record by one-hundredth of a second to 9.77 seconds at the Athens grand prix.

## July

**6 July SINGAPORE**
Twice Olympic 1,500 metres champion Sebastian Coe, head of the London 2012 Olympic bid team, reaps the reward for relentless hard work when London is awarded the Games over long-time favourite Paris. The next day suicide bombers strike London's transport system, killing 52 people.

## August

**6–14 August FINLAND**
Torrential storms interrupt the world championships in Helsinki but fail to deter Olympic 100 metres champion Justin Gatlin, who completes a 100–200 metres gold medal double, while Yelena Isinbayeva sets her 18th world record in the women's pole vault after claiming her first world title.

## September

**12 September UNITED KINGDOM**
At the end of a glorious autumn day at the Oval cricket ground in London, England regain the Ashes by winning their first series against their oldest enemy Australia for 18 years.

## October

**12 October BRAZIL**
Brazil successfully complete a two-year, 10-team, 18-match marathon to qualify for the 2006 soccer World Cup. Under new FIFA rules they no longer qualify automatically as the defending champions.

**26 October UNITED STATES**
The Chicago White Sox win their first baseball World Series since 1917 by defeating the Houston Astros 4–0.

**26 November UNITED KINGDOM**
The New Zealand All Blacks complete only their second grand slam in history by beating Wales, Ireland, England and Scotland on successive Saturdays. They had already reasserted southern hemisphere rugby union supremacy by defeating the British Lions 3–0.

## December

**4 December CROATIA**
Croatia win the Davis Cup final for the first time with a 3–2 victory over the Slovak Republic. They are the first unseeded team to win the men's tennis team event.

# WORLD TIMELINE OF SPORT 2006

## February

**12–26 February ITALY**
Benjamin Raich leads an Austrian clean sweep in the slalom and also wins gold in the giant slalom at the Turin winter Olympic Games. Austrians dominate the Alpine skiing with 14 of the 30 medals.

**18 February ITALY**
Norway's Kjetil André Aamodt becomes the first Alpine skier to win four winter Olympic gold medals with victory in the Turin Games super-G at the age of 34. Half an hour later Croatia's Janica Kostelić matches the feat with her fourth career gold, in the combined event.

## May

**4 May ITALY**
Newspapers publish transcripts of phone calls intercepted in 2004 in which Juventus general director Luciano Moggi tells the head of the referees' association which officials he wants appointed. The Italian federation and magistrates in four cities open investigations involving Juventus, Lazio, Fiorentina and AC Milan.

## June

## July

**4 July GERMANY**
Extra-time strikes from Fabio Grosso and Alessandro Del Piero give Italy a 2–0 win over Germany and a place in the soccer World Cup final. France, who eliminated Brazil in the quarter-finals, defeat Portugal 1–0 in the other semi-final.

**9 July GERMANY**
France captain Zinedine Zidane is sent off in extra time after headbutting Italy's Marco Materazzi in the Berlin World Cup final with the score tied at 1–1. Materazzi had levelled the score after Zidane scored the opening goal. Italy go on to win the penalty shootout 5–3.

## August

**7–13 August SWEDEN**
Portuguese Francis Obikwelu becomes the first man since 1978 to win the European athletics championships 100–200 metres double. Belgium's Kim Gevaert completes the women's double at the Gothenburg championships.

**10 September ITALY**
Michael Schumacher says he will retire at the end of the Formula One season after winning the Italian Grand Prix. It is the 90th career victory for the 37-year-old German.

**24 September IRELAND**
Only six weeks after the death of his wife Heather from cancer, Irishman Darren Clarke helps Europe to an 18½ to 9½ victory over the United States in the Ryder Cup. The win at the K Club is the third in a row for the Europeans.

## October

**23 February ITALY**
Shizuka Arakawa becomes the first Japanese to win an Olympic figure skating title, relegating twice world champion Irina Slutskaya to third place in the women's event.

**2 April JAPAN**
Ethiopian Kenenisa Bekele completes a fifth consecutive long- and short-course cross-country double. The world 5,000 and 10,000 metres record-holder tries to win a sixth long-course title the following year but fails to finish.

**9 June GERMANY**
Hosts Germany, playing without their injured captain Michael Ballack, open the soccer World Cup with an entertaining 4–2 win over Costa Rica in Munich.

**11 June FRANCE**
Despite winning only one game in the opening set, Spaniard Rafael Nadal becomes the first man to beat Roger Federer in a grand slam final. Nadal defeats the Swiss 1–6 6–1 6–4 7–6 at the French Open to record his 60th consecutive match victory on clay.

**27 June GERMANY**
Ronaldo scores a record 15th World Cup goal as Brazil defeat Ghana 3–0 to enter the quarter-finals.

**23 July UNITED KINGDOM**
Tiger Woods wins the British Open by two shots in his first golf major since the death of his father Earl. The American uses his driver only once on a sun-baked Royal Liverpool course, shaping his victory with immaculate iron play.

**27 July FRANCE**
The Swiss-based Phonak cycling team announce that Tour de France winner Floyd Landis of the United States tested positive for excessive amounts of the male sex hormone testosterone after finishing first in the 17th stage.

**21 August UNITED KINGDOM**
Pakistan become the first team to forfeit a cricket test when they refuse to take the field after tea on the fourth day of the fourth test against England at The Oval in London. Their protest follows the umpires' decision to dock them five runs for alleged ball tampering.

**9 September ITALY**
Italy's Serie A soccer season starts two weeks late. Juventus are in Serie B for the first time, on minus 17 points. Fiorentina, Lazio and Reggina stay in the top division with heavy points penalties. AC Milan, docked eight points, are allowed to stay in the Champions League despite being censured by UEFA.

**16 October PAKISTAN**
Pakistan pace bowlers Shoaib Akhtar and Mohammad Asif are withdrawn from the Champions Trophy squad after becoming the first test cricketers to test positive for steroids. Shoaib is suspended for two years and Asif for one before the bans are overturned by a Pakistan Cricket Board tribunal due to 'exceptional circumstances'.

**21 November AUSTRALIA**
Australia's five-times Olympic swimming champion Ian Thorpe retires at the age of 24. Thorpe won three gold medals at the 2000 Sydney Olympics and two more at the 2004 Athens Games. He also won 11 world titles and set 13 world records, including the 200 and 400 metres freestyle marks.

# Additional Photo Credits

## World Timeline of Sport 2000
*pages 362–63*

Mike Blake, 30 January 2000
Rajesh Jantilal, 9 April 2000
Mohsin Raza, 26 May 2000
Tony O'Brien, 2 July 2000
Ruben Sprich, 6 July 2000
Dylan Martinez, 8 July 2000
Kieran Doherty, 9 July 2000
Kai Pfaffenbach, 21 July 2000
Ferran Paredes, 23 July 2000
Kai Pfaffenbach, 15 September 2000
Ian Waldie, 16 September 2000
Mike Blake, 23 September 2000
Andy Clark, 23 September 2000
Gary Hershorn, 25 September 2000
Susumu Toshiyuki, 8 October 2000
Mike Segar, 26 October 2000
Albert Gea, 10 December 2000

## World Timeline of Sport 2001
*pages 364–65*

Mark Baker, 27 January 2001
Duffin McGee, 18 February 2001
Megan Lewis, 27 August 1997
Jayanta Shaw, 15 March 2001
Gary Hershorn, 7 April 2001
Mike Hutchings, 22 April 2001
Stefano Rellandini, 6 June 2001
Kieran Doherty, 9 July 2001
Mark Baker, 14 July 2001
Mark Baker, 29 July 2001
Jason Reed, 6 August 2001
Shaun Best, 9 September 2001
Mike Blake, 5 October 2001
Gary Hershorn, 6 October 2001
Haruyoshi Yamaguchi, 14 October 2001
David Leeds, 30 October 2001
Mike Blake, 4 November 2001
Eriko Sugita, 27 November 2001

## World Timeline of Sport 2002
*pages 366–67*

Mark Baker, 26 January 2002
Colin Braley, 3 February 2002
Jerry Lampen, 8 February 2002
Mike Blake, 17 February 2002
Andy Clark, 24 February 2002
Paul Hanna, 17 February 2002
Andrew Winning, 23 February 2002
Stephen Hird, 14 April 2002
Desmond Boylan, 31 May 2002
Mike Hutchings, 11 April 2000
Gary Hershorn, 8 June 2002
Desmond Boylan, 29 June 2002
Oleg Popov, 30 June 2002
Robert Pratta, 21 July 2002
Jeff J Mitchell, 3 August 2002
Eric Gaillard, 23 July 2002
Kevin Lamarque, 7 September 2002
Xavier Lhospice, 14 September 2002
Darren Staples, 29 September 2002
Sue Ogrocki, 13 October 2002

## World Timeline of Sport 2003
*pages 368–69*

David Gray, 25 January 2003
Mark Baker, 2 March 2003
Mike Hutchings, 23 March 2003
Toby Melville, 13 April 2003
Kevin Lamarque, 22 May 2003
Robert Pratta, 26 June 2003
Tony O'Brien, 24 September 2005
Paul Hanna, 16 July 2003
Jim Tanner, 20 July 2003
Andrea Comas, 25 July 2003
Eric Gaillard, 26 July 2003
Charles Platiau, 24 August 2003
Carlos Barria, 25 August 2003
Jim Ruymen, 14 September 2003
Fabrizio Bensch, 28 September 2003
Bill Hatto, 10 October 2003
Wolfgang Rattay, 12 October 2003
Mike Hutchings, 22 November 2003

## World Timeline of Sport 2004
*pages 370–71*

David Gray, 6 January 2004
Kevin Lamarque, 11 April 2004
Jason O'Brien, 14 April 2004
Lucy Nicholson, 24 April 2004
Mike Finn-Kelsey, 25 April 2004
David Gray, 30 August 2003
Alex Morton, 26 May 2004
Lucy Nicholson, 15 June 2004
Kevin Lamarque, 3 July 2004
Kai Pfaffenbach, 4 July 2004
Stefano Rellandini, 25 July 2004
Jerry Lampen, 23 August 2004
David Gray, 17 August 2004
Mike Blake, 28 August 2004
John Kolesidis, 18 August 2004
Pascal Rossignol, 29 August 2004
John Gress, 12 September 2004
Susan Ragan, 17 September 2004
Peter Jones, 27 October 2004
Jessica Rinaldi, 4 September 2004

## World Timeline of Sport 2005
*pages 372–73*

David Gray, 30 January 2005
Pierre Ducharme, 6 February 2005
Kevin Lamarque, 10 April 2005
Dylan Martinez, 25 May 2005
John Kolesidis, 14 June 2005
Russell Boyce, 19 February 2005
Sergio Moraes, 14 July 2005
Steven Paston, 27 July 2005
Alessandro Bianchi, 11 August 2005
Kieran Doherty, 12 September 2005
Henry Romero, 22 September 2005
Paulo Whitaker, 25 September 2005
Sergio Moraes, 12 October 2005
John Gress, 26 October 2005
Arnd Wiegmann, 17 November 2005
Darren Staples, 3 December 2005
Jeff J Mitchell, 26 November 2005
Nikola Solic, 4 December 2005

## World Timeline of Sport 2006
*pages 374–75*

Leonhard Foeger, 18 February 2006
Wolfgang Rattay, 20 February 2006
David Gray, 24 February 2006
Kimimasa Mayama, 2 April 2006
Daniele La Monaca, 29 June 2006
Kai Pfaffenbach, 9 June 2006
Pascal Rossignol, 11 June 2006
Paulo Whitaker, 27 June 2006
Kieran Doherty, 4 July 2006
Kai Pfaffenbach, 9 July 2006
Robert Galbraith, 23 July 2006
Stefano Rellandini, 20 July 2006
Yves Herman, 8 August 2006
Luke MacGregor, 20 August 2006
Daniele La Monaca, 9 September 2006
Nikola Solic, 10 September 2006
Darren Staples, 24 September 2006
Mohsin Raza, 28 October 2006
Will Burgess, 21 November 2006

# Acknowledgments

## Project Director

**Jassim Ahmad** joined Reuters in 2000 and works in the Media division as Head of Visual Projects, with responsibility for producing photographic books, exhibitions and other visual communications. He also worked on *Reuters – The State of the World*, which has been published as a book in 10 languages and staged as an exhibition over 20 times in 10 countries. Jassim is of British-Indian nationality and is based in Reuters London headquarters.

## Picture Editors

**Catherine Benson** joined the Reuters international picture desk in 2000 from The Guardian newspaper in London. She has been part of the editing team on the daily file as well as major events including two winter Olympics, the Athens summer Olympics, Wimbledon tennis championships, the British Open golf tournament and the UEFA Champions League final.

**Hamish Crooks** spent 11 years working in a variety of roles at Magnum Photos' London office, including co-editing the book *Magnum Football*. He joined Reuters in 2005 to assist in implementing the Reuters Pictures archive website. He has also written sports features for national online newspapers and guest-lectured on photography at universities in the UK.

## Contributing Writers

**John Mehaffey** joined the Reuters Sports Desk in 1981 after working as a general news and political reporter in New Zealand, Australia and England. Since then he has reported on a variety of sports from more than 30 countries, including track and field at six summer Olympic Games. He has attended 10 world athletics championships, the soccer, rugby and cricket World Cups plus the winter Olympics, world championships in amateur boxing, gymnastics and cross-country running, professional boxing, squash, the Wimbledon tennis championships and the U.S. Masters golf. He has also covered the International Olympic Committee and written extensively on sports politics and the problem of drugs in sport.

**Clare Fallon** has been a Reuters journalist since 1982, first in news and economics in London and Rome and, since 1987, on the international Sports Desk in London. She has reported on three summer and three winter Olympic Games, as well as the Auckland and Victoria Commonwealth Games, the 1990 soccer World Cup in Italy and the inaugural Goodwill Games in Moscow in 1985. She has covered world and regional championships in athletics, gymnastics, swimming, Alpine skiing, table tennis and show-jumping as well as numerous editions of the Wimbledon and French Open tennis championships, Davis Cup tennis finals and world and European boxing title fights.

**Special thanks to** Paul Barker, Simon Baskett, Tiziana Barghini, Valerie Bezzina, Roberto Bonzio, Bertrand Boucey, Jonathan Bramley, Adam Bryce, Timothy Collings, Steve Crisp, Ayperi Karabuda Ecer, Dominic Favre (Arc), David Jacobs, Marc Joanny, Angela Kearney, Erik Kirschbaum, Philip Kelly, Gordon Knowles, Paula Leite, Pascal Lietout, Simon Newman, Stefano Paltera, Paul Radford, Gary Regenstreif, Jonne Roriz (Agencia Estado), Peter Schols (Dagblad De Limburger/GPD), Marion Schumann, Alexia Singh, Akio Suga, Leslie D'Souza, Thomas Szlukovenyi, Lewis Tam, Aldrina Thirunagaran, Sara Veness, Richard Whiting and Kimitsu Yogachi.

## Contributing Photographers

This book features images by 249 Reuters and Action Images photographers of 57 different nationalities on rotating locations around the world. The country that follows each name represents the photographer's nationality.

Adrees Latif, United States
Ahmad Masood, Afghanistan
Albert Gea, Spain
Alejandro Ruesga, Spain
Alessandro Bianchi, Italy
Alessandro Garofalo, Italy
Alessia Pierdomenico, Italy
Alex Grimm, Germany
Alex Morton, Britain
Alexandra Beckstein, Germany
Alexandra Beier, Germany
Alfred Cheng Jin, China
Ali Jarekji, Syria
Allen Fredrickson, United States
Aly Song, China
Andrea Comas, Spain
Andreas Meier, Switzerland
Andrew Budd, Britain
Andrew Winning, Britain
Andrew Wong, Britain
Andy Clark, Canada
Anthony Phelps, New Zealand
Anwar Mirza, Pakistan
Arko Datta, India
Arnd Wiegmann, Germany
Babu, India
Bazuki Muhammad, Malaysia
Beawiharta, Indonesia
Bob Martin, Britain
Bobby Yip, Japan
Brandon Malone, Britain
Brendan Mcdermid, United States

Brian Snyder, United States
Bruno Domingos, Brazil
Caren Firouz, Iran
Carlos Barria, Argentina
Charles Platiau, France
Chris Helgren, Canada
Chris Wattie, Canada
Christian Charisius, Argentina
Christopher Herwig, Canada
Claro Cortes IV, Philippines
Claudia Daut, Cuba
Claudio Papi, Italy
Colin Braley, United States
Crispin Thruston, Britain
Damir Sagolj, Bosnia
Dan Chung, Britain
Dan Riedlhuber, Canada
Dani Cardona, Spain
Daniel Munoz, Colombia
Daniele La Monaca, Italy
Danilo Krstanovic, Bosnia
Darren Staples, Britain
Darren Walsh, Britain
David Gray, Australia
David Leeds, United States
David Mercado, Bolivia
David Moir, Britain
David W Cerny, Czech Republic
Desmond Boylan, Ireland
Dimitar Dilkoff, Bulgaria
Duffin McGee, United States
Dylan Martinez, Britain

Eddie Keogh, Britain
Eduardo Munoz, Colombia
Enrique Marcarian, Argentina
Eric Gaillard, France
Eric Miller, United States
Eriko Sugita, Canada
Euan Denholm, Britain
Fabrizio Bensch, Germany
Fadi Alassaad, Lebanon
Fatih Saribas, Turkey
Felix Ordonez Ausin, Spain
Ferran Paredes, Spain
Fran Veale, Ireland
Fred Greaves, United States
Fred Prouser, United States
Gary Cameron, United States
Gary Hershorn, Canada
Giampiero Sposito, Italy
Gopal Chitrakar, Nepal
Grace Liang, China
Grigoris Siamidis, Greece
Grigory Dukor, Russia
Haruyoshi Yamaguchi, Japan
Hazir Reka, Kosovo
Heino Kalis, Germany
Henry Romero, Colombia
Howard Burditt, Zimbabwe
Huan Wei, China
Hugh Gentry, United States
Ian Hodgson, Britain
Ian Waldie, Australia
Jacky Naegelen, France
Jason Lee, China
Jason O'Brien, Australia
Jason Reed, Australia
Jayanta Shaw, India
Jean-Paul Pelissier, France
Jeff J Mitchell, Britain
Jeff Mitchell, United States
Jeff Topping, United States
Jeff Zelevansky, United States
Jerry Lampen, Netherlands
Jessica Rinaldi, United States
Jim Ruymen, United States
Jim Tanner, Britain
John Gress, United States
John Kolesidis, Greece
John Sibley, Britain

Jorge Silva, Mexico
Jose Manuel Ribeiro, Portugal
Jose Miguel Gomez, Colombia
Juan Medina, Argentina
Kai Pfaffenbach, Germany
Kevin Lamarque, United States
Kieran Doherty, Britain
Kim Kyung Hoon, Korea
Kimimasa Mayama, Japan
Kin Cheung, China
Koen van Weel, Netherlands
Laszlo Balogh, Hungary
Lee Mills, Britain
Leon Neal, Britain
Leonhard Foeger, Austrian
Louafi Larbi, Algeria
Lucas Jackson, United States
Lucy Nicholson, Britain
Lucy Pemoni, United States
Luis Cortes, Mexico
Luis Enrique Ascui, Chile
Luke MacGregor, Britain
Marc Koeppelmann, Germany
Marc Serota, United States
Marcelo del Pozo, Spain
Marcos Brindicci, Argentina
Mark Baker, New Zealand
Mark Horsburgh, Australia
Mark Wallheiser, United States
Matt Sullivan, United States
Max Rossi, Italy
Megan Lewis, Australia
Michael Regan, Britain
Michaela Rehle, Germany
Miguel Vidal, Spain
Mike Blake, Canada
Mike Cassese, Canada
Mike Finn-Kelsey, Britain
Mike Hutchings, Britain
Mike Segar, United States
Milan Rasic, Serbia
Miro Kuzmanovic, Austria
Mohsin Raza, Pakistan
Nacho Doce, Spain
Nikola Solic, Croatia
Nir Elias, Israel
Noh Soon-taek, Korea
Ognen Teofilovski, Macedonia

Oleg Popov, Bulgaria
Parth Sanyal, India
Pascal Deschamps, France
Pascal Lauener, Switzerland
Pascal Rossignol, France
Paul Hanna, United States
Paul Vreeker, Netherlands
Paul Zhang, China
Paulo Whitaker, Brazil
Pawel Kopczynski, Poland
Petar Kujundzic, Serbia
Peter Andrews, Poland
Peter Jones, Canada
Peter MacDiarmid, Britain
Peter Muhly, United States
Petr Josek, Czech Republic
Phil Noble, Britain
Philippe Wojazer, France
Pierre Ducharme, United States
R. Marsh Starks, United States
Radu Sigheti, Romania
Rajesh Jantilal, South Africa
Ray Stubblebine, United States
Rebecca Cook, United States
Reinhard Krause, Germany
Ricardo Ordonez, Spain
Richard Carson, United States
Richard Chung, Taiwan
Richard Heathcote, Britain
Rick Wilking, United States
Robert Galbraith, United States
Robert Pratta, France
Ronen Zvulun, Israel
Ruben Sprich, Switzerland
Rupak De Chowdhuri, India
Russell Boyce, Britain
Sean Gardner, United States
Sebastian Derungs, Switzerland
Sergei Karpukhin, Russia
Sergio Moraes, Brazil
Sergio Perez, Spain
Seth Wenig, United States
Shamil Zhumatov, Kazakhstan
Shaun Best, Canada
Siggi Bucher, Switzerland
Simon Baker, New Zealand
Siphiwe Sibeko, South Africa
Stefano Rellandini, Italy

Stephen Hird, Britain
Steve Dipaola, United States
Steve Marcus, United States
Steve Schaefer, United States
Steven Paston, Britain
Stuart Milligan, Australia
Sue Ogrocki, United States
Sukree Sukplang, Thailand
Susan Ragan, United States
Susana Vera, Spain
Susumu Toshiyuki, Japan
Tami Chappell, United States
Thierry Gouegnon, Ivory Coast
Thierry Roge, Belgium
Tiffany Brown, United States
Tim Shaffer, United States
Tim Wimborne, Australia
Toby Melville, Britain
Todd Korol, Canada
Tomas Bravo, Mexico
Tony Gentile, Italy
Tony O'Brien, Britain
Toru Hanai, Japan
Toussaint Kluiters, Netherlands
Umit Bektas, Turkey
Victor Fraile, Spain
Victor Tonelli, France
Vincent Kessler, France
Vincenzo Pinto, Italy
Vivek Prakash, Australia
Will Burgess, Australia
Win McNamee, United States
Wolfgang Rattay, Germany
Xavier Lhospice, France
Yannis Behrakis, Greece
Yaw Bibini, Ghana
Yiorgos Karahalis, Greece
Yuriko Nakao, Japan
Yves Herman, Belgium
Zainal Abd Halim, Malaysia
Zeev Rozen, Israel

# Index